Legal Studies in International, European and Comparative Criminal Law

The main purpose of this book series is to provide sound analyses of major developments in national, EU and international law and case law, as well as insights into court practice and legislative proposals in the areas concerned. The analyses address a broad readership, such as lawyers and practitioners, while also providing guidance for courts. In terms of scope, the series encompasses four main areas, the first of which concerns international criminal law and especially international case law in relevant criminal law subjects. The second addresses international human rights law with a particular focus on the impact of international jurisprudences on national criminal law and criminal justice systems, as well as their interrelations. In turn the third area focuses on European criminal law and case law. Here, particular weight will be attached to studies on European criminal law conducted from a comparative perspective. The fourth and final area presents surveys of comparative criminal law inside and outside Europe. By combining these various aspects, the series especially highlights research aimed at proposing new legal solutions, while focusing on the new challenges of a European area based on high standards of human rights protection.

As a rule, book proposals are subject to peer review, which is carried out by two members of the editorial board in anonymous form.

Lorena Bachmaier Winter • Stefano Ruggeri

Editors

Investigating and Preventing Crime in the Digital Era

New Safeguards, New Rights

Editors
Lorena Bachmaier Winter
Law School
Complutense University Madrid
Madrid, Spain

Stefano Ruggeri
Law Department
Messina University
Messina, Italy

ISSN 2524-8049 ISSN 2524-8057 (electronic)
Legal Studies in International, European and Comparative Criminal Law
ISBN 978-3-031-13954-3 ISBN 978-3-031-13952-9 (eBook)
https://doi.org/10.1007/978-3-031-13952-9

This Springer imprint is published by the registered company Springer Nature Switzerland AG
The registered company address is: Gewerbestrasse 11, 6330 Cham, Switzerland

Preface: The Digital Revolution and Human Rights Challenges

Even if in the field of "technology and law," there is always the risk that some "innovative" analysis might rapidly become outdated because of the speedy evolution of technology, we are convinced that it is worth to assume such risk and try to address the present challenges the digitalization of our lives poses for the law. Only by doing this, it will be possible to understand the future developments and, at the same time, to provide some guidance to the practitioners that have to deal with the problems originated by the use of technological devices by intelligence units, law enforcement and criminal investigators as well as criminals. And, as we all know, the legal solutions in many of these areas are lagging behind.

This is not new. It is well known that much of the technological development in the field of communications technology and the gathering and processing of data has been fostered within the field of national security and the military for preventing attacks and establishing a defensive strategy, but also to be able to counterattack war threats. And in many cases only later, when these technologies have become accessible to the citizens—*e.g.*, the use of drones or the Skype video-communication program—lawmakers have started to adjust legal frameworks to the needs and limits of the digital investigation.

This development has changed completely the way human beings communicate and behave in the present digital world, allowing to obtain a huge amount of data of every individual which provides information of almost every aspect of his or her life. In this new scenario, the challenge may lie in finding the right way to protect the right to privacy of individuals, whatever this may mean in the present world.

The aim of this book is to delve into the impact of the ICTs in the criminal prevention and investigation, by addressing the state of the art of different measures and its implementation in different legal systems vis à vis the protection of human rights. Yet this research not only pursues a diagnostic goal but furthermore aims at providing a reconstruction of this problematic area in light of modern, human rights-oriented notion of criminal justice. This broadens the scope of this investigation, which encompasses both unprecedented safeguards to traditional, or anyway widely recognized individual rights and the emergence of new rights, such as the right to informational self-determination, and the right to information technology privacy, but also new rights as the "neuro-rights" or the "rights in the outer space."

Moreover, although the main focus of this book is the criminal investigation, the field of security, war, and the fight of crime cannot be clearly separated, since they have not only many connecting points, but they increasingly overlap with each other when it comes to criminal activities that pose threats to the national security.

The book includes ten chapters, trying to cover the most recent developments in the area of IT and criminal prevention/investigation, overcoming the national perspectives, although referring when necessary to domestic legal rules. The list of authors has tried to combine young researchers with experience in ICTs (youth in these areas are an added-value), with senior researchers with deep knowledge in cross-border and criminal investigation/prevention field, and areas like aerospatial law.

A common feature of all contributions is the providing of in-depth analysis of the multiple functions of, and consequently of the risks arising from, digital tools, in both fields of crime control and criminal investigation. Some tools prove today almost indispensable for purposes of criminal inquiries, and recourse to them often goes far beyond the limits set out by legal arrangements, and even the constitutional and international law standards. This is the case for such as trojan horses, spywares, and further malwares, which are increasingly used with a view to communication intercepts and search and seizure of digital evidence, as clearly shown by *Diego Foti* and *Viviana Di Nuzzo*, respectively. Moreover, ICTs have gained an increasing role in the area of crime prevention, and unprecedented outcomes can undoubtedly be achieved through instruments such as drones, which, as *Claudio Orlando* pointed out, do not only have enormous advantages for crime detection, but also often prove extremely useful for purposes of crime control. Further tools provide unique information with a view to avoiding criminal actions with huge impact, as *Francesca Pellegrino* highlighted by dealing with multiple potentials of satellites. All in all, the proper management of digital technology plays a key role both in ascertaining past facts with criminal law relevance and in handling new risks that are more and more linked to the cyber-realities. For both these purposes, ICTs are also of the utmost usefulness to information on spatial elements of the physical world which would otherwise be obtained with enormous difficulties. In this context, geolocation stands out as one of the most promising challenges, and the evolution of geographic information and technology has shown its great potential both in crime detection and crime prevention, as held by *Elena Militello*.

The risks arising from ICTs, notwithstanding their extraordinary utility, can however not be underestimated. While recourse to malware provides traditional means of investigation with incomparable capturing potential that magnifies the dangers of interference with the private sphere already existing in the analogical era, further digital tools highlight new risks, particularly due to the implications that can derive from an uncontrolled massive use thereof. This is the case for some surveillance techniques such as automated facial recognition, and even more, emotion facial recognition, which poses difficult problems concerning respect for a number of fundamental rights and freedoms, starting with the rights to privacy and data protection, up to the very presumption of innocence, as widely dealt with by *Isadora Neroni Rezende*. Although such risks can surely not be justified security-based considerations, it would however be an exaggeration to affirm that ICTs endanger a human rights-oriented view of criminal justice. A very challenging task is to examine whether and to what extent digital tools can improve the standards of protection of some fundamental rights and principles by way of reducing certain inevitable shortcomings which can derive from purely human management. *Giulia Lasagni* has undertaken this task by examining pros and contras of Multi-Agent Systems in order to strengthen the efficiency and avoid some biases in the handling of criminal investigations.

Certainly, we can affirm that the outcome of this book has been a joint effort of all contributors, with cross-checks and exchange of peer reviews, which has allowed each of the contributors not only to enrich their chapters, but also to gain knowledge of realities that they were not even aware. In the scientific world, including the legal sciences—whatever this might mean—enhancing knowledge and providing new avenues for understanding reality and thus make possible to address problems, team-work is as much as necessary as in other fields of science. We can only be grateful for the willingness of the contributors to engage in this type of team-work, which has undoubtedly enriched the chapters presented in this book, but even more, has enriched the co-editors.

Therefore, we are glad to present this book to the future readers as a humble but rigorous contribution to the discussion on the need to balance the potential of technology in the criminal prevention and investigation with the protection of our privacy in this continuously changing new digital world. The next challenge to come will be perhaps how to regulate privacy and safety in the metaverse and the ways of prosecuting criminal conducts beyond the physical reality. However, this is still to come. Our aims in this book is to study the interaction of digital investigative measures and the protection of fundamental rights in the criminal prevention and investigation, but still connected to the physical reality.

Madrid, Spain   Lorena Bachmaier Winter
Messina, Italy   Stefano Ruggeri
June 2022

Contents

**Part III   Fact-Finding and Human Rights Challenges in the
            Digital Era**

Part I
Crime Control and Criminal Inquiries in a Digitalised World. New Frontiers

Criminal Investigation, Technological Development, and Digital Tools: Where Are We Heading?

Lorena Bachmaier Winter

Abstract This introductory chapter discusses three aspects that need to be further studied to understand the impact of digitalization and new technologies in the criminal proceedings and to be able to define how criminal procedure should be structured and in which direction it should move. First, the issue of the blurring division between criminal prevention and repression caused and accelerated to a great extent due to the digital shift which claims for a new scheme on the transfer of information from the security and intelligence units to the criminal investigation authorities. Second, the fact that criminal proceedings are becoming more and more transnational, also due to the fact that the internet and the absence of territorial borders in the virtual space have consequences in the way the cross-border criminal investigation is regulated and carried out. And third, because of such 'transnationalisation' of the criminal activities—and criminal assets—with criminal proceedings still bound to domestic rules, it is necessary to rethink the role of criminal law in guaranteeing security in the cyberspace due to the intrinsic limitations of the current normative framework of the criminal procedure. These challenges for the future structure and role of the criminal procedure in the digital society as well as its limits in prosecuting certain cybercrimes are addressed in this chapter.

1 Introduction

The reader should not expect to find in these pages an in-depth or detailed doctrinal analysis—which can be found in the chapters that follow. The purpose of this introductory chapter is humbler. In addition to explaining the reasons that moved us to publish this book, it is aimed at conveying some thoughts that I consider important to bear in mind when we deal with the evolution of the criminal procedure,

L. Bachmaier Winter (✉)
Law Department, Complutense University, Madrid, Spain
e-mail: L.Bachmaier@der.ucm.es

with a particular focus on the change of paradigm that technological progress has generated in this area of law.

The advancement of the information society has created a new context in which new challenges are to be faced in the fight against crime, for perpetrators widely use new technologies, and especially digital communication, in their illicit activities. Criminal groups and individuals, use actively digital tools and platforms for committing crimes. And at the same time, traditional crimes such as fraud, money laundering or harassment—to name just a few—have found an additional stage to expand, the virtual world or cyberspace.

This is a natural reflection of the changes that the so-called 'digital revolution' has produced in our societies. If people are more and more (inter)acting in the digital space, it is to be expected that criminal activities also expand in that same space, which makes it necessary to prosecute them using adequate technological instruments. The statistics of the COVID-19 pandemic confirm this appreciation; the increasing online interaction and decreasing physical movement during this time were mirrored by a higher rate of online crime and a lower rate of criminality in the physical space.[1]

In this scenario, however, not everything runs in favour of crime and criminals. Digital technologies also provide law enforcement agents with efficient tools to trace, detect, prevent, and investigate criminal activities. The real challenge lies in converting the drivers of the new forms of crime into new responses, within a legal framework that strikes the balance between an efficient prevention and prosecution of crime and the respect of human rights of the individuals.

In this regard, one of the main and well-known problems is the fact that the right to privacy is at risk because there is a high probability that it can be encroached by the use of preventive and investigative electronic measures, in the majority of cases without the knowledge and control of the addressee of such measures. An additional reason for concern is that, while the governments' capacity of intrusion in our private lives has increased in an unprecedented way, the pre-conditions and safeguards for such interferences have not been clearly set out neither at a national level in many cases nor at the European level. In fact, as will be shown in the following chapters of this book, regarding the impact of the use of IT investigative tools, the access to digital data and the gathering of e-evidence in criminal investigations, not all jurisdictions have yet enacted precise legal rules on how to carry out digital investigations, which devices can be used for taking evidence, which information can be admitted as evidence at trial, which persons must be informed, and so on.

This book will highlight some of these problems with a particular focus on the impact the lack of appropriate rules and conceptual misunderstandings in the use of IT investigative tools and other digital devices might cause in the sphere of the protection of the fundamental rights in the criminal procedure. Our aim is not to

---

[1] See the Interpol report "Cybercrime Covid-19 Impact" of 2020, available at: https://www.interpol. int/News-and-Events/News/2020/INTERPOL-report-shows-alarming-rate-of-cyberattacks-during-COVID-19.

bridge the gap between law and technology, but to clarify how some technologies are used in the criminal prevention as well as in the criminal procedure so that we can contribute to the discussion on how its use should be regulated.

There are still many other topics related to the IT tools and devices which need a further rethinking. In this introductory chapter, I will briefly draw attention to three aspects that, in my opinion, must be addressed from new and deeper perspectives to achieve a better comprehension and design of a renewed criminal procedure in the digital society. First, the dividing line between criminal prevention and repression which is increasingly being blurred, to a great extent because of the digital shift. Second, the fact that criminal proceedings are becoming more and more transnational, also due to the internet and the detachment the cloud and the communications not bound by physical borders has caused. And third, because of such "transnationalisation" of the criminal activities—and criminal assets–, it is necessary to rethink the tools which are aimed to guarantee security in the cyberspace due to the intrinsic limitations of the current normative framework of the criminal procedure.

2 Surveillance Versus Investigation of Crime: A New Sea Change in the Criminal Fact Finding?

The complexity of these problems is even more evident when we look at the difficulties in differentiating the borders between prevention and criminal investigation/prosecution. It is manifest that the divide between these two areas is more and more unclear. The use of big data in assessing risks, as well as the use of mass surveillance upon electronic communications, as the case *Big Brother Watch* has highlighted,[2] shows how much the new digital scenario has contributed to blurring the frontiers between prevention and crime prosecution. The main challenge for criminal proceedings is now to find ways to prevent that all the information, data, and potential evidentiary materials obtained under surveillance regimes flow into the criminal procedure and circumvent its procedural safeguards.

Traditionally, intelligence actions carried out by the secret services in charge of national security were kept clearly separated from the criminal investigation and outside the legal framework of the criminal procedure.[3] There were good reasons for that: they were considered, at least formally and legally, two separate areas that should not be mixed (*Trennungsprinzip*) and whose fields of action, although in some cases they could come close to each other, should not be confused, since their aims and methods were different. Having suffered in the past abuses of the State

---

[2] *Big Brother Watch and others v the United Kingdom*, Appl. nos. 58170/13, 62322/14 and 24960/15 (ECtHR, Chamber's judgment of 13 September 2018; and Grand Chamber's judgment of 25 May 2021).

[3] See Bachmaier Winter (2012), pp. 46 ff.

through its secret services, oppressing or eliminating certain groups of people (e.g., ethnic groups, religious groups, political opposers etc.), moved European countries towards a strict separation of the areas of criminal justice and secret intelligence.

However, in recent times, intelligence activities for preventive purposes have gradually acquired greater relevance in relation to certain serious criminal phenomena[4]—in particular terrorism, organized crime, cybercrime, and money laundering.[5] Certainly, intelligence has always played a crucial role in the identification, understanding and detection of serious dangers to national security and in the design of strategies to combat terrorism and other threats that might have a severe impact upon the economic, industrial and commercial interests of a country. The change comes from the fact that, at present, these intelligence units have gained more importance and occupy a leading position in the prevention and fight against certain types of crime. Their action is now considered essential.[6]

It has been even stated that the fight against terrorism and organized crime is unthinkable without the analysis carried out by intelligence units before an indication of criminal suspicion becomes concrete.[7]

More specifically, among the various factors that explain the growing role of intelligence units in the prevention and fight of serious crimes, in particular terrorism but also cyberattacks, three should be noted here.

---

[4] See for the German system of cooperation between intelligence and criminal investigation, e.g. Zöller (2020), pp. 79–95.

[5] See, for example the report of the International Commission of Jurists *Assessing Damage, Urging Action. Report of the Eminent Jurists Panel on Terrorism, Counter-Terrorism and Human Rights*, done in Geneva in 2009, p. 67, which can be accessed at http://ejp.icj.org/IMG/EJP-Report.pdf.

[6] See the "Guidelines for Starting an Analytic Unit" published by the International Association of Law Enforcement Intelligence Analysts, Inc. (IALEIA): "A lesson learned by the U.S. on September 11, 2001 was that intelligence is integral to preventing terrorist attacks. Since then, more and more U.S. Police agencies have adopted the intelligence led model, and intelligence units have been established worldwide. Intelligence led policing uses analysis in a pro-active way to effectively target criminal groups and activities. This front-end application allows agencies to assess the needs and resources of the organization and jurisdiction, placing viable alternatives in the hands of decision-makers. Strategic targeting allows the agency to prioritize cases with the highest probability of success". On the change in the objectives of the intelligence services from the Cold War to the present moment, as well as its essential role in preventing terrorist attacks, see Treverton (2009), pp. 15 ff.

[7] As it is set out in the report of the International Commission of Jurists *Assessing Damage, Urging Action...*, cit. in note 5, p. 67: "Intelligence plays an indispensable role in identifying, understanding, and analysing terrorist threats, in providing important hints and leads for criminal investigations and in developing effective strategies to counter terrorism. Good intelligence has always been crucial to preventing, disrupting, or subsequently punishing, criminal activity. What is new is the fact that the work of the intelligence agencies has become the most relevant acts in the panoply of counter-terrorist measures available to governments. This centrality is reflected in expanded powers of intelligence agencies, increasing international cooperation, and greater information sharing." See also, Droste (2002), p. 117.

The first is the technological progress, which has provided intelligence units with access to multiple databases and ultimately with the capacity to process incredibly huge amount of information.[8]

The second is that after obtaining and processing such enormous amount of data for study and analysis purposes, as well as for preventive security aims, it has been realised that it is not only very useful for criminal detection and prosecution, but in a vast majority of cases, it is indispensable to the extent that without such data the criminal justice response could not even be activated. This explains why intelligence units have been created not only in the context of the traditional national security objectives, but also within the financial supervisory institutions—for example, for preventing money laundering and financing of terrorism—as well as at the police level. Thus, the outcome is that in practice several intelligence units deal with prevention of severe crimes, and when it comes to terrorism or cybersecurity, there will occur overlaps that require constant and effective coordination among them.

And in the third place, the increasing role that intelligence information plays in the field of criminal prosecution is also explained by the reforms implemented in substantive criminal law, as a consequence of the expansion of risk criminal offences and the criminalisation of often neutral actions at a very early stage, long before a terrorist act is actually committed.

The foregoing factors, among others, have contributed to blurring the distinction between the preventive and the repressive criminal responses, especially regarding cybersecurity, terrorism and financing of terrorism (but not only in those cases). Hence, there is a partial overlap and interrelation between the activity of the classical national security intelligence services, the financial intelligence units, the police information units, and the criminal investigation authorities, all of them being granted a vast access to data obtained by reporting obligations and surveillance.

This new scenario however does not seem to be sufficiently regulated. It is not clarified which is or should be the role of this new and expanded 'intelligence' in the prevention of crimes. These mechanisms are designed to detect threats and are therefore activated on unknown targets, i.e., they may affect any and every citizen even though when there is no previous suspicion against anyone in particular. This is precisely what has led to questioning the proportionality of such techniques, which intercept and store all communications with the aim of selecting which of them are worth being subjected to further analysis. There is hardly any discussion about the value that bulk interceptions can have for security operations, and about the legitimacy and reasonability of the proactive approach in identifying threats to national security.[9] Unlike criminal investigation, such interference in the citizens' privacy is untargeted and operates upon selectors, without any link to a prior suspicion; which

---

[8] On this amount of data accessible in the information society, the growing interconnection of networks and the tendency to merge the private and public spheres of individuals, see, for example, Schermer (2008), pp. 64 ff.

[9] As recognized in the Report on the Democratic Oversight of Signals Intelligence Agencies, of 15 December 2015, of the Venice Commission, CDL-AD(2015)011, para. 47.

makes it understandable to question if such practices comply with the principle of proportionality, and also raises the very question of whether the test of proportionality should be different as the one applied to single criminal investigations.[10]

It this regard, particular attention must be paid to studying the current caselaw of international courts of human rights (especially the European Court of Human Rights, ECtHR) and leading European constitutional courts to elucidate to what extent their caselaw provides for an adequate protection of human rights against existing mechanisms aimed at preventing risks for national security and cybersecurity, and also to what extent those courts give guidance on the impact that such surveillance measures have on our 'digital privacy'.

Of particular interest in this context is the landmark case *Big Brother Watch* of the ECtHR,[11] which involves questions of compliance of the UK Regulation of Investigatory Powers Act 2000 (RIPA) with the European Convention of Human Rights (ECHR). This was not the first time that the ECtHR dealt with the question of whether intelligence regimes, and the measures that they can carry out to prevent national security risks, were in breach of the European Convention.[12] But this was the first time[13] that the ECtHR assessed the implications of digital mass surveillance mechanisms, because its previous judgments on these matters had a narrower legal or factual scope. The Chamber's judgment on this case was delivered in 2018, and the Grand Chamber's judgment in 2021, upholding what the Chamber had decided three years before.

The Strasbourg Court found that the rules of RIPA on bulk surveillance of telecommunications then applicable were in violation of Articles 8 and 10 of the Convention for lack of sufficient oversight of the entire selection process,

> including the selections of bearer for interception, the selectors and search criteria for filtering intercepted communications and the selection of material for examination by an analysts; and secondly the absence of any real safeguards applicable to the selection of related communications data for examination.[14]

With respect to whether the bulk interception of communications for national security aims was legitimate and necessary in a democratic society, the Court left the assessment and balancing of the interests at stake to the national authorities,

---

[10]On the proportionality principle, see e.g. Alexy (1986), 102 Degener (1985), 43 and Emiliou (1996), 23–24.

[11]ECtHR judgment *Big Brother Watch and others v The United Kingdom*, of 13 September 2018, Appl. nos. 58170/13, 62322/14 and 24960/15; and ECtHR Judgment (GC) of 25 May 2021. On this judgment; see, among others, Bachmaier Winter (2021), pp. 17 ff.

[12]See the ECtHR, *Weber and Saravia v. Germany*, judgment of 29 June 2006, Appl. no. 54934/00; *Liberty and others v the United Kingdom* Appl. no. 58243/00, of 1 July 2008; *Roman Zakharov v Russia* Appl. no. 47143/06 (GC), of 4 December 2015; *Szabó and Vissy v Hungary* Appl. no. 37138/14, of 12 January 2016; *Centrum för Rättvisa v Sweden* Appl. no. 35252/08, of 19 June 2018.

[13]In addition to *Centrum för Rättvisa*, a case which also dealt with a digital mass surveillance regime.

[14]Id. (Chamber), para. 387.

which "enjoy a certain margin of appreciation in choosing the means for achieving the legitimate aim of protecting national security". Nevertheless, the Court explicitly recognized that the reports provided by the British independent reviewer on terrorism legislation and by the Venice Commission show that the operation of a bulk interception regime to discover unknown or unidentified targets "is a valuable means to achieve the legitimate aims pursued, particularly given the current threat level from both global terrorism and serious crime".[15] The Court confirmed that the decision to operate a bulk interception regime to identify unknown targets falls within the State's margin of appreciation.[16]

The ECtHR also concluded that, as the risks of secret surveillance increased so much in the "technological sea change", the safeguards provided in its previous case law assessing strategic surveillance measures (mainly in the cases *Klass* and *Weber and Saravia*) can no longer be considered sufficient. Questions as whether a "prior independent control by a judicial authority should not be a necessary requirement in the system of safeguards" were raised in the dissenting opinions.[17]

Bulk surveillance is thus considered legitimate for national security purposes, and the necessity test is linked to the oversight mechanism. Proportionality is left to the margin of appreciation of the States.

Taking a closer look at the differences between criminal procedure and intelligence regimes, the main difference is that, unlike in the former, in the latter the utility test (how useful this mechanism is for detecting threats for national security) and the necessity test (whether there is a less restrictive measure to achieve the same results) can as a rule not be checked with regard to individual cases, but only on the basis of the data reflected in the internal auditing reports and those prepared by the independent commissioner. The *ex post* control by an independent commissioner shall fulfil this task, although it naturally will not cover all files or records.

The ECtHR was completely aware of this difference. Therefore, it held that the impossibility to determine whether the same preventive aim could have been achieved by other less intrusive means than the bulk interception of communications made it necessary to rely on the assessment made by national lawmakers and on the reports produced by the independent oversight bodies.

The two most distinctive elements in relation to safeguards in the criminal investigation are the requirements of the previous suspicion and the *ex ante* judicial warrant. In the interception of communications within a criminal investigation, the initial control requires a grounded judicial warrant, checking the lawfulness and all the elements of proportionality, considering the existence of a suspicion against an individual. The targeted interception for criminal investigative purposes is subject to

---

[15] Id., para. 386.

[16] Id., para. 314.

[17] See ibid., partly concurring, partly dissenting opinion of Judge Koskelo, joined by Judge Turković, para. 20. The possibility for such a prior mechanism of prior judicial or independent authorisation is illustrated by the Swedish legislation, as seen in the *Centrum för Rättvisa* cited above.

control at all stages by the judicial authority and, in addition, the *ex post* control will be open to the defendant as well as to the adjudicating court.

Of course, the approach in the case of non-targeted surveillance differs completely from the one adopted on targeted interceptions. There is no initial decision based on a previous suspicion simply because there is no target. This is logical once the assessments on suitability and necessity of the measures are accepted. The minimum necessary indications, or the suspicions, that must be present in a criminal case in order to allow a targeted interception of communication are not applicable to the situation of unknown targets being subjected to bulk interceptions.[18]

All these differences call for a ban on allowing the intelligence information to flow without restrictions into the criminal proceedings. However, in practice, this exchange might not be kept under control, precisely in those areas where the intelligence unit is authorized to carry out surveillance measures in the area of prevention of serious crime and terrorism.

3   Digital, Global, and Transnational: Some Notes

The digitalisation has also caused an unprecedented increase of the 'transnationalisation' of the criminal proceedings as well as a 'delocalisation' of evidence, a reality that also requires a new legal approach to overcome the traditional national view of investigative measures.

Regarding the investigation of cybercrime—as well as other types of cross-border crimes—and the impact of the digital data and e-evidence on criminal investigations, very few systems establish rules on how to obtain the digital evidence located abroad or in the cloud.[19] In many cases, there are no rules at a national level about how to carry out computer searches in order to keep them within the proportionality requirements, and also to prevent disclosing confidential information (as for example, lawyer-client privileges).[20] And even when these national rules exist, they offer significant differences between them, and thus the absence of harmonisation can prevent the admissibility of the evidence obtained through online cross-border measures.[21]

Indeed, despite the rules introduced by the CoE Convention on Cybercrime,[22] the legal provisions on access to digital data and ensuring its integrity are still

---

[18] See *Big Brother Watch* (Chamber), para. 317.

[19] For a comparative study at the European Union level see Sieber and Von zur Mühlen (2016). See also Bachmaier Winter (2017), p. 3 ff.; Soares Pereira (2019), p. 248 ff.

[20] On the lawyer-client privilege in a comparative view, see Bachmaier Winter and Thaman (2020), pp. 37 ff.

[21] Bachmaier Winter (2017), pp. 317 ff.

[22] CETS 185, of 23 November 2001.

fragmented at a national level, something which is causing problems for its access and transfer, and also with regard to the admissibility of e-evidence. This is the reason that led to negotiating at the Council of Europe level an adequate legal framework to overcome those obstacles in accessing and using electronic evidence. After almost four years of intense negotiations, finally on the 17 November 2021 the Committee of Ministers of the Council of Europe adopted the Second Additional Protocol to the Budapest Convention on Cybercrime.[23] It is still to be seen to what extent the present problems on accessing electronic evidence will be overcome in the future. For the moment the Second Protocol is open for signature by the CoE member States, and the EU Council has authorised the EU member States to sign it.[24]

Furthermore, in the fields in which the cross-border evidence plays an increasingly important role, it is no longer sufficient to provide for the protection of procedural safeguards at a national level, because the data and the communications electronically stored may be used in a different jurisdiction than that in which those communications took place. The recent developments by the European Commission on the e-evidence Digital Exchange System (e-EDES)—an initiative which is part of the broader Digital Criminal Justice project[25]—includes the establishment of a single electronic platform to exchange the most frequently applied instruments for judicial cooperation. This will enable a reliable transfer of electronic evidence with a view to ensuring its authenticity and integrity. Once such a secure exchange platform is operating, the transfer of e-evidence among the EU Member States will be facilitated, and the checks and safeguards for the integrity and authenticity of the e-evidence will be strengthened. However, the access, the admissibility, and the assessment of the evidence obtained abroad will still be a challenge. Common rules and principles are still to be developed, to guarantee that the protection of human rights will not be lowered by facilitating the transfer of evidence across States.

---

[23] Second Additional Protocol to the Budapest Convention on enhanced cooperation and disclosure of electronic evidence, adopted on 17 November 2021, and opened for signature on 12 May 2022. The rules included in this Protocol aim at providing tools for enhanced co-operation and disclosure of electronic evidence—such as direct cooperation with service providers and registrars, effective means to obtain subscriber information and traffic data, immediate co-operation in emergencies or joint investigations—respecting human rights and rule of law, including data protection rights.

[24] Council Decision (EU) 2022/722, of 5 April 2022 authorizing Member States to sign, in the interest of the European Union, the Second Additional Protocol to the Convention on Cybercrime on enhanced co-operation and disclosure of electronic evidence, O.J. of 11.5.2022, L/134/15.

[25] See the Communication from the Commission "Digitalisation of justice in the European Union. A toolbox of opportunities", Brussels, 2.12.2020, COM(2020) 710 final, accessible at https://eur-lex.europa.eu/legal-content/EN/ALL/?uri=COM:2020:710:FIN.

4   Cybercrime *Versus* Cybersecurity: Criminal Investigation or Resilience?

The digital society poses new challenges for the security of individuals, above all from the points of view of resilience against cyberattacks, preventing crime, and protecting human rights. Cybersecurity is a major concern in our societies, and some figures may illustrate the magnitude of the problem. According to some projections, costs of data breaches will reach $5 trillion annually by 2024, up from $3 trillion in 2015.[26] A recent survey of the EU showed that most people in the EU (55%) are concerned about their data being unlawfully accessed. According to the European Union Agency for Cybersecurity (ENISA) report for 2018,[27] a total of 351,913,075 unique malicious URLs were identified, representing an increase in the number of malicious URLs compared to previous year totalling 282,807,433. Child pornography exchange has increased a 500% during the pandemic.

The European Union Security Strategy, published on 24 July 2020,[28] confirmed that cyber-attacks and cybercrime continue to rise, and security threats are also becoming more complex. They feed on the ability to work cross-border and on inter-connectivity, and they exploit the blurring of the boundaries between the physical and digital worlds; they tend to exploit vulnerable groups, social and economic divergences.[29]

According to the EU institutions, all these areas are to be addressed under one main principle or concept: resilience.[30] Of course, in achieving this specific aspect of resilience, technical, scientific, social, and political layers are to be interlinked. All these aspects need an adequate legal framework and, according to the ENISA Report Conclusions,

> several barriers do exist in Europe and worldwide that hinder access to CTI information, such as the existence of diversified regulatory spaces, the unavailability of reliable incident information and deficiencies in information sharing.

A priority in this context is to study the interactions of cybersecurity, and the connected concept of resilience, and to examine the prosecution of cybercrime and cyberattacks. Regarding cybersecurity, it is necessary to address how the concept of

---

[26] Juniper Research, The Future of Cybercrime & Security (2018), p. 4 ff., accessible at https://www.sciencedirect.com/journal/computer-fraud-and-security.

[27] Regulation (EU) 2019/881 of the European Parliament and of the Council of 17 April 2019 on ENISA (the European Union Agency for Cybersecurity) and on information and communications technology cybersecurity certification and repealing Regulation (EU) No 526/2013 (Cybersecurity Act).

[28] COM(2020) 605 final.

[29] The main areas to be addressed according to the EU strategy are: Cybercrime, the Networks and Information Security (NIS), the EU Defence Agency (EDA), Cyberdefence, in the intergovernmental pillar of the EU.

[30] In this realm, resilience is defined as "the ability to provide and maintain an acceptable level of service in the face of various faults and challenges to normal operation" (ENISA 2011).

resilience can be implemented in all linked areas, as for example through providing a better legal framework, establishing a supranational institutional investigation and prosecution authority, and increasing the public-private partnership to facilitate technical assistance. There is also a need to analyse which impact these actions adopted within the context of cybersecurity by public and/or private entities will have on the criminal investigation of cybercrimes, and how they will share valuable information and evidence for criminal prosecution purposes with law enforcement.

It needs to be further explored what the role of the criminal investigation and prosecution is in the field of cybersecurity, since the objectives of the criminal law and criminal prosecution are not precisely aiming at resilience, but through an effective sanctioning system provide deterrence in the committing of criminal conducts and also give guidance on what are the most precious values of a specific legal order in a certain time. Such aims might function in certain areas but are hardly effective when facing cyberattacks not linked to a concrete territorial jurisdiction or person. The study of the existing barriers is also significant in the criminal justice response, precisely considering that cybercrime is in essence a cross-border crime and evidence might not be easily accessed, which might open the door to use the concept of procedural resilience, as many criminal investigations on cyberattacks/ cybercrimes will hardly lead to the identification of cyber-offenders or to their prosecution and sanction. All this should make us reflect on the application of the principle of mandatory prosecution, as it will be pointless to open a criminal investigation where it is already foreseeable that the perpetrators will never be identified and, if identified, there is hardlyno chance that they will be brought to justice. Finally, there is also an element that needs to be recast within the criminal procedure in fighting cybercrime, which is clearly linked to the actors that provide cybersecurity: the role of public-private cooperation regarding cybersecurity and fighting cybercrime, and the risks that such partnerships may entail.

In these areas, the main current challenge is likely to determine whether the same standards and tools can be deployed in cybersecurity and the prevention of cybercrime, and to which extent it is possible to share information on cyberattacks among States for the purposes of criminal investigation. While a security policy against foreign cyberattacks may stick to the concept of resilience, so that the conflict is not escalated with public attribution and retaliation against the foreign attacker, in the criminal law realm the response should go beyond the resilience territory and reach the prosecution and sanction. The differences in addressing cybersecurity threats in the foreign policy and in criminal law, and when the two areas may converge, must be analysed from a "holistic" or interdisciplinary point of view; criminal proceedings cannot be instituted without taking into account the security policy and the cybersecurity elements.

It goes without saying that the first step to achieve some coherence in the criminal prosecution of cybercrime is to raise awareness of the challenges for security in the present digital society, be conscious that there are overlapping fields of cyberattacks, cyberwar and cybercrime, all encompassed under the broad concept of cybersecurity, and that the boundaries of international law, security and prevention of crime and prosecution and sanctioning of criminal conducts has become less clear.

While at the level of international security we must face the question of how much evidence it is necessary to produce to attribute publicly a cyberattack to another country, at the level of cybercrime it will often be more and more necessary to count with the support of private companies to identify the perpetrator. The various instruments to prevent cyberattacks and to react against them will inevitably be overlapping and even conflicting at times. All these factors require a new approach in the criminal proceedings during the investigation of certain types of cybercrime, where the concept of resilience may also become relevant.

5   Final Remarks

A constant feature in history is that human beings have used and developed technical instruments to face immediate needs. As scientific knowledge advanced, technology also became more and more sophisticated (sometimes raising new needs in mankind), but typically humans were in command of technology and decided its course of action. This might be changing with self-learning machines, which will be capable to take decisions in an independent fashion. The law cannot stay behind technological evolution. And the protection of human rights, which is a especially significant part of the law, must advance at the same pace as the technology if we want the IT society to respect the rule of law and comply with human rights conventions and the essential national and supranational constitutional principles in this realm.

This applies especially to criminal proceedings, where the State can use powerful means against individuals, and even more in a world where AI allows processing data in a measure, and at a speed, that were unimaginable some decades ago. The ever-growing tempo of scientific and technological development, and the immense possibilities that AI offers, cannot but affect the content of this book. Some of the issues that are treated here as novel may perhaps become in a few years matter for the study of the history of criminal procedure.

Even if some of the technological instruments studied in the chapters of this book may become soon outdated, the big challenge of finding a balance between the aim of criminal procedure and the protection of fundamental rights will always be present. The need to become aware of the reach of IT investigative measures in the sphere of privacy—a notion that is very different from the traditional concept of privacy that emerged from the bourgeois pre-industrial society—is today more important than ever. In the era of the IT society, the debate about the principles of necessity and proportionality as criteria to justify and limit interferences with fundamental rights has acquired even more relevance.

This may also be an opportunity to rethink the classical structure and goals of the criminal procedure, in a context where a large amount of evidence is generated without direct connection with the commission of a crime and therefore pre-date the criminal proceedings. This is not a novelty in itself, for many evidentiary sources exist prior to the initiation of a criminal proceedings, and the criminal investigation is aimed precisely at discovering them. After all, something similar occurs in civil procedure, where public or notary documents are produced in the realm of contractual relationships with the intention to create evidence that is prior to and independent from the inception of a future legal suit. But, as far as the theme of this book is concerned, the difference is that electronic data and evidence is often generated and stored without our intervention, without our knowledge, with a pro forma consent (as when we accept cookies in our computer), or with aims totally unrelated to a possible future procedure to establish the criminal liability of a person. Therefore, the collection, storage, and processing of data under bulk surveillance regimes authorized for national security purposes, or public space surveillance for public security aims, needs to be carefully controlled, to prevent that those data end up in the criminal procedure as evidence.

Our lives, including social interaction, financial activities, professional acts, communications, etc., in the vast majority of cases leave a digital trace which is registered. And despite the legal attempts to limit data retention and despite the rules on data protection following the principles of specialty and prior consent, reality shows that there are more "data leaks" and "data hacks" than can be imagined. Accessing those data for purposes of criminal prevention or prosecution must be strictly controlled by a judicial authority, and its use as evidence can only be admitted under a strict control of proportionality.

The core elements of such control are not necessarily changing according to technological development. Even though the transformation of the digital world requires adjustments in the conception and rules of the traditional criminal procedure, the importance and nature of some key notions remain. Understanding the meaning and consequences of the old principles of necessity and proportionality, the balancing of values, is something that goes beyond technology and probably beyond the best algorithmic designs. Already in 1939, Ortega y Gasset wrote that the growth of new knowledge and the loss of wisdom were distinctive signs of the new times. In the Spanish philosopher's view, the techniques invented by men threaten to strangle them;[31] the horizon of human beings, with their fixed animal activities, is always limited, and science is incapable to tell human beings anything vital about themselves.[32]

In any event—as Ortega also predicted—machines will end up self-governing their functioning, and this requires establishing limits on technological development from other instances. This is precisely the challenge that the law faces: to determine such limits, which—as the chapters of this book explain—can be introduced in the software so that technology can directly implement norms on the basis of those legal limits.

We are heading towards an increasingly digital criminal investigation, with greater influence of data obtained for surveillance purposes, and where private actors will even take the lead at the investigative stage and in providing evidence. Despite

---

[31] Ortega y Gasset (1935), in his lecture given at the Complutense University of Madrid on the 20th May 1935, p. 30.

[32] Ortega y Gasset (1939), p. 360 ff.

this new 'procedural scenario', the notions of necessity and proportionality will remain crucial in ensuring procedural safeguards. The concept of proportionality *stricto sensu* will still be the one more difficult to assess, as it has a marked blurred profile. To assess whether this criterion has been met, it will still be necessary to refer to undetermined legal concepts such as the *reasonable proportion* between the gravity of the interference with fundamental rights and the aim pursued; or the *rule of common sense* which seeks to prevent excessive harms that are not justified by the aims. To assess what is 'reasonable' or 'excessive', or what falls within the 'common sense' in the area of interferences with the right to privacy caused by digital surveillance or investigative measures is a *petitio principii*, because the terms of 'adequate balance', 'reasonability', 'common sense' or 'prohibition of excess' are as broad and vague as the principle of proportionality.

Assessing competing legal interests and values in a certain social context, balancing the aims and the gravity of the interference, is a difficult task, up to now left to the judicial argumentation. Nevertheless, in the future we might also see an algorithm undertaking the proportionality assessment. At the present moment we are not still there, but maybe this is where we are heading.

References

Alexy R (1986) A theory of constitutional rights. Oxford University Press, Oxford

Bachmaier Winter L (2012) Información de inteligencia y proceso penal. In: Bachmaier L (ed) Terrorismo, proceso penal y derechos fundamentales. Marcial Pons, Madrid, pp 45–101

Bachmaier Winter L (2017) Remote search of computers under the new Spanish Law of 2015: proportionality principle and the protection of privacy. ZStW 129(1):1–27

Bachmaier Winter L (2021) Proportionality, surveillance and criminal investigation: Strasbourg Court facing Big Brother. In: Billis E, Knust N, Rui P (eds) The principle of proportionality in crime control and criminal justice. Hart, pp 317–335

Bachmaier Winter L, Thaman S (2020) A comparative view of the right to counsel and the protection of attorney-client communications. In: Bachmaier Winter L, Thamn S, Lynn V (eds) The right to counsel and the protection of attorney-client communications in criminal proceedings. Springer, Cham, pp 7–73

Degener W (1985) Grundsatz der Verhältnismäßigkeit und strafprozessuale Zwangsmaßnahme. Duncker & Humblot, Berlin

Droste B (2002) Nachrichtendienste und Sicherheitsbehörden im Kampf gegen Organisierte Kriminalität. Carl Heymans Verlag, Köln

Emiliou N (1996) The principle of proportionality in European law: a comparative study. Kluwer International, London

Ortega y Gasset J (1935) Misión del bibliotecario, reprint by Asoc. Andaluza Bibliotecarios, Málaga, p 1994

Ortega y Gasset J (1939) Meditaciones de la técnica y otros ensayos sobre ciencia y filosofía, reprint by Alianza, Madrid 2000

Schermer BW (2008) Surveillance and privacy in an ubiquitous network society. Amsterdam Law Forum 1(63), 2008–2009:63–76

Sieber U, Von zur Mühlen N (eds) (2016) Access to telecommunication data in criminal justice. Duncker & Humblot, Berlin

Soares Pereira R (2019) O acesso (unilateral e sem recurso a mecanismos de cooperação judiciária internacional) a dados armazenados em sistemas informáticos localizados no estrangeiro. Revista de Estudios Europeos, special issue 1-2019: 246–273

Treverton GF (2009) Intelligence for an age of terror. Cambridge University Press, Cambridge, p 2009

Zöller MA (2020) Die Zusammenarbeit der Nachrichtendienste mit Strafverfolgungsbehörden. In: Dietrich JH, Gärditz KF, Graulich K et al (eds) Nachrichtendienste in vernetzter Sicherheitsarchitektur. Mohr Siebeck, Tübingen, pp 79–95

Geolocation in Crime Detection and Prevention

Elena Militello

Abstract The present chapter aims at depicting the role of geolocation techniques in the criminal justice system. Geolocation is intended as the process of attaching a specific location, through the use of geographic references, to an object or a subject. The chapter analyses the developments in geographic information and technology, from Geographic Information Systems to Global Navigation Satellite Systems, before tackling their current and potential role both in crime detection and in crime prevention.

1 Introduction to the Spatial Dimension of Crime Detection and Prevention

Location is a key attribute to any given human action. Objects and subjects are constantly situated in three-dimensional contexts through height, width and depth, that change and evolve through the fourth dimension, that is time.[1] Even the environments that we consider virtual at the utmost level, emerging from contemporary technological developments, such as artificial intelligence, cybercrimes, cryptocurrencies, cloud computing, or machine learning, cannot prescind from the spatial dimension of their huge underlying assets, from data centres and submarine Internet cables to locations for the production of the energy consumed. The spatial component of phenomena with relevant legal repercussions has too often been disregarded by legal practitioners involved in crime prevention and detection, relegated to mere criminological analyses in the field of environmental criminology.[2]

---

[1] Reichenbach (1958), p. 109 ff.

[2] Environmental Criminology was first born out of a groundbreaking suggestion by Jeffery (1971), suggesting that crime prevention could be enhanced by improving the tactical design of the built

---

E. Militello (✉)
Law Department, University of Messina, Messina, Italy
e-mail: elena.militello@unime.it

© The Author(s), under exclusive license to Springer Nature Switzerland AG 2022
L. Bachmaier Winter, S. Ruggeri (eds.), *Investigating and Preventing Crime in the Digital Era*, Legal Studies in International, European and Comparative Criminal Law 7, https://doi.org/10.1007/978-3-031-13952-9_2

19

The relationship between criminal investigations and spatial data has always been a complex one. On the one hand, investigating bodies have always deployed techniques to identify the location of suspects, starting from a mere stakeout, physically following the suspects to understand their life patterns, and discovering potential sources of evidence, onto traditional surveillance methods such as eavesdropping or, more recently, wiretapping. On the other hand, spatial data analyses and geolocation techniques are increasingly powerful and impact citizens' daily life with the threat of surveillance and criminal profiling.

As technologies evolve ever more rapidly, the bodies in charge of criminal law legislation and judicial investigations struggle to keep their pace. Their ambitious goal is to maintain, at the same time, efficient countering of illicit activities and unwavering protection of citizens' rights. The rights at stake are those connected to personal and family life and liberty, privacy and data protection, against surveillance conducted by private third parties managing citizens' data for business purposes and by law enforcement agencies.[3]

Lawyers and law researchers have long hinted at the potential use that could be made by investigating authorities of state-of-the-art geolocation techniques while underlying the risks for the public community of ever more intruding technologies impacting on the citizens' right to privacy.

However, the hyper-specialization of legal research tends to exclude interdisciplinary approaches aiming at unfolding the functioning of those scientific developments in the field of information and communication technology (ICT) which enable ever more precise geolocation.

It is thus the objective of the present chapter to bridge the gap between law experts and geographic information systems (GIS), to foster a truly cross-subject approach to the role of spatial elements' analysis in the criminal justice system, not only in the investigating phase but also in the efforts toward the prevention of crimes.

The approach will be a comprehensive one, not focusing on national regulation or legislation but instead aimed at providing a departing point, an overview of the geolocation techniques that are currently available in Europe and the United States and their—still underestimated—potential in the criminal justice system.

The pairing of data with their geographical references, both through databases (through geographic information systems) and in a dynamic way (through geo-positioning systems), is nowadays widely available from a technical standpoint. Fundamentally, the different actors in the criminal justice systems need to be aware of the existence of such databases and techniques to tackle individual crimes more swiftly and effectively and to contribute to the building of an "atlas" of crime to deepen their actual knowledge of the systems they operate in.[4]

environment (*e.g.* better lighting or natural visibility in parks or public streets) in which the daily lives of society members unfold. Such tactical design, based on statistical evidence and data, would cause a decrease both in crime rates and in societal fear of crime. This theory was named "Crime Prevention Through Environmental Design" (CPTED).

[3] The legal doctrine literature in this field has extensively developed in the last decade, both in Europe and in the United States. See *e.g.* Vervaele (2014).

[4] The ambition to create an "atlas" of crime is shared by many authors: *e.g.* Turnbull et al. (2000); Besson (2005).

2 Technologies and Techniques Behind Geolocation

The technologies and techniques of geolocation currently available in terms of measurements and digital analyses are impressive and rely on huge amounts of data available in the public sphere or only to experts and investigating bodies.

Preliminarily, a difference must be highlighted, between live spatial tracking (geo-positioning systems—GPS—also known as Global Navigation Satellite System—GNSS) and longitudinal, yet punctual geographic information on how places change throughout time (geographic information systems—GIS).[5]

Geolocation techniques aim to capture how objects are situated in relation to their surrounding environment. This detection might vary in scale and resolution; it could replicate, in scale, distances, and other geographical information, such as altitude and the conditions of the soil.

2.1 *Historical Origins and Development of Geolocation Techniques*

The first tool to be used by humans to track geographic coordinates was cartography, *i.e.* the technique and the art of map-making. To create a map, in brief, meant to men of all eras to represent a three-dimensional topography onto a two-dimensional representation.[6]

The science behind cartography evolved as time went by, from a mere sensory recollection of perceived distances to a proper, Euclidean, accurate scientific measurement. The first cartographers, from ancient times to the Middle Ages and the Renaissance, were usually navigators who, during a navigation effort by the coasts for commercial or military purposes, also took the time to draft a map of the locations they were visiting.[7]

Once human technologies allowed men to detach themselves from the ground and fly, a new wave of geolocation began, with the development of aerial imagery and flights, from the 1940s to contemporary remote or drone sensing.[8] This means that cameras were initially placed on board of flights, starting from the earliest military flights and discovery expeditions. The resulting photos had to be corrected to annul the differential distortion that the lenses and how pictures were taken might have caused in their perspective.

Later, with the widespread use of satellites, aerial imagery with a human on board was quickly substituted by remote sensing, with cameras placed on public or even

---

[5]Longley et al. (2015), pp. 11–13.

[6]Uttal (2000), p. 247 ff; Ignaccolo (2021), pp. 246–251.

[7]Kahlaoui (2018), pp. 50–64.

[8]Trorey (1952), pp. 1–4; Falkner and Dennis (2002), pp. 15–27.

private satellites rotating all around the terrestrial globe at given intervals of time. This produces more accuracy but also a more distant approach, that could be circumvented by the deployment of digital cameras with a record-high resolution, that is the number of pixels across the width and height of the image.

In those same years, satellite navigation systems, capable of dynamically tracking the position of individuals at any given time, started to develop. In 1973, the U.S. Department of Defense kickstarted the Global Positioning System (GPS) project, which became operational with its original name of Navstar GPS in 1993. Satellite navigation systems do not necessarily require an Internet connection, although they are effectively boosted if there is one. The massive spreading of personal devices with both mobile connections and GPS systems in the last 30 years has caused a significant spread in the daily use of geolocating technologies. Currently, mobile phones rely on four concurrent technologies to provide geolocated or "geotagged data": GPS, cell towers, Bluetooth, and wi-fi Internet.

More and more providers and creators of maps, in recent years, have placed great importance on panoramic images taken from street level,[9] which record all three dimensions, including the height of the built environment. This huge capturing effort, amounting to ca. 170 billion photos in 2021, might also cause distress in the privacy of subjects whose houses and faces (but also, in some instances, identity) could be stored indefinitely in the map-making effort, despite countermeasures like the pixelating of portions of images recognized to be human faces, license plates or, in some instances, private abodes, a technique which was earlier on used by human auditors and now by artificial intelligence.[10]

All the aforementioned mapping technologies, however, relied on privately owned software and platforms: an additional step forward in this field was lately made by the introduction of bottom-up, crowdsourced, participatory methods that resulted in community mapping and open-source mapping efforts. This was inserted within scientific literature on the defy to the perceived impartiality of collected data and was named VGI, *i.e.* Volunteered Geographic Information.[11]

It is also useful to briefly refer to the national territorial information systems, *i.e.* the whole system of men, tools, and procedures that allow data acquisition and distribution and that validate them when requested by anyone who needs them for any purpose.

In the United States, there is widespread use of databases that include spatial data. In the criminal justice field, specifically, the Department of Justice provides open data that is available to the public online.[12] The Federal Bureau of Investigation (FBI) has developed a Uniform Crime Reporting (UCR) Program, which includes four data collections: the National Incident-Based Reporting System (NIBRS), the

---

[9] The most famous instance of blanket street-view-image capturing for business purposes is Google Street View: Anguelov et al. (2010), p. 32 ff.

[10] The most recent figures and developments are recollected by Zhang (2021).

[11] Williams (2020), p. 54 ff.

[12] See: www.justice.gov/open/open-data.

Summary Reporting System (SRS), the Law Enforcement Officers Killed and Assaulted (LEOKA) Program, and the Hate Crime Statistics Program, even though not every law enforcement agency provides data to all of these collections.[13]

At the European Union (EU) level, the EU Commission developed its internal GIS, called "GISCO".[14] EU countries are at different levels of development in the collection of spatial data. Certain countries, like Germany, show a high level of interest in this type of data collection.

In Germany, indeed, there is a whole *Bundesamt* (Federal Office) dedicated to the collection of geographic data: the Federal Office for Cartography and Geodesy, *i.e.* the measurement of Earth (*Bundesamt für Kartographie und Geodäsie*).[15]

Other countries, instead, face more hinders in effectively collecting justice data and/or spatial data. For example, in Italy, data is collected mainly by the National Institute of Statistics (ISTAT). A Territorial Information System on Justice (SITG: *Sistema informativo territoriale sulla giustizia*) was activated and later shut down in 2017; its data was sent back to ISTAT.[16]

2.2   The Technologies Behind Geographic Information Systems and Remote Sensing

Spatial data, or "geographic information", is data to which a geographic location, representation, or reference point is associated. It specifies the exact location (either in terms of latitude and longitude or in terms of distance from a specific point) of geographic features, be they manmade or natural, and describes them. Geographic features can be divided into 'point features' like trees, linear features like roads, and 'area features' like cadastral land parcels.

"Geographic Information Systems" (GIS) are computer-based information systems, integrating hardware and software components. They enable the capture, management, analysis, visualization, and display of geo-referenced spatial data from the real world.[17]

GIS, therefore, is a technology to manage data in a way that allows to connect them to maps and to analyse spatial information, by linking tabular data (*i.e.* alphanumerical descriptions, called attributes) to any geographical feature. Data itself is stored in purposed databases (geodatabases), or files, often in a specific format known as Shapefile.

Shapefiles are a specific format of files created by the ESRI company (Environmental Systems Research Institute). Shapefiles are interchangeable among different

---

[13] See: www.fbi.gov/services/cjis/ucr/publications.

[14] See: ec.europa.eu/eurostat/web/gisco.

[15] See: www.bkg.bund.de.

[16] See: www4.istat.it/it/archivio/195710.

[17] Burrough (1986), p. 16.

users (across different GIS software types). Each Shapefile contains several (usually five) sets of data, such as database data (with .dbf as an extension), projection data (.prj), and the geometry itself (.shp). Data collectors, like public entities and even municipalities, if they are diligent, should store and share spatial data in Shapefile format, rather than flatten images (*e.g.* jpg, png), to ensure data interchangeability across different software platforms and users, who might be able to process spatial analyses. Data management and visualizations are achieved through software platforms that enable the processing of information (geoprocessing).

This effort belongs to a broader set of initiatives aiming at sharing raw files and machine-readable data to allow multiple audiences to work on the very same data sources. As a result of this, transparency and cross-disciplinary evaluations might become the norm in the not-so-distant future.

The utility of GIS is multifaceted, as it can be of great help in answering specific questions on a geographical region such as its current state and conditions, the changes over time, the spatial patterns, the query of whether specific conditions occurred in a certain polygon area, the interaction and isolation of different variables.[18]

Data used in GIS contexts is mainly of two types: vector and raster.

Vector data is spatial data that stores locations using Cartesian coordinate locations (latitude and longitude). Vector data can be points, lines, and polygons, and can also record height and time.

Attribute tables are data structured as a defined set of fields, and many rows, each representing an individual data record.

Instead, raster data is spatial data that stores location depending on a single origin point and with a data stream of known width, height, and resolution. This is often used for continuous surfaces and is based on a regular grid of pixels, each with a fixed cell size. Each cell has its numeric value, which can refer to specific attributes (*e.g.* it can indicate the height in a topography).[19]

Once there is a specific set of data, the following step is geoprocessing, which can be defined as the practice of using GIS tools to process, transform, filter, and query GIS data. This phase can be carried out through different types of software, depending on the purpose and the license (*e.g.* ArcGIS, QGIS, GrassGIS).

Geoprocessing itself is conducted through algorithms, often automated through programming languages (frequently the R language or the Python language). Algorithms can be programmed to be chained to one another to answer specific questions.[20]

An early instance thereof, in the United States, in the field of criminal justice, has been CrimeStat, a spatial statistics program led by the National Institute of Justice since 1996.[21]

---

[18]Longley et al. (2015), pp. 31–32.

[19]Yang et al. (2011), p. 3875 ff.

[20]Robins et al. (2003), p. 137 ff.

[21]Levine (2006), p. 41 ff.

Through the geoprocessing phase, the user can create the map documents, with the underlying data that is not data embedded within itself but only referred to in an internal or external storage disk.

Within a specific spatial data analysis, there are often multiple sets—called "layers"—of data, stacked through the "Overlay" function and measuring their space interdependency.[22]

Geoprocessing allows the user to conduct any type of analysis: for example, "hotspot analyses" or "heat maps" that identify clusters of spatial phenomena.[23] An application thereof, in the criminal justice field, can be the "risk terrain modelling", used to identify which features in the environment attract crime (*e.g.* whether proximity to parks with poor lighting conditions is correlated to higher crime rates during specific time windows).[24]

Among more advanced techniques using geographic analysis are remote sensing techniques. It is worth underlining how some of them may help in the reconstruction of specific settings where an event (*e.g.* a crime) occurred. Remote sensing technologies include three-dimensional modelling and point clouds (the three-dimensional reproduction of collections of millions of raw spatial data points), obtained through photogrammetry or LiDAR (light detection and ranging, a three-dimensional laser-scanning which measures the time for the reflected light to return to the receiver to produce three-dimensional point clouds and meshes from drone-based and other image-capturing tools.)[25]

2.3 The Technologies Behind Global Navigation Satellite Systems

Besides the aforementioned technologies aimed at representing geographical features at a given time, different technologies of Global Navigation Satellite Systems (GNSS) were invented, as previously mentioned, to track the geographical position of a moving person or object, their movement, and the corresponding time. Global Positioning System (GPS), as explained above in para. 2.1, is the most famed satellite navigation system, capable of dynamically tracking the position of individuals at any given time.

As mentioned above, GPS was born as a U.S. military tool to provide guidance to army members in their orienteering efforts, as a modern evolution of compasses and stars-based methods to find cardinal directions, with a first satellite launch in 1978 and the first proper use in 1993.[26]

---

[22] Albert and Reginald (1999), p. 7 ff.

[23] Biron et al. (2019), p. 1263 ff.

[24] The technique is explained extensively by its creator in Caplan and Kennedy (2010).

[25] Dong and Chen (2017), p. 19 ff.

[26] Ceruzzi (2018), pp. 105–122.

The U.S. Presidents in charge in those years soon announced that it would become available for more general, civilian use without a charge, first only with lower accuracy to give the U.S. Department of Defense a competitive advantage, and later, since 2000, without such limitation. The fact that such a critical infrastructure for the development of modern-day companies and technologies is government-owned led public competitors to fear that the concession of the civilian use might in the future be revoked by the United States.[27] Therefore, other countries followed with their GNSS since then, including Russia's GLONASS, China's Beidou, and, eventually, in 2016, the European Union's Galileo, operated by the European Union Agency for the Space Programme (EUSPA), which has been fully operating only since 2020.[28]

GNSS systems work thanks to the interaction between satellites, gravitating in predetermined orbits around the Earth; ground stations, making sure that satellites are respecting their given orbits; and receivers in the hands of the users. Every GNSS system needs at least 24 satellites to be able to track directly every part of the Earth's surface at any given moment. The United States also owns ten additional emergency satellites, to address any potential issue that may arise. In addition to the already listed four complete sets of GNSS (GPS, GLONASS, Beidou, and Galileo), also India and Japan have recently entered the GNSS race, respectively with seven and two satellites.[29]

Once GPS started being used for civilian purposes, at first, there was the need for a specific tracking device to be attached to the asset one wished to follow, *e.g.* a suspect's car. Nowadays, and since the spreading of the availability of mobile phones, instead, every device has a built-in GPS, not only allowing the communication company to know where the phone is located, constantly, but also, in contemporary smartphones, to automatically (with a one-time opt-in authorization click when the person first turns on the phone) geotag their documents and pictures, embedding within the document, as one of their attributes, the latitude, and longitude where it was taken.[30] The same goes with other types of location services, those which are needed for many apps downloaded on a phone. However, the person can always decide to locate herself in a different place than that where the picture was taken (in that case, the actual location remains saved as metadata within the mobile phone or stored in the cloud computing system but will not pop up in the app). This entails that the voluntary geolocation of a subject in a place cannot be tantamount to proper tracking, in terms of guaranteeing that the subject was in a specific place at a specific time.

The proper tracking can only be carried out through the geolocation systems installed in devices used nowadays. They can be of four types, often operating simultaneously: besides the GPS, the Bluetooth technology (BLE), the Wi-Fi

---

[27] *Ibidem,* pp. 157–172.

[28] See: www.euspa.europa.eu/european-space/galileo/What-Galileo.

[29] Kumar et al. (2021) p. 3 ff.

[30] Faqir (2013), p. 433 ff.

technology, and network-based geolocation, based on cell towers. Each of the last three can be deactivated by the device user, when they are not using the services related to that technology but, together, they can act as a proxy for a location tracker of the device at any given time.[31]

Briefly, all geolocation services use some kind of triangulation technology: the distance of a specific asset, receiver, or tracker, is calculated by crossing the distance from at least three points through electromagnetic radio signals. These points are: satellites in the case of GPS, Wi-Fi hotspots or wireless access points in the case of Wi-Fi, cell towers in the case of network-based geolocation, and other Bluetooth beacons in the case of BLE.[32] GPS, Wi-Fi, and mobile networks all operate by sending radio signals, which travel at the speed of light. Thus, they can calculate precise locations through a system of more than accurate timing. GNSS satellites, in particular, are furnished with the most accurate human-made clocks, the so-called "atomic clocks". Their timing is constantly shared with ground receivers after being adjusted to take into account the effects of their microscopically higher slowness, as compared to clocks on Earth, due to the lesser gravity at the satellites' orbit and consequently to the relativity theory, stating that gravity curves time and space.

The four abovementioned different systems work together dynamically, allowing users to take advantage of the optimal technology at each location, meaning that a tracker will find the most precise geolocation technology available at any given time: it might start trying, at first, to geolocate an asset (*e.g.* a mobile phone) via Bluetooth and, if that fails, it might proceed through GPS or eventually through Wi-Fi or mobile networks. For example, this use of subsequent geolocation technologies in case of failure of the previous has been tested, during these last pandemic years, in some COVID-19 contact-tracing apps. They would resort to cell towers in the case of failure by the primary technology, *i.e.* Bluetooth.[33]

3 Geolocation as a Tool for Crime Detection

The use of Geographic Information Systems (GIS) and Global Navigation Satellite Systems (GNSS) in the practice of criminal enforcement agencies in the past 20 years has led to the birth of the term "geospatial law enforcement."[34]

An increasing number of law enforcement agencies and prosecutors' offices all around the world has either trained some members of the workforce to become crime

---

[31] Roxin et al. (2007), pp. 1–9.

[32] *Ibidem.*

[33] González-Cabañas et al. (2021), p. 1093 ff.

[34] *E.g.* Dhingra (2019).

analysts or hired some *ex novo*.[35] The most common use is that of tracking devices through GNSS systems but crime analysts also strongly rely upon GIS technologies for mapping, routing and data analysis tasks. GIS, as explained above, can provide— at the same time—insight into demographics, historical imagery, and visualization of sites where initial contacts with the police occurred, crime scenes, and sites for the disposal of crime-related materials. Whether an agency is investigating repetitive crimes with lone-wolf perpetrators or sophisticated criminal organizations, they can employ forensic GIS to analyse crime patterns, manage special operations, and understand trends and patterns.[36]

In this Chapter, the term "crime detection" will be employed broadly, to encompass any activity related to the uncovering of a previously committed criminal act, the verification of reported *notitiae criminis*, and the acquisition of evidence needed to identify and, subsequently, prosecute crime perpetrators.

The United States was a pioneer in the field. In 1997, the US National Institute of Justice (NIJ) set up the Crime Mapping Research Center (CMRC) to promote research, evaluation, development, and dissemination of GIS technology.[37] Earlier, criminal law enforcement agencies already used spatial analysis to analyse the *modus operandi* of crime perpetrators, but they did so not through advanced technologies but by employing paper pans, pins, and sticky notes. The widening of gaps in unequal development between States or regions or even agencies may lead to unintended consequences. Those agencies that do not evolve and adapt to new technologies risk continuing to operate with a persisting lower efficacy of crime countering measures, which also impacts quality-of-life indicators for the inhabitants' communities.[38]

Among the potential uses of crime mapping, this Chapter highlights some in crime detection and countering, after a crime has been committed, through phone tracking and GPS but also GIS; and some in crime prevention, before a specific crime occurs and to care for the whole affected community. It refers to "successful" examples of the use of geolocation techniques in countering crimes every time that the use of mapping was instrumental in problem-solving, prevention, and enforcement efforts. It may also improve internal police processes in terms of investigating, identifying problems, or allocating staff. Even more importantly, it can lead to the identification, apprehension, or prosecution of suspects.[39]

The use of GIS and GPS information within a specific investigation might cause issues in admitting and using evidence, considering that it is a new type of evidence, and its reliability must be granted to be the linchpin of convictions.

---

[35] See, for official US data in 2008: bja.ojp.gov/sites/g/files/xyckuh186/files/Publications/Vera-CrimeAnalysts.pdf.

[36] Elmes et al. (2014), pp. 19–38.

[37] See the U.S. Office of Justice Programs' website: www.ojp.gov/pdffiles1/nij/178919.pdf.

[38] Baraka and Murimi (2019), p. 36 ff.

[39] Early instances of such applications are collected in La Vigne and Wartell (1998), vol 1, pp. 3–14.

In the United States, the Fourth Amendment[40] enshrines the right of individuals against unreasonable searches and seizures by public authorities, protected by the exclusionary rule, with the impossibility to introduce illegally obtained evidence at trial.[41] The word "search" hints at hunting for something related to crime, while the word "seizure" refers to the public authorities taking possession of the results of the search.[42] Among public authorities, law enforcement authorities are clearly included when acting in the context of a criminal investigation.

The protection awarded by the Fourth Amendment encompasses a wide range of situations within criminal proceedings. The traditional interpretation of the text of the norm requires that the warrant contains a determination by an independent judge or magistrate that there is probable cause to believe that a specific crime has been committed.[43]

Only then can a search or seizure be legitimately carried out and its results can later be admitted into evidence. In all cases requiring the processing and computing of large amounts of data, the "specificity" of a crime can be questioned. Not only were the words used in the text quite general, but the Supreme Court also interpreted them extensively: they are interpreted to encompass any intrusion by public authorities within the private sphere of citizens, *i.e.* where they have a "reasonable expectation of privacy."[44] An important corollary is the "third-party doctrine": there is no subjective expectation of privacy in what we disclose to someone else, a third party, like a mobile network service provider if they later reveal it to public authorities.[45] The scope of application of the Fourth Amendment today comprises body searches, the searching of places, computer searches, wiretapping, as well as arrests, considered as a seizure of the body.[46]

In light of the development of modern technologies that allow for continuous monitoring, more and more cases arose—across all jurisdictions—of the collection of criminal evidence through the use of GPS and cell phone location techniques. Individuals are continuously revealing their location to their wireless carriers through both these technologies, to perform the essential functions of a "smartphone."[47]

In these recent instances, however, the extent of any reasonable expectation of privacy is deeply limited, as third-party providers (and, indirectly, law enforcement)

---

[40] U.S. Constitution, IV Amendment: "The right of the people to be secure in their persons, houses, papers, and effects, against unreasonable searches and seizures, shall not be violated, and no warrants shall issue, but upon probable cause, supported by oath or affirmation, and particularly describing the place to be searched, and the persons or things to be seized."

[41] Schlesinger (1977), p. 50 ff.

[42] Taslitz (2009), p. 2 ff.

[43] LaFave (2020), vol 2, pp. 3–24.

[44] U.S. Supreme Court, *Katz v. United States*, 389 U.S. 347 (1967). Wilkins (1987), p. 1087 ff.

[45] Kerr (2009), p. 561 ff.

[46] LaFave (2020); Militello (2020), p. 54 ff.

[47] U.S. Supreme Court, *Carpenter v. United States*, 585 U.S. (2018). Wilson (2021), p. 155 ff.

can know everything about a person through their data. Every bit and piece of data might be insignificant on its own, but it constitutes a sort of "mosaic" when all of them are pieced together.[48]

GNSS can also be valuable when used by law enforcement agencies as a personal locator to avoid the completion or the worsening of consequences of certain crimes. This is especially true in cases of missing persons or of abductions, especially child abduction, as is usually done by tracking one's phone or, more recently, other types of personal belonging to which commercial tags using Bluetooth technologies are attached. In the United States, there is an interesting nationwide system of real-time alerts not only on extreme weather conditions but also on missing or abducted children (so-called Amber alerts) that pop up on the phone of people who are in the area where the child went missing or where the abductor is suspected to be going, to collect as many eyewitness testimonies as possible.[49]

Finally, not only live movements but also a chronology of location crowdsourced data are nowadays almost always stored by third-party providers like providers of map apps (*e.g.* Google Maps) or physical activity tracking (like Strava) on mobile phones.[50] If correctly recovered from a device and safely stored during a forensic investigation, such GPS evidence (of the location of the suspect and/or of victims) and track points could hold major evidentiary value for a case both in terms of alibis and in terms of conviction.[51]

Setting aside dynamic tracking like GNSS, as concerns geographic information in the form of aerial imagery, the U.S. Supreme Court has long taken the stance to exclude any reasonable expectation of privacy in cases of "environmental surveillance."[52] They developed a theory of "open fields", allowing for aerial surveillance through drones, helicopters, or satellites (despite the obvious differences among them in terms of resolution of images). A further step was allowing flying thermoscanners to look for drugs (as marijuana growing sites are often equipped with heat lamps to maintain the room's temperature higher than the outside) or to check if there's anybody alive in a dangerous situation.[53] However, some lower courts recently opened up to a higher protection standard, stating that *de facto* law enforcement may need a warrant to conduct a massive aerial surveillance program.[54]

An even stronger approach to privacy concerns than the U.S. one is the one taken by the Council of Europe's Convention on Human Rights and by the European

---

[48] See especially the concurring opinion of U.S. Supreme Court's Justice Sonia Sotomayor, to the decision in the case known as *United States v. Jones*, 565 US (2012). Kerr (2012), p. 312 ff.

[49] Griffin and Miller 2008 p. 159 ff.

[50] Wolfson and Lease (2011), pp. 1–10.

[51] McKenna et al. (2018), p. 591 ff.

[52] U.S. Supreme Court, *Dow Chemical Co. v. United States*, 106 S. Ct. 1819 (1986).

[53] U.S. Supreme Court, *Kyllo v. United States*, 533 U.S. 27 (2001).

[54] U.S. Court of Appeals, *Leaders of a Beautiful Struggle v. Baltimore Police Department*, 456 F. Supp. 3d at 702–03 (4. Cir 2020), reheard *en banc* 2 F.4th 330 (fourth Cir. 2021). Ferguson (2021); Wilson (2021), p 155 ff. However, its principle was declined to extend by a Pennsylvania District Court in *United States v. Bowers*, W.D.Pa., October 11, 2021, 548 F.Supp.3d 504.

Union's Nice Charter on Fundamental Rights. In both Charters, Article 8 enshrines people's right to respect for their private and family life, home, and communications, whereas interference with this right by public authorities is only allowed for lawful reasons, such as for the protection of national security or economic wellbeing, public safety, health or morals, rights and freedoms of others, or prevention of other crimes.

Hence, the human and fundamental right to privacy enshrined in both aforementioned Charters should be respected against any threat of invasion, coming either from technological devices such as smartphones or mobile apps or from the use of location data more generally.[55]

Within this wider framework, many of the issues arising out of the use of geolocated data can be set and inserted into the legal context.

Creators of GIS data layers must also be aware of confidential and sensitive data and of the need to take precautions to protect victims' rights and privacy or confidentiality.[56] An ever-growing line of research of GIS experts is social media data mining, both following geotagged photos or other geotagged social media data (GSMD) as location metadata are considered a valuable proxy for tracking human movement.[57] This is an evolution, through cutting-edge technologies, of the theory of "Social Network Analysis", typically employed by investigators to "analyse criminal networks, investigate the relations among criminals, and evaluate the effectiveness of law enforcement interventions aimed at disrupting criminal networks."[58]

An interesting field is that of combining location data, usually considered as external records, with text mining techniques to assess the sentiment of whoever writes a social media post, to identify those responsible for crimes, especially Twitter announcements of attacks by terrorist forces.[59] Geotagged data might be used to locate a person at a certain time or to prove an alibi.

However, they are quite easy to amend or forge: in most social media there is the possibility of tagging oneself later on a previous picture, through chosen or automatic geotagging (people can be in one country and tag themselves in a different one simply by typing in the "Location" field a different place). There are also people who are conscious about sharing their data. They may only use browsers' incognito mode settings[60] or refuse to allow geotagging as individuals are not under an obligation to disclose non-essential location data to service providers; at the same time, specific locations like social venues or natural parks, may request visitors to remain off geotagged photos for reputation or preservation purposes.[61]

---

[55] ECtHR, *Uzun v Germany*, Judgment of 2 September 2010, Appl no 35623/05.

[56] *E.g.* Bu-Pasha et al. (2016), p. 312 ff.

[57] Hawelka et al. (2014), p. 260 ff; Lemieux (2015), p. 3 ff.

[58] Cavallaro et al. (2020), p. 8 ff.

[59] Keyvanpour et al. (2011), p. 872 ff; Al-Zaidy et al. (2012), p. 147 ff; Al-Saif and Al-Dossari (2018), p. 377.

[60] Panneck (2019), p. 511 ff.

[61] Holson (2018).

A wider perspective of the types of crimes in which the help of non-dynamic geolocation techniques might be useful include: construction abuses, by showing where building contractors disregarded urban planning laws and committed crimes that can be seen from above (like expanding a building's allowed volume or surface or building in a protected area where it would be altogether forbidden to add any building);[62] pollution and environmental crimes for the effects of pollution on the aerial views; cybercrimes, when linked to the IP address (although it can be altered through VPNs); tax crimes and money laundering, when matching geotagged data in social media with the officially declared income would cause a suspicion; apprehending fugitives on the run or hiding for long years, who need to find hiding places in remote locations; graphical display of trial evidence; autodialling systems of alert placed on law enforcement transportation means; breaking alibis through cell phone mapping; matching repeat or serial offenders with crime locations by letting patterns emerge.[63]

Finally, in a wide array of other types of crimes, additionally, the use of technical geographic, and architectural knowledge is proving instrumental in "geoforensic" studies, *i.e.* in finding or reconstructing crime scenes.

On the one hand, some authors began talking of a new field of work that is known as "forensic geoarchaeology".[64] One interesting example thereof is the possibility to understand where alive or dead bodies are hiding either through satellite images that show the change in terrains over the years, in cases of clandestine or mass graves, or if corpses were hidden by burying them within a different material like concrete (through scanners that perceive the difference in materials, usually placed on drones),[65] or through infrared scanners that may be useful in cases of missing persons.[66]

On the other hand, a new tool is "forensic architecture", which allows for crime scene reconstruction not through manual measurements and the traditional, diagrammatic, often incomplete representations of crime scenes.

The 3D scanning methods (as the LiDAR-based scanners mentioned in the previous paragraph) started being used to allow for a more complete digital, scaled, three-dimensional representation of a crime scene (so-called "forensic mapping"), where first responders often lack the time and clarity of mind to treat the scene properly.[67] They might be equipped with technologies that record the entire scene and allow users to later transfer it in a digital format. These scanning methods are improving at a record pace, with the ever-increasing availability and user-

---

[62] Saviano and Tondo (2021).

[63] King (2019).

[64] Goldberg and MacPhail (2006), pp. 286–294.

[65] Lockwood and Masters (2021), p 1770 ff.

[66] Barone et al. (2021), p. 2 ff.

[67] See *e.g.* the U.S. government's National Institute of Standards and Technology website: www.nist.gov/news-events/news/2020/03/spotlight-navigating-first-responders-through-unfamiliar-spaces-laser-light.

friendliness of low-cost computing power and capture platforms and artificial intelligence and machine learning-augmented processing tools. Interesting case studies have already been realized, from the reconstruction of car wrecking accidents[68] to the ambitious effort of an architectural non-profit organization to obtain a detailed chronological (in a second-by-second sequence) reconstruction of the blast explosion that occurred in August 2020 in the port of Beirut, Lebanon.[69]

As to the question of whether geolocation data based on GIS platforms can be used as digital evidence, the answer seems to be positive. In the United States, there is a strong reliance on the criteria set forth by the Supreme Court in analysing scientific evidence in the *Frye* and *Daubert* judgments.[70] In Italy, a recent judgment by the Supreme Court of Cassation—in a case related to the violation of building regulations—has stated that Earth-based remote sensing systems, aerial photographs, and topographical data stored in a GIS platform (like data extracted from Google Earth) are documentary evidence that can be fully used (as long as their authenticity is ensured) since they "represent facts, people or things."[71]

In conclusion, in the past, investigators used to physically pin on a board with a paper map all the relevant information that was in any way connected to a location on a map. Then, they would employ physical woollen threads they used to find overlapping regions and areas of interest, especially in repeat crimes to find these patterns.

Nowadays, investigators have the possibility of analysing these data at a much faster pace and with much more precise results of the analysis, less subject to physical mistakes. They can create different simulations and combine different sets of data to verify whether the hypothesis is sound or not. Without physically looking at data pinpointed on a map, investigators risk missing details, patterns, and connections and this explains why spatial analysis and spatiality itself are so important in modern criminal investigations. Different datasets with different provenance coexist, from emergency calls for police service to victims reporting data to reports by policemen on patrol. It is of the essence that this data be collected upfront by every agency in a stable, reliable, and consistent manner with a high degree of interoperability (through the transversal use of the same categories and measurement units to avoid needing to clean up the data on the back end and unnecessary delays.

Cooperation is also fundamental, both in the sense that the different neighbouring jurisdictions shall collaborate in the creation of maps, and in terms of inter-agency cooperation, as can be the case between the police and the fire department in arson cases.

---

[68] McFadden (2017).

[69] The video of the reconstruction is available online at: forensic-architecture.org/investigation/beirut-port-explosion.

[70] *Frye v. United States*, 293 F. 1013 (D.C. Cir. 1923); *Daubert v. Merrell Dow Pharmaceuticals, Inc.,* 509 U.S. 579 (1993).

[71] Italian Court of Cassation, third section, 19 October 2017, n. 48178, with a comment by La Selva (2018).

Finally, another requirement is the funding, as law enforcement agencies need to be able to access this software and turn them into a user-friendly interface, to spend years educating and training police officers and prosecutors in these specific IT functions that are GIS-related or, if they outsource the crime analysis function, to rely on external providers which of course must respect the highest possible standards.

Technological advancements need to always be paired with the emotional intelligence, instinct, and experience of law enforcement agents with a deep knowledge of the territory and its dynamics. At the same time, if properly dosed, data-driven policies and GIS systems might help look at things differently, identify patterns, and avoid structural or personal biases due to long-standing knowledge of a certain city area, which could also result in a fairer administration of justice.[72]

4 Potential Roles for Geolocation in Crime Prevention and Recidivism Reduction

Crime prevention has always been grounded on the role of data, especially spatial data, starting from the 1829 ground-breaking theories of an Italian sociologist, Adriano Balbi, and a French lawyer, Andre-Michel Guerry.[73] The two researchers believed that crime prevention should be based upon verifiable data. They innovated the field by using data from the French census to explain recidivism rates.

Data-driven crime prevention became mainstream in the United States in the last 15 years, earlier than in Europe.[74]

The use of geographic information has been deemed useful to identify criminal justice trends and draft new policies, even more than it has been used to solve specific crimes, as highlighted in the previous paragraph.

GIS software gives police officers and policymakers the ability to highlight crime hot spots or different aspects of a crime on a map in different regions or neighbourhoods. By doing so, they help contextualize data and gain insight into the reasons behind a higher occurrence of crimes in a certain area following in the footsteps of the above mentioned earlier approach of so-called Crime Prevention Through Environmental Design (CPTED).[75] A GIS technique used to identify what features in the environment attract crime is "risk terrain modelling" ("RTM"), developed by the Rutgers Center on Public Security (RCPS) by analysing hotspot data of where crime rates are higher and which physical features of the built environment are more frequent in high-risk areas or blocks.[76]

---

[72] Nobles (2010), pp. 205–220.

[73] Wang (2012), p. 159.

[74] Chainey and Ratcliffe (2005), pp. 1–11.

[75] Jeffery (1971), p. 498 ff. See *supra*, fn 2.

[76] *Supra*, fn 15.

In an analysis dating back to 2000, the potential of GIS data was highlighted in evaluating, among others, the impact of drug crackdown operations, mapping campus violence, sketching gun violence trends, setting up neighbourhood watch programs, predicting residential break-in patterns, preventing construction site crimes, including typical mafia boycotts.[77]

More recently, the analysis of social media posts through location tracking has become an ever-common method used by law enforcement agencies to take pre-emptive actions.[78] Even for tracing suspects or criminals in terrorism-related cases, location tracking of their social media or phone records often appears instrumental in ensuring that crimes be not brought to worse consequences.[79]

Shifting the focus away from crime control and onto policymakers concerned with peaceful cohabitation of citizens, these techniques, if properly understood and deployed, might avoid hazardous concentrations of intersections, thus reducing traffic violations and increasing street crime avoidance, but also urban plans on the positioning of streetlights, public transportation bus stops or the creation of apps allowing citizens to verify the crime statistics in one's proximity (*e.g.* to decide where to reside as a single woman) or even showing the "safest path home". The inherent risk of creating a list of areas or cities to be avoided is producing the unintended effect of worsening the prejudices towards certain cities or parts of a city.[80]

Much of the criminological analysis known as geographic criminology or "CrimeGIS"[81] depends on the availability of updated databases in any given territory. In the United States, the Justice Mapping Center (JMC) uses more data to make informed decisions on the future of the criminal justice system.[82] CompStat 2.0., a software used by the New York Police Department, publicly released its data.[83] Other projects, like Columbia University's "Million Dollar Blocks", help highlight the structural injustices and flaws of contemporary criminal justice by showing which communities are paying the highest price, in a blatantly disproportionate measure. [84]

Another potential use of geolocation techniques besides crime detection that may curb recidivism is one concerning precautionary measures, the post-conviction phase, and penitentiary law, *i.e.* electronic monitoring.

This makes use of geofencing technologies. Geofencing uses GPS (or other technologies like Radio Frequency Identification—RFID) to create a virtual

---

[77] All cases collected by La Vigne and Wartell (1998), Vol 2.

[78] Chaturvedi (2019).

[79] Bard (2016), p. 731 ff.

[80] Viswanath and Basu (2015), p. 45 ff.

[81] Rosner (2017), pp. 25–44.

[82] Weisburd et al. (2009), pp. 3–31.

[83] The software was available online within the U.S. borders at compstat.nypdonline.org.

[84] For the "Million dollar blocks" project by Columbia's Spatial Information Design lab see: c4sr. columbia.edu/projects/million-dollar-blocks. Kurgan and Cadora (2006).

geographic boundary, which can be set to enable software to trigger a response when a tracked device (usually a mobile phone) enters or leaves a particular area. This is commercially used by business owners to keep track of the customers frequently accessing their facilities for customised marketing purposes but also by local municipalities wishing to gather evidence on the most used routes or public spaces.[85]

Shifting to criminal procedure systems, among the conditions for pretrial release or for parole, which are a way for a convicted individual to avoid prison time through alternative ways of punishment, one can agree to GPS electronic surveillance. One of the main concerns over the granting of house detention or parole motions is often that public controls are never sufficient to avoid that the subject may flee or reiterate their crimes. In several countries, there is a piece of legislation on the deployment of ankle monitors on suspects or convicted criminals. The first such instance was the United States' Community Control Programs ever since the early '90s.

In Italy, Art. 275-*bis* of the Italian Code of Criminal Procedure (It.c.c.p.) was inserted in 2000 to foresee an ankle monitor ("*braccialetto elettronico*") within precautionary measures in addition to house arrests.[86] More recently, a 2019 reform on the crimes of stalking and family abuses included among the norms on removal from the family home (Art. 282-*bis*, para. VI, It.c.c.p.) and restraining or protection orders (Art. 282-ter, para. I, It.c.c.p.) also the possibility of electronic monitoring. In these cases, it would take the form of proximity tracking through a double geolocation device: an ankle bracelet on the offender and a transmitter to be carried around by the victim.[87]

Another example of the use of ankle monitors is that applied to certain categories of offenders, namely sex offenders, together with their insertion in a national registry.[88]

In this case, too, the observer is left wondering how the voluntariness of the consent to enter such an agreement might be assessed, especially in programs aimed at rehabilitation, like probation and drug court agreements.

Additionally, better tools of spatial analysis of crime patterns contribute to the spreading of "digital predictive justice", with all their related risks: extracting future trends out of an analysis of where crimes had occurred in the past.[89] On this note, criminal profiling in the context of facial profiling was recently banned by the EU Parliament of the European Union, at the same time as a non-binding resolution also calls for a ban on AI-based predictive policing.[90]

---

[85] Rodriguez Garzon et al. (2019), pp. 1184–1187.

[86] It. Law Decree 341/2000.

[87] Amato (2019), pp. 64–65. Recent Italian cases where the use of this new legislative tool was publicly made known can be found in Parma, Venice, Catania.

[88] Troshynski (2017), p. 103 ff.

[89] The term was coined in Garapon and Lassègue (2018).

[90] Heikkilä (2021).

This brings the perspective from micro-tools and person-based infrastructures to city-wide surveillance systems, which are even more extreme and at a broader scale of analysis.

Besides the threat of securitization of our societies, the use of big data and predictive policing is often structurally unjust, and algorithms may be racially biased. This led some scholars to talk of "coded inequity", due to how algorithms perpetuate the unjust structure of the contexts in which they are written.[91]

Some general prevention surveillance programs, like China's "citizens' score", are of particular concern for civil liberties, even though they might have been intended as a special prevention tool. It is aimed at threatening the person responsible for even a minor crime with the possibility that the consequences of that action might be reflected in one's chances to conduct a normal life, *e.g.* buying a house or travelling by train within the country.[92]

5   Conclusions

Almost no one may nowadays doubt that technologies are increasingly intertwined among each other but also with people's lives, jobs, and social interactions. This creates a dichotomy between the compelling need to guarantee individuals' privacy and that to guarantee stable and reliable connections through the newest and most advanced technology, leaving no one behind.

In contemporary societies, data is fundamental. Even more so, spatial data has become essential. Evidence-based policymaking has become the standard to which many legal systems aspire. There are unimaginable amounts of data circulating, spatial data in particular, but not as much in many criminal justice systems. It is often reiterated how crime and criminals easily overcome political and geographical boundaries, thus also leaving their traces to law enforcement agencies who are ready to address them.

However, there is a widespread fear of the development of a "culture of surveillance"[93] in such a digitally advanced world: it is often highlighted how modern individuals disclose every single shade, crack, or leak of their personality to their technological devices, thus creating a breakdown between the public and the private sphere.

The long-standing need, for criminal justice systems, to strike a balance between individuals' privacy and data protection rights expands in the cutting-edge realm of geographic information systems.

---

[91] As explained in Benjamin (2019).

[92] CBS News (2018).

[93] The term is taken from Lyon (2018). See also Zuboff (2019), p. 30 ff.

This delicate balance should serve, at the same time, as an enabler of liberty, on the one hand, and as a warranty for security and the national interest in targeting crimes, on the other hand.[94]

Throughout the present chapter, we have analysed two geolocation techniques that are on the verge of fame in criminal justice: GPS, which has been vastly used by law enforcement agencies and analysed in detail in scholarly literature for its immediate threat of degenerating into surveillance; and GIS, which is a newer addition to investigating tools and can contribute greatly to cope with the complex factors that influence the emergence and location of crimes, but which is highly dependent on existing records system at each participating law enforcement agency. The possibility of sharing anonymized crime data with the community and creating real-time multiple alerts to intervene directly on crime scenes might engender a higher commitment of the local communities in terms of community policing and a renewed sense of trust in the institutions.

The integrity of judicial authorities, in terms of free assessment of evidence and of their role as *periti peritorum* (experts among the experts), reminds us of the importance for judges and law practitioners to understand and navigate the implications of contemporary spatial technologies, without deferring judgments to the appointed experts in an uncritical way.

A suggestion emerging from the analysis of modern geolocation techniques might be to foster evidence-based, data-driven risk assessment in crime prevention and policing, focusing on places that enable crime instead of on people as crime authors, as the supporters of the theory of Crime Prevention Through Environmental Design (CPTED) have been suggesting for decades.[95]

Be it detecting anomalies in crime scenes, cross-border crimes, highlighting patterns, or facilitating search and rescue, geospatial analytics and artificial intelligence together can facilitate decision-making and give law enforcement agencies the chance to draw certain conclusions and become more proactive.

Artificial intelligence applied to geolocation techniques may allow law enforcement agencies to re-enact all possible reconstructions of a crime scene and select those which appear to be in line with all existing clues. Then, data mining might allow machines to process big data at a speed rate that is unfathomable to humans and cross existing databases to highlight any unruly or unpredictable element which might constitute a clue.[96]

The issue remains as to the potential sources of error as well as to risks of discrimination and machine bias,[97] although algorithm bias is less felt in mere geographic analyses than in behaviour-predicting software.

---

[94] Quattrocolo (2020), p. 44 ff.

[95] Since Jeffery (1971), on which see *supra* fn 2.

[96] Gless (2020), p. 195 ff.

[97] See, for a wide recollection of the issues linked to potential machine biases and algorithmic justice, Završnik (2021), p. 623 ff.

Faced with the wary threat of widespread surveillance, our societies are left wondering whether the mere existence of cutting-edge technologies, ever more intrusive as to their computing power, justifies their use in criminal procedure contexts, infringing upon the fundamental rights of individuals.

The provisional response is that the criminal justice system cannot turn away from the newest tools but there is a need to spread awareness concerning the intrusion capacity of these ever-evolving instruments and the reduction of the physical scope of our reasonable expectations of privacy, and that is the role for legal practitioners.

References

Albert WS, Reginald GG (1999) The use of spatial cognitive abilities in geographical information systems: the map overlay operation. Trans GIS 3(1):7–21

Al-Saif H, Al-Dossari H (2018) Detecting and classifying crimes from Arabic twitter posts using text mining techniques. Int J Adv Comput Sci Appl 10:377–387

Al-Zaidy R, Fung BC, Youssef AM, Fortin F (2012) Mining criminal networks from unstructured text documents. Digit Investig 3-4:147–160

Amato G (2019) Stalking: su utilizzo braccialetto elettronico l'incognita risorse. Guida al Diritto 4: 64–65

Anguelov D et al (2010) Google street view: capturing the world at street level. Computer 43(6): 32–38

Baraka GE, Murimi SK (2019) Stuck in the past with push-pins on paper maps: challenges of transition from manual to computerized crime mapping and analysis in Kenya. Int J Police Sci Manage 21(1):36–47

Bard J (2016) Unpacking the Dirtbox: confronting cell phone location tracking with the fourth amendment. Boston Coll Law Rev 57:731

Barone PM, Di Maggio RM, Mesturini S (2021) Forensic geoarchaeology in the search for missing persons. Forensic Sci 1

Benjamin R (2019) Race after technology: shining light on the new Jim code. How biased are our algorithms?. Institute for Advanced Study. www.ias.edu/ideas/race-after-technology

Besson J-L (2005) Les cartes du crime. Presses Universitaires de France, Paris

Biron K, Mansoor W, Miniaoui S, Atalla S, Mukhtar H, Bin Hashim KF (2019) Data science tools for crime investigation, archival, and analysis. In: 2019 IEEE SmartWorld, Ubiquitous Intelligence & Computing, Advanced & Trusted Computing, Scalable Computing & Communications, Cloud & Big Data Computing, Internet of People and Smart City Innovation, pp 1263–1266

Bu-Pasha S, Alén-Savikko A, Mäkinen J, Guinness R, Korpisaari P (2016) EU law perspectives on location data privacy in smartphones and informed consent for transparency. Eur Data Protect Law Rev 2(3):312–323

Burrough P (1986) Principles of geographical information systems for land resources assessment. Clarendon Press, Oxford

Caplan JM, Kennedy LW (2010) Risk terrain modeling manual: theoretical framework and technical steps of spatial risk assessment for crime analysis. Rutgers Center on Public Security, Newark

Cavallaro L, Ficara A, De Meo P, Fiumara G, Catanese S, Bagdasar O et al (2020) Disrupting resilient criminal networks through data analysis: the case of Sicilian mafia. PLoS One 15:8

CBS News (2018) China's behavior monitoring system bars some from travel, purchasing property. www.cbsnews.com

Ceruzzi PE (2018) GPS. IEEE, Piscataway

Chainey S, Ratcliffe J (2005) GIS and crime mapping. Wiley, Hoboken

Chaturvedi A (2019) Role of GIS and emerging technologies in crime detection and prevention. Geospatial world. www.geospatialworld.net

Dhingra A (2019) GIS helps in effective analysis of crime patterns. Geospatial world. www.geospatialworld.net

Dong P, Chen Q (2017) LiDAR remote sensing and applications. CRC Press, Boca Raton

Elmes GA, Roedl G, Conley J (2014) Forensic GIS. The role of geospatial technologies for investigating crime and providing evidence. Springer, Dordrecht

Falkner E, Dennis M (2002) Aerial mapping: methods and applications. Lewis, Boca Raton

Faqir R (2013) The use of technology of global positioning system (GPS) in Criminal investigation & right to privacy under the constitution and criminal legislations in Jordan: legal analysis study. Revue internationale de droit pénal 84:433–462

Ferguson AG (2021) Facial recognition and the fourth amendment. Minn Law Rev 105:1105–1207

Garapon A, Lassègue J (2018) Justice digitale: Révolution graphique et rupture anthropologique. Presses universitaires de France, Paris

Gless S (2020) AI in the courtroom: a comparative analysis of machine evidence in criminal trials. Georgetown J Int Law 51:195

Goldberg P, MacPhail R (2006) Practical and theoretical geoarchaeology. Blackwell Publishing, Malden

González-Cabañas J, Cuevas A, Cuevas R, Maier M (2021) Digital contact tracing: large-scale geolocation data as an alternative to bluetooth-based apps failure. Electronics 10(9):1093

Griffin T, Miller MK (2008) Child abduction, AMBER alert, and crime control theater. Crim Justice Rev 33(2):159–176

Hawelka B, Sitko I, Beinat E, Sobolevsky S, Kazakopoulos P, Ratti C (2014) Geo-located twitter as proxy for global mobility patterns. Cartogr Geogr Inf Sci 41(3):260–271

Heikkilä M (2021) European Parliament calls for a ban on facial recognition. Politico. www.politico.eu

Holson LM (2018) Is geotagging on Instagram ruining natural wonders? Some Say Yes. The New York Times. https://www.nytimes.com/2018/11/29/travel/instagram-geotagging-environ ment.html

Ignaccolo C (2021) Mapping practices for a cosmopolitan world. In: Schröder J, Carta M, Scaffidi F, Contato A (eds) Cosmopolitan Habitat. De Gruyter, Berlin, pp 246–251

Jeffery CR (1971) Crime prevention through environmental design. Am Behav Sci 14(4):598

Kahlaoui T (2018) Creating the Mediterranean: maps and the Islamic imagination. Brill, Leiden/Boston

Kerr OS (2009) The case for the third-party doctrine. Mich Law Rev 107(4):561–602

Kerr OS (2012) The mosaic theory of the fourth amendment. Mich Law Rev 111(3):311–354

Keyvanpour MR, Javideh M, Ebrahimi MR (2011) Detecting and investigating crime by means of data mining: a general crime matching framework. Proc Comput Sci 3:872–880

King M (2019) How mapping technology can help catch killers. ESRI Malaysia. esrimalaysia.com

Kumar A, Kumar S, Lal P, Saikia P, Srivastava PK, Petropoulos GP (2021) Introduction to GPS/GNSS technology. GPS and GNSS technology. Geosciences:3–20

Kurgan L, Cadora E (2006) Architecture and justice. www.c4sr.columbia.edu

La Selva P (2018) I fotogrammi di Google Earth sono prove documentali: dalla Cassazione Penale al T.A.R. Calabria. Ius in itinere. www.iusinitinere.it

La Vigne NG, Wartell J (eds) (1998) Crime mapping case studies: successes in the field, 2nd edn 2000. Police Executive Research Forum (PERF), Washington DC

LaFave W (2020) Search and seizure: a treatise on the fourth amendment, vol 6, 6th edn. Thomson Reuters/West, Eagan

Lemieux AM (2015) Geotagged photos: a useful tool for criminological research? Crime Sci 4:3

Levine N (2006) Crime mapping and the CrimeStat program. Geogr Anal 38(1):41–56

Lockwood E, Masters P (2021) Application of viewshed analysis and probability mapping for search area determination based on the moors murders on Saddleworth moor, the United Kingdom. J Forensic Sci 66(5):1770–1787

Longley PA et al (eds) (2015) Geographic information systems & science, 4th edn. Wiley, Hoboken

Lyon D (2018) The culture of surveillance. Polity Press, Cambridge (UK)

McFadden C (2017) Building a Solid Case: Forensic Mapping (and Ghost Clouds). Xyht. www. xyht.com

McKenna AT, Gaudion AC, Evans JL (2018) The role of satellites and smart devices: data surprises and security, privacy, and regulatory challenges. Penn State Law Rev 123:591

Militello E (2020) Criminal investigations on corporate liability: a comparative account on Italy and the United States. Pacini, Pisa

Nobles MR (2010) Using geographic information systems to study race, crime, and policing. In: Rice SK, White MD (eds) Race, ethnicity, and policing: new and essential readings. New York University Press, New York, pp 205–220

Panneck T (2019) Incognito mode is in the constitution note. Minn Law Rev 104:511–552

Quattrocolo S (2020) Artificial intelligence, computational modelling and criminal proceedings. A framework for a European legal discussion. Springer, Cham

Reichenbach H (1958) The philosophy of space and time. Dover Publications, New York

Robins A, Rountree J, Rountree N (2003) Learning and teaching programming: a review and discussion. Comput Sci Educ 13(2):137–172

Rodriguez Garzon S, Pöllabauer T, Zickau S, Küpper A (2019) Interactive design of geofences for proactive location-based services in smart cities. In: 2019 IEEE SmartWorld 1184–1187. ieeexplore.ieee.org

Rosner H-J (2017) "CrimeGIS". Geographische Informationssysteme in der Kriminologie. In: Kerner H-J, Kinzig H, Wulf R (eds) Kriminologie Und Strafvollzug. Institut für Kriminologie der Universität Tübingen, Tübingen

Roxin A, Gaber J, Wack M, Nait-Sidi-Moh A (2007) Survey of wireless geolocation techniques. In: 2007 IEEE Globecom workshops. IEEE, Washington, DC, pp 1–9

Saviano R, Tondo L (2021) Buried in concrete: how the mafia made a killing from the destruction of Italy's south. The Guardian. www.theguardian.com

Schlesinger SR (1977) Exclusionary injustice: the problem of illegally obtained evidence. Marcel Dekker, New York

Taslitz AE (2009) Reconstructing the fourth amendment. A history of search and seizure, 1789–1868. New York University Press, New York

Trorey LG (1952) Handbook of aerial mapping and photogrammetry. Cambridge University Press, Cambridge

Troshynski EI (2017) "Stalked by the state": GPS surveillance technology and sex offender parolees. Kriminologisches J 49(2):103–119

Turnbull LS, Hendrix EH, Dent BD (2000) Atlas of crime: mapping the criminal landscape. Oryx Press, Phoenix

Uttal DH (2000) Seeing the big picture: map use and the development of spatial cognition. Dev Sci 3(3):247–264

Vervaele J (2014) Surveillance and criminal investigation: blurring of thresholds and boundaries in the criminal justice system? In: Gutwirth S, Leenes R, De Hert P (eds) Reloading data protection: multidisciplinary insights and contemporary challenges. Springer, Cham, pp 115–128

Viswanath K, Basu A (2015) SafetiPin: an innovative mobile app to collect data on women's safety in Indian cities. Gend Dev 23(1):45–60

Wang F (2012) Why police and policing need GIS: an overview. Ann GIS 18(3):159–171

Weisburd D, Bernasco W, Bruinsma GJN (eds) (2009) Putting crime in its place. Units of analysis in geographic criminology. Springer, New York

Wilkins RG (1987) Defining the "reasonable expectation of privacy": an emerging tripartite analysis. Vanderbilt Law Rev 40:1077–1128

Williams S (2020) Data action: using data for public good. MIT Press, Cambridge

Wilson TH (2021) The mosaic theory's two steps: surveying carpenter in the lower courts. Tex Law Rev Online 99:155–182

Wolfson SM, Lease M (2011) Look before you leap: legal pitfalls of crowdsourcing. Proc Am Soc Inf Sci Technol 48(1):1–10

Yang L, Meng X, Zhang X (2011) SRTM DEM and its application advances. Int J Remote Sens 32(14):3875–3896

Završnik A (2021) Algorithmic justice: algorithms and big data in criminal justice settings. EU J Criminol 18(5):623–642

Zhang M (2021) You can have your home blurred for privacy in Google Street View photos. PetaPixel. www.petapixel.com

Zuboff S (2019) The age of surveillance capitalism: the fight for a human future at the new frontier of power. Public Affairs, New York

Big Data and Satellites: Between Safety of Airspace and Criminal Liability

Francesca Pellegrino

Abstract Every day, the surface of the Earth is observed and monitored by hundreds of artificial satellites operating in orbit at different altitudes and collecting very large quantities of heterogeneous data. The analysis and multi-purpose use of these data are among the great challanges in an increasingly digital society. Satellites can affect safety, security, cybersecurity and sustainable development of transport. The application of United Nations Outer Space Treaties is necessary to resolve issues of legal responsibility in that regard.

1 Introduction

This paper aims to provide an analysis of the legal framework of satellite data and their use for criminal purposes. The adverse impact of this illegal use (security) can affect both airspace and outer space safety.

After an introduction about the concept of safety, security and sustainable development of satellite navigation, the analysis focuses on relationship between satellites and airspace safety and later moves to criminal liability and cyberspace security in outer space.

2 A Brief Overview of the Use of Satellite Data

The use of telecommunication satellites has continued to increase since their first launch, in the 1960s.

F. Pellegrino (✉)
Law Department, University of Messina, Messina, Italy
e-mail: francesca.pellegrino@unime.it

© The Author(s), under exclusive license to Springer Nature Switzerland AG 2022   43
L. Bachmaier Winter, S. Ruggeri (eds.), *Investigating and Preventing Crime in the Digital Era*, Legal Studies in International, European and Comparative Criminal Law 7, https://doi.org/10.1007/978-3-031-13952-9_3

Every day, the surface of the Earth is observed and monitored by hundreds of artificial satellites operating at different altitudes, frequencies, registering changes related to land use, crop growth, floods, soil moisture etc.

Due to the increasing number of these satellites in orbit, very large quantities of heterogeneous data are collected.[1] In fact, satellites are the best instrument for providing telecommunications services, nationally and globally, thanks to their extraordinary data-storage capacity.

The processing and analysis of these very large data are among the great challenges in an increasingly digital society. This data is applicable in transportation, marine sciences, navy, agriculture, safety, security, healthcare, education, communications, forestry and is collected thanks to Earth Observation (EO) programmes. The European Union's Earth observation programme is called Copernicus.[2] Satellites included in this programme are among the world's largest producers of data in the world, especially for border/marine surveillance and external emergency management.

High-precision data are provided for the Galileo satellites. Galileo is the European Union's Global Navigation Satellite System (GNSS),[3] currently in progress, created by the European Union, through the European Space Agency (ESA)[4] and operated by the European Union Agency for the Space Programme (EUSPA)[5] for civil uses. The first Galileo test satellite (GIOVE-A)[6] was launched in 2004 and since 2010 Galileo satellites started transmitting their signals, relayed by ground transmitters, enabling many high-quality services.

---

[1] Re and Ruggeri (2007).

[2] Copernicus is the European Union's Earth Observation programme, coordinated and managed by the European Commission in partnership with the EU Member States, the European Space Agency (ESA) and EU agencies. It has been established by Regulation (EU) No 377/2014 of the European Parliament and of the Council of 3 April 2014, repealing Regulation (EU) No 911/2010. See Cinquepalmi (2019), pp. 63, 142 ff.

[3] Global Navigation Satellite System (GNSS) refers to a constellation of satellites providing signals from space that transmit positioning and timing data to receivers. According to the *Global Navigation Satellite System (GNSS) Manual* (Doc 9849) of ICAO, it is a key element of the Communications, Navigation, and Surveillance/Air Traffic Management (CNS/ATM) systems, as well as a foundation upon which States can deliver improved aeronautical navigation services. See Stipo (1997), pp. 673 ff.; Milde (2008), p. 201; Masutti (2009), pp. 37 ff.; Bassi (2009), pp. 903 ff.

[4] ESA is an intergovernmental organisation, established in 1975, composed of 22 Member States, dedicated to the exploration of space. See USA International Business Publications (ed) (2006); Orlandi (2014), pp. 23 ff.

[5] *EUSPA* ensures that Europe meets its GNSS objectives and that the public benefits from European GNSS. It also supports the development of applications based on Galileo, EGNOS, Copernicus etc.

[6] GIOVE-A (Galileo In-Orbit Validation Element-A) is the first element of the Galileo In-Orbit Validation phase. This pilot satellite marked the very first step towards Europe's new global navigation satellite system. See Re and Ruggeri (2007), pp. 291 ff.

Galileo started offering Early Operational Capability (EOC)[7] on 2016. Since 2020, there are 26 launched satellites in the constellation. Once this constellation reaches Full Operational Capability (FOC) it will consist of 30 satellites (including three active spare satellites), positioned in three circular Medium Earth Orbit (MEO)[8] planes, at an altitude of 23,000 km above the Earth. The full Galileo constellation is expected by 2022.

Satellite telecommunications can play a fundamental role to offer the secure and reliable connectivity required for safety related communications and connections, with a wide coverage, including oceanic areas, at high altitudes where ground-based systems are less effective or totally inactive.

The use of artificial satellites, in particular of Galileo satellites, allows all modes of transport to profit considerably from the implementation of autonomous on-board positioning systems. For example, to establish their exact position in the airspace, airplanes transmit a signal to a constellation of satellites. These coordinates provide a global flight tracking service and allow air traffic controllers to ensure safety and security in the skies.

Earth observation data collected via satellites are also used to monitor and assess the status of the natural environment. The application of satellite data in supporting natural risks, like fires, floods or storms, is well known.

Additionally, Earth observation satellites provide very important data on climate changes, taken from measurements of the movement or melting glaciers and other parameters.

For the time being, very few laws allow for the use of satellite data in a monitoring context under legislation. Despite this shortcoming, systematic archiving of satellite images can be of particular relevance for the legal systems. They could in theory also provide regulators or courts with accurate evidence not otherwise available.

The employment of these satellites affects safety, security and also cybersecurity.

If some satellite passes too near to others, the collision risk in the outer space is very relevant. When the approaching satellites are both manoeuvrable, coordination between them is essential. But when they are operated by agencies from different countries, the coordination can be very complex.

In addition, collisions with space debris[9] in low Earth orbit have become a hazard to satellites: there are millions of pieces of space junk floating throughout space at high speeds. Most orbital debris include human-generated objects, such as pieces of space craft, tiny flecks of paint from spacecrafts, parts of rockets, space objects that are no longer working or are the result of explosions in orbit.

---

[7] The *Early Operational Capability* (*EOC*) milestone marks the *first operational* deployment of the system.

[8] Medium Earth Orbit comprises a wide range of orbits anywhere between LEO and GEO. It is used by a variety of satellites with many different applications.

[9] Ancis (2005), p. 913; Pellegrino (2018), pp. 117 ff.

Therefore, the ESA is developing a collision avoidance system aimed to prevent imminent collisions and reduce the risk of incidents.

In the security field, law enforcement agencies or authorities can benefit from the use of satellites not only in law enforcement actions, but also for logistical purposes. In fact, thanks to satellite surveillance, these bodies can track the movements of suspected criminals on the ground, at sea and in the sky and identify illegal trafficking of goods and smuggling of human beings.

There are currently no information security standards to protect data gathered by satellites and no governing body to regulate and ensure them from cyberattacks. Without common standards, satellites, which are just computer-controlled machines, can be easily hacked. If hackers took control of the Big Data collected by these satellites, the consequences could be catastrophic.

Common standard at international level could be developed and adopted in the future—something which should be welcomed—but it is not easy to enforce them between States, also because there are differences between civil and common law systems.

3   The Concept of Safety, Security and Sustainable Development of Satellite Navigation

In the Italian common language, only the term '*sicurezza*' is used to refer to all measures and practices taken to preserve the life, health, and bodily integrity of individuals. On the contrary, two different terms, safety and security, are used in the English language. But there is more: a third meaning of safety, considered the new safety frontier, is the "sustainable development".

In the field of transport, safety refers to the measures and rules aimed to prevent accidents and incidents involving ships, aircrafts, cars, trains and artificial satellites, against unintended threats. But considering that, in this sector, a zero-incident condition is not attainable for hazards that cannot be eliminated, safety means freedom from "unacceptable risk". This objective can be achieved by the man-machine-environment system, a method to identify the causes of accidents, based on close relationship between human beings, work place/work environment and machines.

As in airspace, also in outer space, it is necessary to ensure that there are no close approaches between satellites and between them and other space objects. Measures to prevent such collisions and to avoid accidents and incidents are included in the concept of safety.

Satellite communications, at the same time, allow to improve safety and security on the ground and, in particular, to ensure safe and secure Air Traffic Management both in airspace and in outer space.

On the contrary, security refers to all the actions taken to protect navigation and transport (at sea, in air and in outer space) against acts of unlawful interference, by a combination of measures and (human and material) resources.

After the 11 September attacks,[10] the category of unlawful acts also includes the use of an aircraft—or other means of transport or space object—as weapons of mass destruction.

In outer space, artificial satellites and other space objects are required to observe a general prohibition on the placement of weapons of mass destruction in this space.

In fact, according to Article IV of the 1967 Outer Space Treaty (OST) on *"Principles Governing the Activities of States in the Exploration and Use of Outer Space, including the Moon and Other Celestial Bodies"*,[11] States Parties undertook *"not to place in orbit around the Earth any objects carrying nuclear weapons or any other kinds of weapons of mass destruction, install such weapons on celestial bodies, or station such weapons in outer space in any other manner"*.[12]

Cybersecurity, as a special branch of security, includes all measures taken to protect a computer system against unauthorized access/attack, cybercrime or other criminal use. Therefore, it includes all measures taken to keep electronic information confidential and safe from damage or theft or cyberattacks that use disguised email as a weapon (phishing, hacking and spoofing).[13]

The third meaning of safety refers to the sustainable development. The traditional definition[14] of sustainable development is contained in the United Nations document called "Our common future" (also called *Brundtland Report*), according to which it is a new development model that meets the needs of the current generations, without compromising the ability of future generations to meet their own needs (principle of intergenerational equity). In fact, the most significant aspect of sustainability is planning for the next generations.

This definition has been criticized, because it is only focused upon human requirements, without regard to the needs of all living species.

Actually, this is no single accepted definition of sustainability at international level. Another well-known definition is based on the balance of three different dimensions (or pillars): economic, social and environmental. This defining framework has been lastly maintained till today and accepted by the 2030 Agenda for

---

[10] *Inter alia*, see Hampton (2011).

[11] The *London, Moscow* and Washington Treaty was opened for signature by the three depository Governments (the Russian Federation, the United Kingdom and the United States of America) in January 1967, and entered into force in October 1967. See Cheng (2004); Marchisio (2018), pp. 205 ff.

[12] For a commentary, see Froehlich (2017), pp. 39 ff. See also Reynolds and Merges (1998).

[13] Phishing is where scammers will send you emails that try to get sensitive information out of you. Hacking means that a hacker has actually gained full access to your e-mail account. Spoofing is when someone makes an email appear as if it was sent from somewhere, it wasn't like your own email address. Pellegrino (2009), pp. 40 ff.

[14] Pellegrino (2013), p. 13 ff.; Borowy (2014), pp. 1 ff.

Sustainable Development,[15] which bothered to identify and classify the objectives of sustainable development (goals).[16]

Verily, the use of satellite data is a powerful tool for sustainable development purposes in outer space, in airspace, at sea and on the ground.

On the one hand, outer space is itself a natural environment that should not be polluted[17] and used by States, except in compliance with a strict implementation of the rules. On the other, for example, artificial satellites are seen as a means of fighting deforestation or climate change on Earth.

4 The International Legal Regime of the Geostationary Orbit and Satellite Telecommunications

Most of telecommunication satellites are placed in geostationary orbit (GEO),[18] a circular orbit around the Earth having a period of revolution of 24 h.

It is estimated that there are currently around 4450 satellites in this orbit.[19] This situation indicates the high degree of saturation of the Earth's orbit. It is a permanent but limited resource. Therefore, its unlimited use is not possible.

Initially, the only rule applicable to this orbit was based on a "first-come, first-served" technique (corresponding to the Roman Law principle "*prior in tempore, potior in iure*") that allowed a *de facto* appropriation by the first-comers, mostly the developed countries. This *de facto* appropriation is allowed by international space law[20] and international telecommunications law.

As regarding the legal regime,[21] considerable disagreements, however, arose between those countries who considered the geostationary orbit an integral part of

---

[15] The 2030 Agenda for Sustainable Development was adopted by the U.N. General Assembly on 25 September 2015 (Resolution 70/1). Leal Filho and Tortato (2019).

[16] It is focused around achieving 17 goals (including water, energy, urbanization, climate, oceans, transport, science and technology) to provide a shared blueprint for peace and prosperity for people and the planet. For a commentary, see Kanie and Biermann (2017); Nhamo et al. (2021), pp. 3 ff.

[17] According to Article I of the OST Treaty: "*The exploration and use of outer space, including the moon and other celestial bodies, shall be carried out for the benefit and in the interests of all countries [...] Outer space, including the moon and other celestial bodies, shall be free for exploration and use by all States without discrimination of any kind, on a basis of equality and in accordance with international law, and there shall be free access to all areas of celestial bodies*". For a commentary, see Tan (2000), pp. 177 ff.

[18] In particular, it is a circular orbit above the equatorial plane in which the period of a satellite's sidereal revolution is equal to the period of sidereal rotation of earth and the satellite moves in the same direction of Earth's rotation. See Ramakrishnan (2019).

[19] Source: *Space Foundation (Italic)*- 2021.

[20] Apfel (1988).

[21] Leanza (2011), pp. 653 ff.

outer space,[22] with consequent applicability of cosmic law rules,[23] and those who excluded this legal classification, considering it as falling within state sovereignty.[24]

According to the principle of freedom of space, as enshrined in the Outer Space Treaty, both orbits and frequencies [25] are considered *res communis*, i.e. common heritage of mankind. This legal nature in itself precludes any sovereignty acquirement by States.[26]

In particular, Article 1 of this Treaty stresses that the exploration and use of outer space *"shall be carried out for the benefit and in the interests of all countries, irrespective of their degree of economic or scientific development, and shall be the province of all mankind"*. It also means freedom of scientific investigation in outer space.

According to Article II of the OST, outer space, including the Moon and other celestial bodies, *"is not subject to national appropriation by claim of sovereignty, by means of use or occupation, or by any other means"*.

In other words, the exploration and use of outer space are not within the state jurisdiction.[27]

In respect to liability for outer space activities,[28] Article VI of the Outer Space Treaty imposes State responsibility for all national activities in outer space and for ensuring that all activities in outer space comply with the Treaty provisions.

Article VI of the same Treaty, therefore, imposes responsibility on each State for space traffic management involving the space activities of its nationals.

The scope of State responsibility for space traffic management is deduced from Article VII of the Outer Space Treaty. The latter reads as follows: *"Each State Party to the Treaty that launches or procures the launching of an object into outer space, including the Moon and other celestial bodies, and each State Party from whose territory or facility an object is launched, is internationally liable for damage to another State Party to the Treaty or to its natural or juridical persons by such object or its component parts on the Earth, in air space or in outer space, including the Moon and other celestial bodies"*.[29]

According to Article VIII of the OST, the State of registry of the object launched into outer space (manned space object)[30] shall retain jurisdiction and control over such object or element and over any persons thereof, while it is in outer space or on a celestial body, or in the high seas, or in another place beyond the limits of the jurisdiction of any State.

---

[22] Vereshchetin (2006).

[23] Durante (1993); Cheng (1997); Lyall and Larsen (2009).

[24] See Oduntan (2012), p. 174 ff.

[25] Masson-Zwaan (2015), pp. 59 ff. See Oberst (2010).

[26] Wassenberg (1991).

[27] Csabafi (1971).

[28] Böckstiegel(1987); Ravillon (2004).

[29] Spada (1983), pp. 699 ff.; Pedrazzi (2008).

[30] Gorbie (1982), pp. 81 ff.; Hobe (2007).

Other rules of cosmic law are contained in the following treaties: Agreement on the Rescue of Astronauts, the Return of Astronauts and the Return of Objects Launched into Outer Space (1968);[31] Convention on International Liability for Damage Caused by Space Objects (1972);[32] Convention on Registration of Objects Launched into Outer Space (1976);[33] Agreement Governing the Activities of States on the Moon and Other Celestial Bodies (1979).[34]

In particular, the Rescue Agreement introduced measures to recover fallen space objects, on the basis of an obligation which comes under the launching State.

Subsequently, the above-mentioned Liability Convention introduced a two-tier liability system on each launching State. On the one hand, a strict liability for damage caused by its space object on the surface of the Earth or to aircraft in flight (Article II). On the other hand, a fault-based liability for damages caused into outer space to other space objects,[35] including persons and/or property on board (Article III).

Later, the Registration Convention introduced a central register of objects launched into outer space, established and maintained, on a mandatory basis, by the Secretary-General.

The Moon Agreement, reaffirming the prohibition of all military use of celestial bodies, stated that the latter represent the common heritage of mankind.[36]

In addition to the aforementioned treaties, which constitute the legal framework (*Corpus Juris spatialis*) for space activities, the rules of cosmic law are supplemented by more specific rules of international telecommunications law, in particular by the 1973 International Telecommunication Convention (Málaga-Torremolinos Convention)[37] on the rational use of the radio frequency spectrum and the GEO. It defines geostationary satellite orbit and frequency bands for satellite communications as limited natural resources.[38] Orbit and radio waves should be used respecting the freedom of the other States.

In this regard, it is useful to refer to Article 33 of Málaga Convention, according to which: "*In using frequency bands for space radio services Members shall bear in*

---

[31] The Agreement entered into force in December 1968. Golda (1993), pp. 198 ff.; Andem (1998); Lafferranderie and Marchisio (2011).

[32] It entered into force on 1 September 1972. See De Sena (1990), p. 294 ff.; Bender (1997).

[33] The Registration Agreement entered into force on 15 September 1976.

[34] The Moon Agreement entered into force in July 1984. For a commentary, see Gestri (1989), p. 502 ff.; von der Dunk (2007), pp. 91 ff.; Gangale (2008), pp. 1 ss.; Hofmann (2010); Li (2010); Tanoguchi (2010).

[35] Crisafulli (89-92/1984), pp. 44 ff.

[36] Buxton (2004), pp. 689 ff.

[37] The Málaga-Torremolinos Convention, signed on 25 October 1973, entered into force on January 1, 1975. For a commentary, see Fernandez-Shaw (1974), pp. 25, 2, 21 ff. See also Smith (1987), pp. 12, 285 ff.; Thompson (1996), pp. 280 ff.

[38] The "orbit/spectrum resource" depends on whether satellites are assigned both a space on the geostationary orbit and a frequency on the radio spectrum. For updates, see Rothblatt (1982), pp. 56 ff.

mind that radio frequencies and the geostationary satellite orbit are limited natural resources, that they must be used efficiently and economically so that countries or groups of countries may have equitable access to both in conformity with the provisions of the Radio Regulations according to their needs and the technical facilities at their disposal".

The international community also felt the need to entrust regulation, planning and coordination of the geostationary orbit and radio frequencies to the International Telecommunication Union (ITU),[39] a specialized agency of the United Nations, responsible for all matters related to information and communication technologies.

The subsequent World Administrative Radio Conference for the Planning of the Broadcasting-Satellite Service (WARC SAT-77)[40] made it compulsory to register radio frequencies, in accordance with frequency allotment and assignment plans, developed by the ITU.

Therefore, the opinion expressed at the UN level by the equatorial countries— embodied in the Bogotà Declaration of 3 December 1976[41]—that the segments of geostationary orbit would be part of the territory over which equatorial States exercise their national sovereignty, has been ignored.

In fact, the Nairobi Convention of 6 November 1982,[42] which repealed the previous Málaga-Torremolinos Convention, reaffirmed the qualification of the geostationary orbit (and relative frequency bands) as limited natural resources. Therefore, the latter must be used taking into account the interests of all States, especially developing countries, intended to use them in the future.

In this perspective, the ITU has developed a plan to allow any country equitable access[43] to the aforementioned resources, enabling each State to locate at least one satellite in the GEO orbit, in addition to the relative frequency band. Obviously, this is an exception to the traditional allocation rule "first-come first-served",[44] allowing all States (or groups of States) the opportunity to meet their needs.

---

[39] ITU is a specialized agency of the United Nations, based in Geneva, which is responsible for defining standards in telecommunications and the use of radio waves. For the ITU history, see Balbi and Fickers (2020).

[40] This Conference took place in Geneva, in 1977. The subsequent 1979 World Administrative Radio Conference (WARC-79) remains one of the most significant conferences in ITU history. Most of the decisions taken at WARC-79 are still applicable, including regulation of the world's radio spectrum and satellite industry and standards that improve operation through cooperation. For updates, see Smith (1985), pp. 229 ff.; Smith (1985–1986), p. 227.

[41] By the *Declaration* of the First Meeting of Equatorial Countries (*Bogotá Declaration*), seven equatorial countries (Colombia, the Republic of Congo, Ecuador, Indonesia, Kenya, Uganda and Zaire) affirmed their sovereignty over the portion of geostationary orbit over their territory. An eighth State, Brazil, has signed the Bogotá Declaration as an observer. Gabon and Somalia joined in later.

[42] One of the major objectives of this Conference was the revision of the International Telecommunication Convention.

[43] Varmer (1987), pp. 175 ff.

[44] Finch (1986), p. 7, 788.

In the light of this legal evolution, it seems no longer doubtful that geostationary orbit has to be considered an integral part of outer space, having the nature of *"res communis omnim"*, with the consequent obligation for all States no to prevent others countries to use it at the same time.

Other rules are enshrined in most recent international agreements, such as the International Space Station Intergovernmental Agreement (IGA), signed on 29 January 1998.[45] According to Article 1 of this agreement, its purpose is to ensure: *"a long term international co-operative framework on the basis of genuine partnership, for the detailed design, development, operation, and utilization of a permanently inhabited civil Space Station for peaceful purposes, in accordance with international law"*.

As regards secondary legislation, the ITU Radio Regulations[46] states that radio frequencies and any associated orbits must be used *"rationally, efficiently and economically, [..] so that countries or groups of countries may have equitable access to those orbits and frequencies, taking into account the special needs of the developing countries and the geographical situation of particular countries"*.

Under this Regulation, the principle "first-come, first-served" has been replaced by the principle of equal and fair access[47] to these resources and rational use of the radio-frequency spectrum and geostationary satellite orbits.

Within this legal framework, mention has to be made to the role of soft law norms, such as the principles of the United Nations Committee on the Peaceful Uses of Outer Space (COPUOS),[48] contained in the following documents: International Direct Television Broadcasting, adopted in 1982,[49] Remote Sensing Principles, adopted in 1986,[50] Use of Nuclear Power Sources in Outer Space, adopted in 1992,[51] International Cooperation in the Exploration and Use of Outer Space for the Benefit and in the Interest of All States, Taking into Particular Account the Needs of Developing Countries, international cooperation in the exploration and use of Space, with particular reference to the needs of developing countries, adopted in 1996.[52]

---

[45] Agreement signed at Washington by the fifteen governments involved in the Space Station project and entered into force in January 29, 1998.

[46] The 2020 edition of the ITU Radio Regulations entered into force on 1 January 2021.

[47] See Petroni (2016), pp. 127 ff.

[48] The *COPUOS* was set up by the General Assembly in 1959 to govern the exploration and use of space for the benefit of all humanity: for peace, security and development. Gorbiel (1984), p. 206.

[49] UN Resolution RES 37/92 (*"Principles Governing the Use by States of Artificial Earth Satellites for International Direct Television Broadcasting"*), 1982.

[50] UN Resolution RES 41/65 (*"Principles relating to remote sensing of the Earth from outer space"*), 1986.

[51] UN Resolution RES 47/68 (*"Principles Relevant to the Use of Nuclear Power Sources in Outer Space"*), 1992.

[52] General Assembly Resolution A/RES/51/122 (*"Declaration on International Cooperation in the Exploration and Use of Outer Space for the Benefit and in the Interest of All States, Taking into Particular Account the Needs of Developing Countries"*), General Assembly 51st session, 1996.

5   Relationship Between Satellites and Airspace Safety

There is a very close relationship between the use of artificial satellites and airspace safety. Satellite communications have an important role to play in the ATM (Air Traffic Management) infrastructure both in Europe and in the wider world. First of all, ATM can benefit from low Earth orbit satellites, while providing high bandwidth and faster data transfer speed. Satellite communications improve Air Traffic Services (ATS) over congested continental areas and remote areas, allowing safer, more efficient, and sustainable traffic management operations.

In fact, by using satellite-based VHF systems providing voice and datalink services, air traffic controllers can communicate with aircraft flying in oceanic and remote airspace at the same frequency as with aircraft flying in continental airspace.

Satellite Data-Link Services (DLS),[53] already used for oceanic and remote regions, can also be used anywhere. Thanks to satellite communications, controllers are able to reduce the minimum separation between aircraft, ensuring safety, optimizing traffic and so reducing CO_2 emissions.

Furthermore, the continuous increase of traffic for both general aviation and new domains (e.g. UAVs)[54] represents a major challenge for ATM systems, required to manage a large amount of data and, at the same time, to ensure an improved level of both safety and security, including environmental protection. These goals are pursued by the Single European Sky (SES),[55] a European Commission initiative that seeks to reform the European air traffic management system through a series of actions carried out also on a technological level.

---

[53] Datalink services (DLS) are regulated by Commission Regulation (EC) No. 29/2009 of 16 January 2009 laying down requirements on data link services for the Single *European* Sky.

[54] See Masutti (2007), pp. 783 ff.; Franchi (2010), pp. 732 ff. and 1213 ff.; La Torre (2012), pp. 553 ff.

[55] The Single European Sky (*SES*) is an ambitious initiative launched by the European Commission in 2004 to reform the architecture of European Air Traffic Management (ATM) system. Its aim is to reduce the cost of air traffic service provision and increasing Europe's capacity to meet forecast growth in demand for air traffic. For the creation of a SES, the European Commission submitted three legislative packages. The first SES package includes SES Framework Regulation (EC) No. 549/2004 (laying down the framework for the creation of the SES), Air Navigation Services Regulation (EC) No. 550/2004 (on the provision of air navigation services for the SES), Airspace Regulation (EC) No. 551/2004 (on the organisation and use of the airspace in the SES), Interoperability Regulation (EC) No. 552/2004 (on the interoperability of the European Air Traffic Management network). The second package (SES II) is composed of Regulation (EC) No. 1070/2009 amending SES I Regulations (EC) No. 549/2004, (EC) No. 550/2004, (EC); No. 551/2004 and (EC) No. 552/2004 to improve the performance and sustainability of the European aviation transport system. The third Package (SES II+) is composed of a proposal for a Regulation of the European Parliament and of the Council on the implementation of the Single European Sky (recast) and Proposal for a Regulation of the European Parliament and of the Council amending Regulation (EU) 2018/1139 as regards the capacity of the European Union Aviation Safety Agency to act as Performance Review Body of the Single European Sky. See Crespo (2011); Trovò (2011), p. 24; Hartman and Boscoianu (2015), pp. 97 ff.

In this context, the optimisation of information and communications technologies are particularly relevant for airport capacity, safety, performance, environmental impact, efficiency and quality of service.

The project "SESAR" is one of the most ambitious modernisation projects, launched by the European Union with the aim to contribute to the implementation of the Single European Sky.

On 7 December 2015, the European Commission published a comprehensive European Aviation Strategy[56] for implementing a new Air Traffic Management concept, including administrative, operational and technical reach and for contributing to safer, shorter, cleaner and cheaper flights.

To support such an ambitious objective, Single European Sky ATM Research (SESAR) programme[57] has been introduced to improve ATM performance by modernising and harmonising its technological systems within Europe and develop the ATM Master Plan,[58] which identifies the essential operational and technological changes required to achieve improvements in terms of safety and security, operational efficiency and capacity.

In particular, during the flight, data is being exchanged between cockpit crew, Air Operations Center (AOC) and ATC (Air Traffic Control)/ATFM (Air Traffic Flow Management).[59] This exchange of information allows deviation in the flight path. A planned flight trajectory can experience changes during the flight, due to weather-related problems, military airspace block or other constraints and restrictions.

But the current exchange of data is based on an old flight plan system that contains numerous shortcomings, such as no automated flight plan updates. In addition, to address growing traffic, increasing operational efficiency and improving safety standards,[60] new instruments are needed.

To this end, SESAR has recognised a technological modernisation of the air-ground/air-traffic service (ATS) datalink as an essential stage towards Trajectory Based Operations (TBO).[61] Through TBO, flight plans will be continually updated during flight to maintain an optimal trajectory to destination, allowing air traffic

---

[56] Communication from the Commission to the European Parliament, the Council, the European Economic and Social Committee and the Committee of the Regions. *An Aviation Strategy for Europe*—Brussels, 7.12.2015 COM (2015) 598 final.

[57] *Single European Sky ATM Research (SESAR)* is a collaborative project to completely overhaul European airspace and its air traffic management (ATM). Ingratoci (2009), pp. 485 ff.

[58] European ATM Master Plan Digitalising Europe's Aviation Infrastructure, edition 2020. It is the main planning tool for ATM modernisation across Europe and defines the development and deployment priorities needed to deliver the Single European Sky ATM Research (SESAR) vision.

[59] ATFM is the regulation of air traffic in order to avoid exceeding airport or air traffic control capacity in handling traffic, and to ensure that available capacity is used efficiently.

[60] Pelton and Jakhu (2010).

[61] Trajectory Based Operations (TBO) is an air traffic management (ATM) concept that enhances strategic planning of aircraft flows to reduce capacity-to-demand imbalances in the National Airspace System (NAS), and provides tools to air traffic management personnel and controllers to help expedite aircraft movement between origin and destination.

control to offer better routes and maximize airport and airspace capacity. The combined effect will be less fuel burn, lower CO_2 emissions, reduced delays.

Without the satellite system, the air traffic service would be blind.

6 Criminal Liability in Outer Space

The first mention of criminal liability in an outer space environment can be found in the Draft Convention on Manned Space Flight,[62] which calls for principles of liability and responsibility laid down in the OST and the Rescue Agreement. In particular, Article III of the draft Convention gives jurisdiction in relation to a manned space object to the State of registry, while Article IV devolves responsibility for the spacecraft and all persons onboard to the commander. In turn, all members of the crew are accountable to the Director of Manned Space Flight Operations in charge. By this measure, the draft Convention skillfully and unequivocally identifies the 'chain of command'.[63]

In addition, this document makes clear that criminal conduct on aircraft under international air law can also provide a useful model for future space law initiatives, especially in the field of space tourism. Nevertheless, in the event of serious crimes committed during a long duration spaceflight, the approach followed by the draft Convention on Manned Space Flight would provide greater protection both for the crew and the defendant's rights.

For historical and political reasons, criminal behaviors on aircraft were focused on hijacking, sabotage, unlawful seizure of aircraft and terrorism attack. The concept of security was already included in the 1944 Chicago Convention[64] and, in particular, in Annex 17[65] to the same instrument, but was later developed by other conventions.

---

[62] Draft Convention on Manned Space Flight (1990), elaborated by the Institute for Air and Space Law, Cologne University; the Institute of State and Law, Academy of Sciences of the USSR; the Research and Study of Space Law and Policy Center, University of Mississippi. For a commentary, see Böckstiegel (1992), pp. 7 ff.

[63] The chain of command is the formal line of authority, communication, and responsibility/accountability within an organization. It lays out a company's lines of authority and decision-making power. By utilizing this chain, the principle of unity of command is maintained. See Borkowski (2011).

[64] Convention on International Civil Aviation (also known as *Chicago Convention*) was signed on 7 December 1944 by 52 States and went into effect on April 4, 1947. See Kehrer (2019), pp. 30, 178 ff.

[65] In fact, Annex 17 to the Convention on International Civil Aviation contains Standards and Recommended Practices (SARPs) on *Security—Safeguarding International Civil Aviation against Acts of Unlawful Interference*. SARPs for international aviation security were first adopted by the ICAO Council in March 1974. See Abeyratne (1997), pp. 245 ff.

The 1963 Tokyo Convention[66] applies to offences and certain other acts committed on board a civil aircraft. According to this international text, the commander may exercise the power to disembark a person if he has good reason to believe that this person has committed, or is about to commit, an act of unlawful interference and if this measure is necessary to protect the security of the aircraft or of persons or property on board, or to maintain the order and discipline (Article 12).

The Tokyo Convention has been improved by other international treaties, such as the 1970 Hague Convention for the Suppression of Unlawful Seizure[67] and the 1971 Montreal Convention for the Suppression of Unlawful Acts Against the Safety of Civil Aviation.[68]

Certainly, there are difficulties to simply apply these international rules to space activities, such as space tourism, considering that the above-mentioned conventions have been elaborated having exclusive regard to civil aviation and aircraft. In addition, the concepts of sovereignty and allocation of liability, that are applicable to international space law, are very different from those adopted in aviation law. Therefore, it is not easy to propose a wide interpretation or amendments of these conventions to cover activities in outer space.

Other rules on criminal liability derive from the specific legal framework regulating the International Space Station (ISS).[69] a modular (habitable) space station, located in Low Earth Orbit (LEO).[70] The ISS has been established by means of an Intergovernmental Agreement (IGA)[71] which contains specific provisions relating to crimes committed onboard the station (Article 22). In contrast to the Outer Space Treaty and the above-mentioned Draft Convention, the IGA applies the criminal rules of the State of the astronaut's nationality.

---

[66] The Convention on *Offences and Certain Other Acts Committed on Board Aircraft*, commonly called the Tokyo Convention, is an international Treaty, concluded at Tokyo on 14 September 1963. It entered into force on 4 December 1969. See Jacchia (1969).

[67] The Convention for the Suppression of Unlawful Seizure of Aircraft (Hague Hijacking Convention) was adopted on 10 March 1988 end entered into force on 1 March 1992. See Poulantzas (1971), pp. 25 ff.

[68] Signed at Montreal on 23 September 1971. It came into force on 26 January 1973. See Crivellaro (1972), p. 13.

[69] The International Space Station is a co-operative programme between Europe, the United States, Russia, Canada and Japan for the joint development, operation and utilisation of a permanently inhabited Space Station in low Earth orbit. It is a multinational collaborative project involving five participating space agencies: NASA (United States), Roscosmos (Russia), JAXA (Japan), ESA (Europe) and CSA (Canada). See Panella (1991), p. 195 ss.

[70] Low Earth orbit (LEO) is an orbit that is relatively close to Earth's surface. It is normally at an altitude of less than 1000 km above Earth.

[71] It is an international Treaty signed on 29 January 1998 by the fifteen governments involved in the Space Station project. This key government-level document establishes "*a long term international co-operative framework, on the basis of genuine partnership, for the detailed design, development, operation, and utilisation of a permanently inhabited civil Space Station for peaceful purposes, in accordance with international law*" (Article 1). See Benkö et al. (1993), p. 233; Böckstiegel (2001); Benkö and Schrogl (2005).

The second paragraph of Article 22 of the IGA provides that the States signatory to this Agreement may exercise criminal jurisdiction over personnel on any flight element in orbit when they are their respective nationals. This means that if an Italian commits a crime against a French astronaut in a module that was registered to Japan, the Italian criminal law would be applicable, and Italy would have responsibility for criminal jurisdiction.

The same paragraph specifies that prosecution involves any misconduct that *"(a) affects the life or safety of a national of another Partner State or (b) occurs in or on, or causes damage to the flight element of another party"*.

In addition, there is a separate Code of Conduct for the International Space Station Crew (ISS CCoC).[72] applicable to all ISS crewmembers from the time they are assigned to the station by the competent astronaut management body.

This Code establishes a clear chain of command on-orbit, close relationships between ground and on-orbit management, and provides the ISS commander with specific authority and responsibility to enforce safety, security and crew rescue procedures. A large number of regulations, that cover each stage of the mission, are also binding for the individual crewmember.

This Code is supported by a number of individual policies. Cooperating agencies recognise that their astronauts' conduct may be subject to control not only by their own personnel policy, but also by rules developed by the ISS partnership.

The challenges of regulating crew conduct differ depending on the nature of the mission. In the field of space tourism, the problem is how to manage a large number of people with different temperaments, who are in space for a short time and for recreational reasons.

The administration of justice on long time spaceflight and interplanetary missions is obviously more complicated and could have serious impact upon the crew and the mission's success.

The issue of criminality in outer space must be addressed proactively *(ex ante)* as part of the planning stage of an interplanetary mission, and not managing reactively *(ex post)* an event that could adversely affect the mission and maybe even the lives of the crew.

---

[72]This Code of Conduct is part of the Electronic Code of Federal Regulations (e-CFR), Title 14—Aeronautics and Space, Chapter V—National Aeronautics and Space Administration, part 1214—Space Flight, Subpart 1214.4—International Space Station Crew, paragraph 1214.403 *Code of Conduct for the International Space Station Crew*. It sets forth minimum standards for NASA-provided International Space Station crewmembers.

7 Cyberspace Security Legal Framework and Outer Space

In recent times, modern society has become dependent on new technological and digital domains. Essential systems—such as air and maritime transport, weather monitoring, communications, defence—rely on space infrastructure, including satellites, data links and ground stations.

Space operations are totally dependent on cyberspace and the very sophisticated space systems are attractive for hackers. As any other digitized infrastructure, also satellites and other space-based objects are vulnerable to cyberattacks. Moreover, some space systems are old, created before cybersecurity became a priority.

Due to the close relationship between space activities and cyberspace since access to both outer space and cyberspace is made possible only through the development of technology, space law can be used as a model to build a mandatory legal system for cyberspace.

Nevertheless, regulation in cyberspace is still lacking, especially at international level. Few national space legislations have expressly addressed the need to meet cybersecurity requirements. Hence, lacking express cybersecurity requirements enshrined in both international and national laws, it would seem that no cybersecurity obligations would directly apply to space actors. Therefore, national and international recommendations and guidelines (*soft law* instruments) currently mainly represent the legal framework for coordinating bodies of both areas.

The situation is different at the European level. Although the Lisbon Treaty introduced a specific and shared competence of the EU for space under Article 189, paragraph 2 of the TFEU, the EU cannot harmonize the laws and regulations of the Member States when it comes to space activities ("*excluding any harmonisation of the laws and regulations of the Member States*"). Indeed, even though the recent Regulation (EU) 2021/696 of 28 April 2021 (EU Space Programme Regulation)[73] addresses the issue of cybersecurity, it deals only with relation to the EU programmes Galileo, EGNOS, Copernicus etc.

However, changes have been made to the EU cybersecurity regulatory framework with direct impact to the space sector, thanks to a directive, a legislative act much more flexible than regulation, since it sets out a goal that all EU Member States must achieve. Directive (EU) 2016/1148[74] is the first step of EU-wide cybersecurity legislation towards the creation of a common perspective in the Union in this sector. It introduces measures for a high common level of security of Networks and Information Systems (NIS) across all EU Countries.

---

[73] Regulation (EU) 2021/696 of the European Parliament and of the Council of 28 April 2021 establishing the Union Space Programme and the European Union Agency for the Space Programme and repealing Regulations (EU) No 912/2010, (EU) No 1285/2013 and (EU) No 377/2014 and Decision No 541/2014/EU (*OJ L 170, 12.5.2021, p. 69–148*).

[74] Directive (EU) 2016/1148 of the European Parliament and of the Council of 6 July 2016 concerning measures for a high common level of security of network and information systems across the Union (*OJ L 194, 19.7.2016, p. 1–30*). For a commentary, Sabella (2017), pp. 139 ff.; Salamone (2017), pp. 69 ff.

The reliability and security of networks and information systems are essential to economic and societal activities and, in particular, to the functioning of the internal market, but the existing capabilities are insufficient to ensure a high level of security.

This Directive thus attempts to increase cyber resilience by forcing the EU States to adopt national cybersecurity strategies and designate their national authorities for cybersecurity. In particular, Member States are required

> to increase their preparedness and improve their cooperation with each other, and by requiring operators of critical infrastructures, such as energy, transport, and key providers of information society services (e-commerce platforms, social networks, etc), as well as public administrations to adopt appropriate steps to manage security risks and report serious incidents to the national competent authorities.[75]

This legal framework not only requires compliance with certain security requirements, but also introduces an obligation to notify incidents with a relevant impact on the networks and information systems of the public administration entities, critical infrastructure operators, essential services operators and digital service providers, considering that security incidents have an increasing impact and frequency and might have serious consequences on the regular functioning of the society and cause damages to human life.

The NIS Directive has also indicated the specific sectors concerned by these provisions and required the Member States to identify the Operators of Essential Services (OESs) for each area.

Another type of actors is the Digital Service Providers (DSPs), namely cloud computing service, online marketplace and online search engines. Both entities are forced to reach a certain level of cybersecurity and report any incident, but the difference between OESs and DSPs have not been clarified in the defining provisions.

Another important measure introduced by the NIS Directive consists of a system of information-sharing and incident-reporting based on the national Computer Security Incident Response Team (CSIRT),[76] coordinated by the European Network and Information Security Agency (ENISA)[77] and the newly founded Cooperation Group.

---

[75] So reads the Explanatory Memorandum *Accompanying the* Proposal for a Directive of the European Parliament and of the Council concerning measures to ensure a high common level of network and information security across the Union—COM/2013/048 final - 2013/0027 (COD).

[76] CSIRT (Computer Security Incident Response Team) is the national structure responsible for monitoring, intercepting, analyzing and responding to cyber threats. For more details, *it is worthwhile to mention Handbook for Computer Security Incident Response Teams (CSIRTs)*, a document that describes how CSIRTs interact with other organizations and manage sensitive information. In addition, operational and technical issues are addressed, such as security, equipment and staffing considerations.

[77] The European Network and Information Security Agency (ENISA) is a EU Agency that provides practical advice and solutions for the public and private sector in EU Member States and for the EU institutions. In particular, it assists EU countries in the development of National Cyber Security Strategies. It is at the heart of a pan-European collaboration network of CSIRTs.

With regard to sanctions, there is no distinction between the public and private persons, considering that all must be subject to penalties in case of very serious infringements.

By the subsequent Regulation (EU) 2019/881[78] (Cybersecurity Act), the ENISA has acquired a strategic role in promoting cybersecurity in the Union, in particular by helping the Member States to implement the NIS Directive. Subsequently, the COVID-19 crisis has accelerated the processes of digitalization of our society. It follows that the creation of a safe and secure European digital environment is now imperative.

In this context, the Commission has proposed a revision[79] of Directive 2016/ 1148, despite the fact that, at the time of its publication, this act was very ambitious in the aim of EU legislator. It focused on the transnational nature of threats related to network and information systems and services, but soon became apparent the inability to intervene or to report an incident. On the one hand, the measures identified in this Directive seemed outdated, not taking into account technological changes occurred in the meantime. On the other hand, since the European legislator adopted a directive, the level of discretion of the Member States remained very high.

As appears from the Explanatory Memorandum of the above-mentioned NIS2 proposal, these gaps of the NIS Directive and the practical difficulties in applying its requirements have led the Commission to start the revision process.

The proposed Directive states that Member States are required to adopt regulatory measures and a national cybersecurity strategy defining appropriate policy with the aim to achieve a high common level of cybersecurity within the Union. Member States are also required to put in place national cybersecurity crisis management frameworks, by designating national competent authorities responsible for the management of relevant cybersecurity incidents and crises.

This proposal extends the scope of the current NIS Directive by including all medium and large companies in selected sectors, leaving some flexibility for Member States to identify smaller entities with a high security risk profile. In general, small entities are excluded from the scope of the proposal, except for providers of electronic communications networks or publicity electronic communications services.

The distinction between OESs and DSPs has been completely deleted, considering that both categories are required to comply with the new provisions. The scope of this proposal is wide. It should apply to certain public or private essential entities

---

[78] Regulation (EU) 2019/881 of the European Parliament and of the Council of 17 April 2019 on ENISA (the European Union Agency for Cybersecurity) and on information and communications technology cybersecurity certification and repealing Regulation (EU) No 526/2013 (Cybersecurity Act) (*OJ L 151, 7.6.2019, p. 15–69*). See Loré and Musacchio (2021).

[79] Proposal for a Directive of the European Parliament and of the Council on measures for a high common level of cybersecurity across the Union, repealing Directive (EU) 2016/1148, Brussels, 16.12.2020, COM (2020) 823 final, 2020/0359(COD).

operating in the sectors listed in Annex I[80] (essential) and in Annex II[81] (important). The most notable difference between them is the supervisory and penalty regimes. Both essential and important entities are considered to be under the jurisdiction of the Member State in which they provide their services.

Regarding the harmonisation of the national systems, the proposal's provisions establish an increased control over the Member States through supervision measures and enforcement based on administrative sanctions, even in case of failure to report incidents.

Finally, it is worthwhile to mention other EU documents elaborated to enhance the system: the new EU's Cybersecurity Strategy,[82] that accompanies the proposal for the NIS2 Directive, the Proposal for a Directive on the Resilience of Critical Entities (RCE Directive),[83] and the Digital Europe Programme.[84]

8 Final Remarks

This study has revolved around three thematic areas, closely linked one to the others, namely: big data collected by satellites, airspace safety and criminal liability for activities carried out in outer space.

Space safety and satellites vulnerability are, respectively, among the greatest global challenges and threats of this century.

---

[80]The sectors listed in Annex I are: energy, transport, banking, financial market, infrastructures, heath, drinking water, waste water, digital infrastructure, public administration and space.

[81]The sectors listed in Annex II are: postal and courier services, waste management, manufacture, production and distribution of chemicals, food production, processing and distribution, manufacturing and digital providers.

[82]The EU's Cybersecurity Strategy in the Digital Decade was adopted on 16 December 2020 by the European Commission and EEAS (*European External Action Service)* to reinforce the EU's diplomatic response to cyberattacks, allowing to impose targeted sanctions to deter and respond to cyberattacks which constitute an external threat to the EU or its Member States. See Brighi (2019), pp. 35 ff.

[83]Proposal for a Directive of the European Parliament and of the Council on the resilience of critical entities –COM/2020/829 final. The RCE Directive expands the scope and deepens the 2008 European Critical Infrastructure (ECI) Directive. It covers ten sectors, namely energy, transport, banking, financial market infrastructures, health, drinking water, wastewater, digital infrastructure, public administration and space.

[84]The Digital Europe Programme is a new EU funding programme focused on bringing digital technology to businesses, citizens and public administrations. The European Commission has proposed this new programme, within the framework of the 2021–2027 MFF (Multiannual Financial Framework), to support the deployment and optimal use of the digital capacities that underpin innovation in areas of public interest and business, considering that economies and societies depend increasingly on digital capacities.

Regarding the safety issue, the international rules contained in the *Corpus juris spatialis*[85] are fully applicable to artificial satellites to ensure safety in outer space, in addition to the rules of the international telecommunications law.[86]

Regarding the second issue, faced with shortages of detailed space law rules in the field of space security and criminal liability, the doctrine tried to extend to satellites the international instruments—such as the Tokyo Convention, the Aja Convention and the Montreal Convention—adopted in order to safeguard civil aviation against acts of unlawful interference.

But this extension of the scope of the above-mentioned conventions is not easy, considering that this legislation has been designed for aircraft and navigation within the airspace. Satellites—as well known—differ greatly from aircrafts. In addition, the discipline applicable in the airspace is very different from the legal regime for outer space.[87]

A shortcoming is also present in the field of satellite cybersecurity, as far as international law is concerned. The international community has only published non-binding guidelines and recommendations in this field. On the contrary, in terms of European Union law, binding rules derives from the NIS Directive, supplemented and supported by soft law documents.

Despite the importance of space policy at EU level, however, legislation in this field is not yet properly developed neither at national nor at EU at national level.

In conclusion, having analysed the legal system in the sector of satellite safety, security and cybersecurity, a very fragmented and deficient regulatory framework emerges clearly, due to the difficulty for the law to keep up with the high-tech that develops *at an* ever faster rate, accelerated by the pandemic, highlighting a number of new problems, not always resolvable—in the face of this lack of regulation—by a broad interpretation of existing legislation.

References

Abeyratne R (1997) Terror in the skies. Approaches to controlling unlawful interference with civil aviation. Int J Polit Cult Soc 11(2):245 ff
Abeyratne R (2002) Frontiers of aerospace law. Ashgate Publishing, Farnham, Surrey
Ancis L (2005) Responsabilità per danni causati da *space debris* sulla superficie terrestre. Diritto dei trasporti, pp 913 ff
Andem MN (1998) The 1968 rescue agreement and the commercialisation of outer space activities during the 21st century: some reflections: proceedings forty-first colloquium on the law of outer space. American Institute of Aeronautics and Astronautics, Melbourne
Apfel NH (1988) Space law. Watts, New York

---

[85] See also Zhukov and Kolosov (1984); Marchisio (1990); Peyrefitte (1993); Cheng (1997); Böckstiegel et al. (2002); Dempsey (2004); Diederiks-Vershoor and Kopal (2008).

[86] For more details, see Uchenna (2018).

[87] See Back Impallomeni (1990), pp. 258 ff.; Francioni and Pocar (1993); Abeyratne (2002).

Back Impallomeni E (1990) Spazio aereo e spazio extra-atmosferico. In: Enciclopedia del diritto, XLIII, Giuffrè, Milan, pp 258 ff

Balbi G, Fickers A (eds) (2020) History of the international telecommunication union (ITU). Transnational techno-diplomacy from the telegraph to the internet. Walter De Gruyter, Berlin/Boston

Bassi N (2009) Modelli di servizi pubblici planetari: i casi di Intelsat e del Global Navigation Satellite System. Rivista trimestrale di diritto pubblico, pp 903 ff

Bender R (1997) Space transportation liability: national and international aspects, Alphen an den Rijn. Kluwer Law International, Netherlands

Benkö M, Schrogl KU (eds) (2005) Space law: current problems and perspectives for future regulation. Utrecht, Netherlands

Benkö M, Schrogl KU, De Graaff W (eds) (1993) International space law in the making: current issues in the UN Committee on the peaceful uses of outer space (forum for air and space law). Editions Frontières, Gif-sur-Yvette, pp 1–18

Böckstiegel KH (1987) Space law: changes and expectations at the turn to commercial space activities. Kluwer Law and Taxation Publishers Deventer, The Netherlands

Böckstiegel KH (ed) (1992) Manned Space Flight Legal Aspects in the Light of Scientific and Technical Development. Proceedings of an International Colloquium Cologne, May 20–22, 1992 organized by the Institute of Air and Space Law University of Cologne, Carl Heymanns Verlag, Köln, Berlin, Bonn, Münch, 1993

Böckstiegel KH (2001) (ed) *Luft-un Weltraumrechet im 21 Jahrhundert - air and space law in the 21st century (Liber Amicorum)*. Carl Heymanns Verlag, Cologne

Böckstiegel KH, Benkö M, Hobe S (2002) Space law: basic legal documents. Eleven International Publishing, The Hague

Borkowski N (2011) Organizational behavior in health care. Jones and Bartlett Publishers, Sudbury

Borowy I (2014) Defining sustainable development for our common future: a history of the world commission on environment and development (Brundtland Commission). Routledge, Taylor & Francis, London

Brighi R (2019) Vulnerabilità e sicurezza: un'analisi informatico-giuridica di concetti in evoluzione. Notizie di Politica, pp 35–45

Buxton CR (2004) Property in outer space: the common heritage of mankind principle vs. the first in time, first in right, rule of property. J Air Law Commer 69(4):689–707

Cheng B (1997) Studies in international space law. Clarendon Press, Oxford

Cheng B (2004) Studies in international space law. Clarendon Press, Oxford

Cinquepalmi F (2019) Regulation (EU) no 377/2014 establishing the Copernicus Programme: from the Baveno Manifesto to the present EU legislative framework for land and urban observation. Rivista della cooperazione giuridica internazionale, pp 142–147

Crespo DC (2011) Achieving the single European sky: goals and challenges, Alphen aan den Rijn. Kluwer Law International, Netherlands

Crisafulli S (89–92/1984) In tema di risarcimento dei danni causati da oggetti spaziali. Diritto aereo, pp 44–75

Crivellaro A (1972) Ancora sulla cosiddetta pirateria aerea: il testo definitivo della Convenzione dell'Aja. Giurisprudenza italiana IV:13–32

Csabafi IA (1971) The concept of state jurisdiction in international space law: a study in the progressive development of space law in the United Nations. Martinus Nijhoff Publishers, The Hague

De Sena P (1990) Questioni in tema di responsabilità internazionale per attività spaziali. Rivista diritto internazionale, pp 294–319

Dempsey PS (2004) Space law. Oceana Publications, Dobbs Ferry, New York

Diederiks-Vershoor IH, Kopal V (2008) An introduction to space law, Alphen aan den Rijn, 3rd edn. Kluwer Law Intrrenational, Netherlands

Durante F (1993) *Diritto cosmico*. Enciclopedia giuridica Treccani, Roma

Fernandez-Shaw F (1974) The New International Telecommunication Convention (ITC) of Malaga-Torremolinos (1973). EBU Rev pp 21–26

Finch MJ (1986) Limited space: allocating the Geostationaiy orbit. Northwest J Int Law Bus:788–802

Franchi B (2010) Aeromobili senza pilota (UAV): inquadramento giuridico e profili di responsabilità. Responsabilità civile e previdenza, pp 732–751

Francioni F, Pocar F (eds) (1993) Il regime internazionale dello spazio. Giuffré, Milan

Froehlich A (ed) (2017) A fresh view on the outer space treaty. Springer, Berlin, pp 39 ff

Gangale T (2008) Myths of the moon agreement. In: Proceedings of the AIAA Space 2008 Conference and Exposition, 9–11 September 2008, San Diego

Gestri M (1989) Portata e limiti del principio dell'uso pacifico nel diritto dello spazio. Comunità internazionale, pp 502–534

Golda C (1993) Navigazione e attività umana nello spazio: problemi giuridici. Diritto marittimo, pp 198–210

Gorbie A (1982) Space objects in international law. Diritto aereo, pp 81–91

Gorbiel A (1984) Outer space in international law. Int Lawyer 18(1):206–210

Hampton W (2011) September 11, 2001, Attack on the New York City. Candlewick Press, Somerville, Massachusetts

Hartman N, Boscoianu M (2015) Single European sky – the transformation of the aviation industry based on the dynamic capabilities. INCAS Bulletin 7(1):97–109

Hobe S (2007) Spacecraft, satellites, and space objects. In: Max Planck Encyclopedia of Public International Law, Heidelberg

Hofmann M (2010) Moon and celestial bodies. In: Max Planck Encyclopedia of Public International Law, Heidelberg

Ingratoci C (2009) Verso un sistema europeo di nuova generazione per la gestione del traffico aereo: l'impresa comune SESAR. In: Rizzo MP (ed) La gestione del traffico aereo: profili di diritto internazionale, comunitario ed interno. Milan, Giuffré, pp 485–526

Jacchia RA (1969) La Convenzione di Tokyo 1963 nell'ordinamento italiano. Diritto aereo, pp 1–19

Kanie N, Biermann F (eds) (2017) *Governing through goals: sustainable development goals as governance innovation.* The MIT Press, Cambridge

Kehrer T (2019) Closing the liability loophole: the liability convention and the future of conflict in space. Chic J Int Law:178–215

La Torre U (2012) La navigazione degli UAV: un'occasione di riflessione sull'art. 965 c. nav. In tema di danni a terzi sulla superficie. Rivista del diritto della navigazione, pp 553–575

Lafferranderie G, Marchisio S (eds) (2011) The astronauts and rescue agreement: lessons learned. ESA/ECSL Publications, Martinus Nijhoff Publishers, The Hague

Leal Filho W, Tortato U (eds) (2019) Universities and sustainable communities: meeting the goals of the Agenda 2030. Springer, Berlin

Leanza U (2011) Lo stato dell'arte nel regime giuridico dello spazio cosmico. Rivista di diritto della navigazione, pp 653–673

Li S (2010) Some considerations on establishing an international regime on exploration and use of the natural resources of the moon and other celestial bodies. In: Proceedings of the Fifty-Third Colloquium on the Law of Outer Space. International Astronautical Conference, Prague

Loré F, Musacchio P (2021) Cybersecurity e protezione dei dati personali ai tempi dell' "accountability: verso un cambio di prospettiva?. Amministrativ@mente, n. 1

Lyall F, Larsen PB (2009) Space law. A treatise. Taylor & Francis, Ashgate, Surrey

Marchisio S (1990) Il diritto internazionale dello spazio. ASI/CNR, Rome

Marchisio S (2018) Il Trattato sullo spazio del 1967: passato, presente e futuro. Rivista di diritto internazionale, pp 205–213

Masson-Zwaan T (2015) Orbits and frequencies: the legal context. In: Hofmann (ed) Dispute Settlement in the Area of Space Communication. 2nd Luxembourg Workshop on Space and Satellite Communication Law. Bloomsbury Publishing, Luxembourg, pp 59–68

Masutti A (2007) Prospettive di regolamentazione dell'uso dei velivoli senza pilota (UAV) nello spazio aereo comune. Diritto dei trasporti, pp 783–799

Masutti A (2009) GNSS: the Basic Principles for a European Legal Framework on TPL, in Policy aspects of thirdparty liability in satellite navigation. ESPI, Vienna Report, pp 37–48

Milde M (2008) International air law and ICAO. Eleven International Publishing, The Hague

Nhamo G, Togo M, Dube K (eds) (2021) Sustainable development goals for society. Vol. 1: selected topics of global of global relevance. Springer, Berlin

Oberst G (2010) Workshop on Space and Satellite Communication Law Efficient Use of Orbits and Frequencies

Oduntan G (2012) Sovereignty and jurisdiction in airspace and outer space: legal criteria for spatial delimitation. Routledge, Taylor & Francis, Abingdon

Orlandi M (2014) Le competenze dell'Unione europea nel settore dello spazio. Rivista della cooperazione giuridica internazionale, pp 23–48

Panella L (1991) La registrazione della stazione spaziale internazionale. Comunità internazionale, pp 195–215

Pedrazzi M (2008) Outer space, liability for damage. Max Planck Encyclopedia of Public International Law, Heidelberg-Oxford

Pellegrino F (2009) Sviluppo sostenibile dei trasporti marittimi comunitari. Giuffrè, Milan

Pellegrino F (ed) (2013) Sviluppo sostenibile dei trasporti marittimi nel Mediterraneo. Edizioni Scientifiche Italiane, Napoli

Pellegrino F (2018) Space Debris. Ordine Internazionale e Diritti Umani (OIDU), pp 117–126

Pelton JN, Jakhu RM (2010) Space safety regulations and standards. Elsevier, Amsterdam

Petroni G (2016) L'accesso delle Regioni europee ai servizi satellitari. Amministrare, pp 127–146

Peyrefitte L (1993) Droit de l'espace. Dalloz, Paris

Poulantzas NM (1971) The Hague convention for the suppression of unlawful seizure of aircraft. In: Netherlands International Law Review. Springer, Berlin

Ramakrishnan S (2019) Enhancing satellite navigation for low earth and geostationary orbit missions. Stanford University

Ravillon L (ed) (2004) Droit des activités spatiales: Adaptation aux phénomènes de commercialisation et de privatization. Litec, Paris

Re E, Ruggeri M (eds) (2007) Satellite communications and navigation systems. Springer, Berlin

Reynolds G, Merges R (1998) Outer space: problems of law and policy, 2nd edn. Westview Press, Boulder, Colorado

Rothblatt MA (1982) Satellite communication and spectrum allocation. Am J Int Law 76(1):56–77

Sabella PM (2017) Il fenomeno del "cybercrime" nello spazio giuridico contemporaneo. Prevenzione e repressione degli illeciti penali connessi all'utilizzo di Internet per fini di terrorismo, tra esigenze di sicurezza e rispetto dei diritti fondamentali. Informatica e diritto, pp 139–176

Salamone LVM (2017) La disciplina del "cyberspace" alla luce della direttiva europea sulla sicurezza delle reti e dell'informazione: contesto normativo nazionale di riferimento, ruolo dell'"intelligence" e prospettive "de iure condendo". In: federalismi.it, pp 2–69

Smith ML (1985) Space WARC 1985: the quest for equitable access. Boston Univ Int Law J 3:229–255

Smith ML (1985–1986) Space law/space WARC: an analysis of the space law issues raised at the 1985 ITU World Administrative Radio Conference on the Geostationary Orbit. Houston J Int Law, 8

Smith ML (1987) The orbit/spectrum resource and the technology of satellite telecommunications: an overview. Rutgers Comput Technol Law J 12:285–304

Spada M (1983) Indennizzo per i danni causati da oggetti spaziali. Comunità internazionale, pp 699–705

Stipo F (1997) Disciplina del "Sistema Globale di Navigazione Satellitare" (GNSS). Giurisprudenza di merito, pp 673–682

Tan D (2000) Towards a new regime for the protection of outer space as the "province of all mankind". Yale J Int Law 25:177–179

Tanoguchi F (2010) A consideration on an international regime of the moon agreement. In: Proceedings of the Fifty-Third Colloquium on the Law of Outer Space, International Astronautical Conference, Prague

Thompson JC (1996) Space for rent: the international telecommunications union, space law, and orbit/Spectrum leasing. J Air Law Commer 62:280 ff

Trovò L (2011) Il processo d'integrazione degli spazi aerei europei: dalla riorganizzazione in blocchi funzionali verso la globalizzazione dell'Air Traffic Management (ATM). In: Rivista di diritto dell'economia dei trasporti e dell'ambiente, Giureta, pp 439–462

Uchenna J O (2018) International telecommunications law and policy. Cambridge University Press, Cambridge

USA International Business Publications (ed) (2006) European Space Agency Handbook. Washington

Varmer O (1987) The third World's search for equitable access to the geostationary satellite orbit. ILSA J Int Law 11:175–197

Vereshchetin VS (2006) Outer space. In: Max Planck Encyclopedia of Public International Law, Heidelberg-Oxford

Von der Dunk FG (2007) The moon agreement and the prospect of commercial exploitation of lunar resources. Ann Air Space Law 32:91–113

Wassenberg HA (1991) Principles of outer space law in hindsight. Martinus Nijhoff Publishers, The Hague

Zhukov GP, Kolosov UM (1984) International space law. Praeger Publisher, New York

Facial Recognition for Preventive Purposes: The Human Rights Implications of Detecting Emotions in Public Spaces

Isadora Neroni Rezende

Abstract Police departments are increasingly relying on surveillance technologies to tackle public security issues in smart cities. Automated facial recognition is deployed in public spaces for real-time identification of suspects and warranted individuals. In some cases, law enforcement is going even further by exploiting also emotion recognition technologies. In preventive operations indeed, emotion facial recognition (EFR) is being used to infer individuals' inner affective states from traits like facial muscle movements. In this way, law enforcement aims to obtain insightful hints on unknown persons acting suspiciously in public or strategic venues (e.g. train stations, airports). While the employment of such tools still seems to be relegated to dystopian scenarios, it is already a reality in some parts of the world. Hence, there emerges a need to explore their compatibility with the European human rights framework. The Chapter undertakes this task and examines whether and how EFR can be considered compliant with the rights to privacy and data protection, the freedom of thought and the presumption of innocence.

1 Introduction

Cities worldwide are undergoing a radical shift towards digitization, a process that is often reconnected to the adoption of smart city strategies. At its core, indeed, the smart city paradigm—often described as fuzzy and elusive—implies the integration of digital technologies in urban infrastructure to achieve a more efficient and sustainable exploitation of available resources.[1] Unsurprisingly, one of the most

---

Isadora Neroni Rezende is a PhD Candidate in Law, Science and Technology—Rights of the Internet of Everything.

---

[1] Albino et al. (2015), p. 2 ff.; Kummitha and Crutzen (2017), pp. 43, 45.

I. Neroni Rezende (✉)
Department of Legal Studies, University of Bologna, Bologna, Italy
e-mail: isadora.neroni2@unibo.it

© The Author(s), under exclusive license to Springer Nature Switzerland AG 2022
L. Bachmaier Winter, S. Ruggeri (eds.), *Investigating and Preventing Crime in the Digital Era*, Legal Studies in International, European and Comparative Criminal Law 7, https://doi.org/10.1007/978-3-031-13952-9_4

crucial domains of implementation of digital technologies in smart cities is public security: in some parts of the world, being "smart" for a city basically equates to being "safe".[2] Against this background, private companies' efforts in marketing security technologies seem to have conveniently met the demands of law enforcement agencies, always in search of "smarter" strategies for crime prevention and early detection.[3]

Among these instruments, Automated Facial Recognition (AFR) certainly plays a decisive role, in both preventive and investigative activities. As well known, AFR involves the automated processing of digital facial images for the purposes of identifying, authenticating and classifying individuals.[4] Despite their invasiveness from a privacy and data protection standpoint,[5] in the last few years facial recognition technologies have gained big traction in both law enforcement and commercial domains.

On the one hand, indeed, different smartphone applications and banking services now rely on facial recognition to authenticate their users and unlock access to their services.

On the other, law enforcement is increasingly deploying facial recognition in public places and strategic venues (e.g. airports, train stations) to identify known or warranted individuals, specifically inserted in prepopulated watchlists.[6] Even in this context, however, the uses of AFR technologies widely differ around the world. China, for instance, is often mentioned as a worrying example of the unfettered use of facial recognition, which is often relied upon to catch jaywalkers and petty crime offenders.[7] In the United States, facial recognition has sparked an intense public and regulatory debate. In the wake of protests against police brutality and racism, big corporations such as Amazon, IBM and Microsoft have also set out a temporary moratorium on software sales to law enforcement[8]; nonetheless, tech start-ups—like the infamous Clearview AI—keep on providing their services to hundreds of local police departments across the country.[9] In Europe, finally, the advent of facial recognition in the security domain seems to advance at a slower pace, as when compared to Asia and North America. Instances of law enforcement agencies in the

---

[2]Marat and Sutton (2021), p. 248.

[3]On the potentialities of AI applications in law enforcement and criminal justice, see Lasagni, in this volume; Caianiello (2021).

[4]Adapted from Article 29 Data Protection Working Party (2012), p. 2. For an overview of face recognition technologies, their functioning, issues and implications see Berle (2020), pp. 1–17.

[5]Facial recognition technologies indeed process biometric data, a special category of personal data. On the notion of biometric data, see generally Kindt (2018).

[6]See, e.g., BBC News (2018).

[7]Notably, in China AFR is used to catch jaywalkers. See Liao (2018).

[8]Heilweil (2020).

[9]Clearview AI is an US-based tech company which provides facial recognition services. Notably, the app developed by Clearview runs its software not only on government-held images, but also on people's pictures scraped by social media network. On the matter see Neroni Rezende (2020).

European Union using the technology are sporadic, but steadily growing.[10] Often cited examples of pilot projects comprise the ones conducted by the Hamburg and Berlin Police,[11] or that at the Zaventem airport in Brussels.[12]

As if AFR was not worrying privacy activists enough, law enforcement agencies worldwide are starting to go even further, coupling its deployment with emotion recognition technologies. Specifically, the latter build on affective computing[13] and AI to sense and acquire information about human emotional life.[14] A wide range of physiological inputs—such as facial movements, vocal tone, gait, respiration, heart rate, gaze direction—can be processed by machine learning algorithms to infer people's affective inner states.[15] When these tools are combined with facial recognition software, the system is designed to deduce the individual's emotional condition primarily from her facial muscle movements.

At the moment, the applications of Emotion Facial Recognition (EFR) are varied in the security context.[16] Within criminal proceedings, EFR is being tested to detect liars during police interrogations: Often marketed as more refined descendants of polygraph machines,[17] software like CM Cross, EmoKit, Miaodong and Sage Data rely on facial expression images, vocal tone, heart rate and similar datapoints to determine interviewees' emotions during police questionings.[18]

On the other hand, "early warning" systems are leveraged by the police in preventive activities to spot suspicious individuals in public venues. One famous example is the US Transportation Security Authority's 2003 Screening Passengers by Observation Techniques (SPOT) program, which in the aftermath of 9/11 aimed to find terrorists by scrutinizing airline passengers displaying fear or stress.[19] In China, instead, a research paper published by the Hubei Police Academy examines the value of facial expression to identify "dangerous people" and "high-risk groups" who do not have prior criminal records. The author of this research proposes to build a database of video images of offenders before and after they have committed crimes, in order to train an algorithm to pick up individuals involved in illicit undertakings.[20] In this kind of situations indeed, the claim is that offenders suffer high psychological pressure and cannot really hide their true inner states.[21] The

---

[10] O'Flaherty (2020), p. 170.

[11] See, e.g., Raab (2019).

[12] Peeters (2020).

[13] Affective computing comprises both "the creation of and interaction with machine systems that sense, recognize, respond to, and influence emotions". See Daily et al. (2017), p. 213.

[14] Mc Stay (2020), p. 1.

[15] Article 19 (2021), p. 15.

[16] On different applications beyond the security domain, see Mc Stay (2020).

[17] On lie detectors and their implications in criminal proceedings, see Lasagni (2021).

[18] Article 19 (2021), p. 21.

[19] Crawford (2021).

[20] Article 19 (2021), 19.

[21] *Id.*

reasoning behind preventive EFR systems already finds application in different software like Alpha Hawkeye, CM Cross, Joyware and Shenzhen Anshibao, which specifically detects light vibrations on faces and bodies to infer mental— and especially aggressive—states.[22] While it is evident that Chinese-based companies are heavily betting on the success of these tools, it should be highlighted that European law enforcement authorities are not immune to the charm of EFR. For instance, it is noteworthy to mention the Horizon 2020-funded iBorderCrtl program shortly trialed in Hungary, Latvia, and Greece.[23] With the aim of ensuring faster and more efficient border controls, AI-equipped cameras scanned travelers' faces for signs of deception while they responded to border-security agents'.[24]

In light of such growing interest towards these technologies in the security context and beyond, this contribution proposes a wide-ranging assessment of the use of EFR in public places for the purposes of law enforcement. This analysis is very topical, considering that the Proposal for a Regulation of the European Parliament and of the Council Laying Down Harmonised Rules on Artificial Intelligence (Artificial Intelligence Act) is now undergoing the ordinary legislative procedure.[25] That is why, before setting the terms of the investigation, an overall picture of the rules that have been put forward in this prospective piece of legislation, in relation to both AFR and emotion recognition technologies, will be presented.

2 Facial and Emotion Recognition Technologies in the EU Proposed AI Regulation

Recital 38 of the newly proposed Artificial Intelligence Act (hereinafter "the Proposal") highlights the significant degree of intrusion on fundamental rights—such as privacy and data protection, effective remedy and fair trial rights—caused by the use of AI systems in the law enforcement context. Because of the power imbalance that exists between public authorities and individuals that could be subject to surveillance,[26] the Proposal classifies these systems as "high-risk" when employed in this

---

[22] Id.

[23] iBorderCrtl (2016). Critically assessed by Sánchez-Monedero and Dencik (2020).

[24] Article 19 (2021), p. 19. See also Gallagher and Jona (2019).

[25] Proposal for a Regulation of the European Parliament and of the Council Laying Down Harmonised Rules on Artificial Intelligence (Artificial Intelligence Act) and Amending Certain Union Legislative Acts, COM/2021/206 final. Critically assessed by Vaele and Borgesius (2021); Papakostantinou and De Hert (2021).

[26] Malgieri and Ienca note indeed that the scheme of classification of high-risk AI system seems to revolve around three main criteria: (i) the type of AI system; (ii) its domain of application and (iii) its human target. This implies that if AI systems featuring limited risks are employed in very sensitive contexts and used for practices falling under the unbearable risk list they would be prohibited. This mechanism emerges clearly in the case of EFR that is labelled as low-risk when employed, for instance, in the commercial context, and as high-risk when used in law enforcement

domain, thereby submitting them to a "stricter" regime in terms of obligations impending on manufacturers. The Recital enumerates different kinds of technologies that fall within this discipline, including individual risk assessments software, lie detectors and 'deep fakes' tools.

While emotion *facial* recognition in itself is not specifically tackled in the Proposal, two of its building technologies (AFR and emotion recognition technologies) are.[27] AFR is defined by the Proposal as "remote biometric identification system", a notion that, according to the proposal, should be interpreted functionally so as to refer to "an AI system for the purpose of identifying natural persons at a distance through the comparison of a person's biometric data with the biometric data contained in a reference database, and without prior knowledge of the user of the AI system whether the person will be present and can be identified".[28] A distinction is made between real-time and post biometric identification, where the former identifies systems involving the use of "live" or "near-live" materials, such as CCTV footage. This kind of application is regulated at Article 5 of the Proposal, which lists (tendentially) prohibited AI practices. Using a negative formulation, the provision bans the use of AFR in publicly accessible[29] places for law enforcement purposes, unless specific conditions apply.

While observing the principle of strict necessity, AFR should be deployed only for the following grounds: (i) the targeted search for specific potential victims of crime, including missing children; (ii) the prevention of a specific, substantial and imminent threat to the life or physical safety of natural persons or of a terrorist attack; (iii) the detection, investigation and prosecution of a serious criminal offence for which the European Arrest Warrant does not demand the so-called dual criminality requirement.[30] In addition, the provision lays down further parameters—inspired by a risk-based approach informing the whole Proposal—that should guide users' case-by-case assessments on the opportunity of the deploying live facial recognition. These are: (a) the nature of the situation giving rise to the possible use, in particular

---

or education. See Malgieri and Ienca (2021). The Consultative Committee on the 108+ Convention has also highlighted the sensitivity of the law enforcement context, also in light of the power asymmetries between public authorities and data subjects. See Consultative Committee of the Convention for the Protection of Individuals with regard to Automatic Processing of Personal Data (2021).

[27] It should be noted that biometric *identification* systems should not be conflated with biometric *classification* ones. Generally speaking, facial recognition technologies may have three different purposes: (i) verification/authentication; (ii) identification; (iii) classification/categorization. For an overview, see Castelvecchi (2020).

[28] Art. 3(36) of the Proposal.

[29] See Recital 9 of the Proposal for a notion of "publicly accessible place".

[30] See Art. 2(2) of the Framework Decision 2002/584/JHA: Council Framework Decision of 13 June 2002 on the European arrest warrant and the surrender procedures between Member States—Statements made by certain Member States on the adoption of the Framework Decision, OJ L 190, 18.7.2002, p. 1–20.

the seriousness, probability and scale of the harm caused in the absence of the use of the system; (b) the consequences of the use of the system for the rights and freedoms of all persons concerned, in particular the seriousness, probability and scale of those consequences.

Importantly, Article 5(2) of the Proposal also recalls the applicability of the proportionality principle, with specific regard to temporal, geographic and personal limitations in the use of the technology. In any case, implementation of the AFR in publicly accessible places for law enforcement purposes should be subject to the prior authorization of a judicial or independent administrative authority, on the basis of a "reasoned request" including objective evidence or clear indications so as to the necessity and proportionality of its deployment.

For situations of urgency, the use of the system may be commenced without a prior authorization, and a subsequent intervention of an independent authority is allowed only during or after the use. Finally, the Proposal leaves a space for national regulation on the matter by Member States, which are called on to provide for detailed national rules for the request, issuance and exercise of necessary authorizations, the criminal offences legitimizing the use of the technology and the authorities that could use such systems.[31]

Furthermore, emotion recognition technologies are explicitly comprised into the scope of the Regulation under Article 1(c) of the Proposal. They are defined as an "AI system for the purpose of identifying or inferring emotions or intentions of natural persons on the basis of their biometric data".[32] Differently from live AFR, (biometric) emotion recognition *per se* is not targeted by many provisions in the Proposal. Depending on the functionalities concretely embedded in the system, EFR applications may be subject to different layers of rules in the framework of the Regulation. The Proposal only regulates a specific instance of facial recognition technologies in the law enforcement domain, namely those that perform strict identification operations by comparing biometric inputs with templates pre-stored in dedicated watchlist databases (i.e. the so-called "one to many" comparison). Software processing facial images data may then fall within this regime only if it integrates this kind of functionality, and this applies also to EFR systems. As known, however, EFR and more broadly biometric categorization systems do not always involve identification of targeted individuals.[33]

---

[31] Cf. Article 10 the Directive (EU) 2016/680 of the European Parliament and of the Council of 27 April 2016 on the protection of natural persons with regard to the processing of personal data by competent authorities for the purposes of the prevention, investigation, detection or prosecution of criminal offences or the execution of criminal penalties, and on the free movement of such data, and repealing Council Framework Decision 2008/977/JHA, OJ L 119, 4.5.2016, pp. 89–131 (the Police Directive).

[32] Art. 3(34) of the Proposal.

[33] See note 27 for an overview of different facial recognition systems.

When these applications are often leveraged in the commercial context, for instance, individuals' singling out is not always foreseen.[34] On the opposite, identification is key to many—if not all—activities of law enforcement authorities.[35] In EFR policing uses, one-to-many identification may not a direct function of the software, but it is certainly an objective pursued by law enforcement agencies employing such systems—and it may be performed "manually" at a subsequent moment. That is, identification may be carried out first-hand by human police officers having stopped the individual targeted by the software. In this latter case, EFR would not strictly fall within the scope of the rules laid down at Article 5 of the Regulation. Nonetheless, as it will be also argued later on, where identification objectives are still pursued, it would still be appropriate to apply this regime.[36]

Emotion recognition is lastly mentioned at Article 52 of the Proposal, which foresees transparency obligations for certain AI systems. Because of the specific nature of law enforcement activities, when emotion recognition tools are available for the public to report a criminal offence, the provision excludes that technology providers should design the systems in such a way that individuals are aware of their interaction with the artificial agent.[37]

In conclusion, it is noteworthy to mention that Article 2(4) of the Proposal foresees a significant limitation to the scope of the Regulation in specific law enforcement scenarios. In derogation to the rules laid down in Article 2(1)(c) of the Proposal, Article 2(4) exempts public authorities in a third country or international organizations from complying with the standards set out in the Regulation, provided that these entities use AI systems in the framework of international agreements for law enforcement and judicial cooperation with the Union or more Member States.

Regrettably, this provision seems to ignore the hierarchy of the sources of the law within the EU system.[38] While international agreements concluded by the Union need to respect EU Treaties but not secondary law, those autonomously concluded by Member States are entirely subject to the principle of the primacy of EU law. Hence, it seems difficult to understand how a Regulation could exempt public authorities from respecting European human rights standards (enshrined in EU primary law) in extraterritorial operations carried out in the framework of international agreements to which the Union is not a party. A reversal of the hierarchy of EU

---

[34] In this case emotion facial recognition technologies are also referred to as "soft biometrics". See McStay (2020), p. 4. Examples of this kind of applications involve EFR embedded in billboards and shopping malls cameras to register people's emotional reactions to adverts displayed in public venues.

[35] Kotsoglou and Oswald (2020), p. 87; Neroni Rezende (2020), pp. 382–383.

[36] Below, Sect. 5.

[37] Art 52(1) of the Proposal. Under Art. 52(2), this applies also to biometric classification.

[38] On the position of the international agreements concluded by the Union within the hierarchy of the sources of EU law, see Adam and Tizzano (2014), pp. 149–156.

legal sources appears here to be at play, and this dangerously creates a hole in the application of human rights safeguards in these extraterritorial scenarios.

3   Which Room for Emotion Facial Recognition in Europe?

Given that the use of EFR technologies is increasing worldwide, and instances of its application have also been witnessed in Europe,[39] it seems appropriate to engage in a legal assessment of the technology against the European human rights framework, comprising both the Charter of Fundamental Rights of the EU (CFREU) and the European Convention of Human Rights (ECHR).[40] Our analysis will be articulated in two steps. First, the question of whether EFR can at all be deemed to be compatible with the CFREU and the ECHR will be addressed. This Section will examine the first conditions set out by Article 52(1) CFREU to justify the interferences on CFREU rights, and will mainly revolve around the "essence of the right" criterion. The second Section will then shift the focus to the proportionality test only, to see whether, regardless of the outcome of the first evaluation, EFR can be considered compliant with these further requirements of Article 52 CFREU.

The analysis will mainly take preventive activities of law enforcement in public urban spaces as a reference setting. As suggested, normative benchmarks for this assessment will leverage the rights to privacy and data protection, given the strict inapplicability of other fair trial rights in the preventive phase.[41] This choice presents several advantages. Firstly, both rights apply to data-driven preventive activities of security agencies by explicit legislative provision, i.e. Article 1(1) of the Directive 2016/680/EU (the Police Directive).[42] Secondly, privacy and data protection present strong conceptual links with other fundamental rights—even in the criminal context—as the former are often framed as instrumental rights.[43] This is true for instance with regard to the freedom of thought that, as we will see, is also called into question by emotion recognition technologies. The freedom of thought and the right to privacy seem to revolve specifically around the protection of *thoughts* when it comes to preserving the inner self of the individual. Certainly, the association of these entitlements to mere (involuntary) emotions may not seem totally fitting. As a premise for the assessment, however, it can be argued that emotions are actually very like thoughts. The link between emotions and thoughts has indeed been explored

---

[39] See, e.g., European Parliament (2021).

[40] The European framework has been rightly described as a multilevel system of protection of fundamental rights. See Kostoris (2018), p. 68 ff.

[41] Cf. Neroni Rezende (2021), p. 375, note 63. On the qualification of data stemming from EFR processing as personal data and thus the applicability of the EU data protection framework, see Ienca and Malgieri (2021).

[42] See, e.g., Art. 1(1) of the Police Directive.

[43] Rouvroy and Poullet (2009), p. 50; Hildebrandt (2010), pp. 36–37.

from both a philosophical and cognitive perspective.[44] Given the similarities between the two, it is reasonable to assess the impact of EFR against the abovementioned rights, whose span of protection should equally cover thoughts and emotions alike.

Finally, the rights to privacy and data protection share a "common concern" with the presumption of innocence, that is the protection of the individual against undue stigmatization. While this fair trial right is not specifically designed for the preventive phase, a strong upholding of these other "kindred rights" may achieve an anticipated application or coverage in this domain as well. From this perspective, one last Section will explore the possible tensions between the use of EFR technologies and the rationale behind the presumption of innocence.

4 Lawfulness, General Interest and the Interest of the Rights at Stake

4.1 Lawfulness and General Interest

First of all, when assessing the legitimacy of a measure limiting fundamental rights, the existence of a legal basis should be verified. Indeed, the need for a legal basis grounding (and framing) the encroachments upon the rights protected emerges clearly both at the level of primary and secondary legislation in the EU. This is echoed at Article 8(2) of the Convention, which should be taken into consideration in light of the so-called "equivalence clause" (Article 52(3) CFREU). At the level of secondary law, the lawfulness requirement is one of the foundational principles of EU legislation on data protection, and it is indeed recalled by Article 4(1)(a) of the Police Directive. The use of EFR technologies should then be explicitly foreseen in a further legal basis of national or EU law.[45] This text should in particular determine the grounds and purposes of the implied data processing operations, pursuant to the purpose limitation principle, another tenet of EU data protection law.[46]

Interpreting the lawfulness principle in compliance with the jurisprudence of the ECtHR, the "quality of the law" doctrine should also be taken into account. For this requirement to be satisfied, the Court demands that the legal basis in question is at once "foreseeable" and "accessible".[47] The quality of the law requirement has also

---

[44] In philosophy, see Nussbaum (2001), p. 33. In cognitive research, see Feldman Barrett (2017), pp. 1–23; Science Daily (2017).

[45] Noteworthily, Recital 41 of the Proposal for the AI Regulation excludes that the latter can be understood as providing for a legal basis for the use of the technologies and related data processing operations tackled in the text.

[46] Art. 4(1)(b) of the Police Directive.

[47] For a very detailed reconstruction of how the case law of the ECtHR and CJEU evolved in this respect, see De Hert and Malgieri (2020).

been examined within the specific context of preventive and covert surveillance measures.[48] The ECtHR has specified that here the meaning of foreseeability is not the same as in other domains. Specifically, "foreseeability" means that the law should simply be clear enough to inform citizens of the *circumstances* in and the *conditions* upon which public authorities are empowered to resort to these measures.[49] In particular, the legal basis for surveillance should precisely frame the margin of discretion afforded to public authorities in resorting to these tools, as safeguard to potential abuses.

A second requirement to be met refers to the general objectives pursued with the use of the surveillance tool. This criterion has never posed significant challenges in the law enforcement context, and the same goes for EFR technologies. On the one hand indeed, Article 8(2) of the ECHR explicitly mentions national security, public safety and prevention and prosecution of crimes as legitimate aims justifying encroachments upon the right to private life. On the other, the CJEU has recognized the prevention, investigation and prosecution of criminal offences and the protection of national security as objectives of general interests under the Charter.[50]

4.2   Essence of the Right

If these cumulative criteria are satisfied, the analysis should then turn to the "essence of the right" requirement. Because of its vagueness, this criterion has been subject to significant doctrinal and jurisprudential analysis, both at the EU and national level. For instance, Brkan defines it as "the untouchable core or inner circle of a fundamental right that cannot be diminished, restricted or interfered with".[51] The roots of the concepts are often traced back in the German legal system, where Article 19(2) of the Constitution provides that "[i]n no case may the essence [*Wesensgehalt*] of a basic right be affected".[52] While the notion has made inroads in other Member States' constitutional settings, the CJEU had its first recourse to the essence of the

---

[48] See, e.g. ECtHR, *Roman Zakharov v Russia*, judgement of 4 December 2015, Appl. No.47143/ 06, para. 229; ECtHR, *Big Brother Watch and others v the United Kingdom*, judgement of 13 September 2018, Appl. Nos. 58170/13, 62322/14 and 24960/15, para. 306.

[49] ECtHR, Grand Chamber, *Big Brother Watch and Others v United Kingdom*, judgement of 25 May 2021, Appl. Nos. 58170/13, 62322/14 and 24960/15, para. 333; ECtHR, *Zackarov v Russia*, para. 229; ECtHR, *Malone v the United Kingdom*, judgement of 2 August 1984, Appl. No.8691/79, para. 67; ECtHR, *Huvig v France*, judgement of 24 April 1990, Appl. No.11105/84, para. 29; ECtHR, *Kruslin v France*, judgement of 24 April 1990, Appl. No.11801/85, para. 30; ECtHR, *Rotaru v Romania*, judgement of 4 May 2000, Appl. No. 28341/95 para. 55; ECtHR, *Weber and Saravia v Germany*, judgement of 29 June 2006, Appl. No.54934/00, para. 93;

[50] Cf. CJEU, *Digital Rights Ireland and Others*, judgement of 8 April 2014, Joined Cases C-293/12 and C-594/12, paras. 41–42; CJEU, *La Quadrature du Net and Others*, judgement of 6 October 2020, Joined Cases C-511/18, C-512/18, C-520/18, para. 122.

[51] Brkan (2018), p. 333.

[52] *Id.*, p. 339; Ojanen (2016), p. 324.

right in the landmarking case *Nold*. There, the Court recognized fundamental rights as being part of Community (now Union) law and underlined that these can be limited only "on condition that the *substance* of these rights is left untouched".[53] In absence of any binding text of primary law, the Court gradually developed this autonomous concept[54] while taking inspiration from both national constitutional traditions of Member States[55] and the case law of the ECtHR.[56] As a crowning of this jurisprudential path, the "substance" of rights was then translated into the Charter with a different wording, becoming the "essence".

Despite this final acknowledgement in EU primary law, the "essence of the right" criterion has long been subject to diverging interpretations. In particular, two doctrines have been counterposed: the relative (or exclusionary) theory and the absolute (or integrative) one. The difference between the two revolves around the relationship of the "essence of the right" with the proportionality assessment. On the one hand, the proponents of the absolute theory conceive the essence of the right as being completely independent from the proportionality principle. The starting point is that fundamental rights are conceptualized as being composed of a nucleus, and a peripheral part which can be restricted exclusively under certain conditions.[57] The proportionality test would thus apply only to peripherical limitations to fundamental rights, being the core of the right absolutely immune from such restrictions, even in presence of powerful overriding reasons.[58] On the other hand, the relative theory tends to merge the "essence of the right" criterion and proportionality assessments. Essence has only a declarative value because the legitimacy of *any* interference can be assessed through the lens of proportionality. In the EU legal framework, a literal interpretation of Article 52 CFREU suggests that an absolutist approach is preferred.[59] From the *Digital Rights Ireland* judgement onwards, indeed, the case law of the CJEU has made increasing references to this criterion and confirmed the latter interpretative perspective.[60]

While seemingly of a pure doctrinal nature, this discussion has undeniable practical consequences in the case at hand. The implications of an absolutist conception of the "essence of the right" parameter have first become tangible in the *Schrems* case. Here the CJEU annulled the Safe Harbor scheme only based on a

---

[53] CJEU, *Nold v Commission*, judgement of 14 May 1974, Case C-4/73, para. 14 [emphasis added].

[54] Brkan (2018), p. 347.

[55] *Id.*, pp. 341–344.

[56] *Id.*, pp. 348–349 (discussing the inconsistency of the interpretation and application of the notion in the ECtHR's jurisprudence).

[57] *Id.*, p. 336.

[58] *Id.*

[59] Brkan (2018), p. 360. As for the ECHR, a similar stance is proposed by Rivers (2006), pp. 184–185.

[60] *Compare* CJEU, *Digital Rights*, paras. 39–40; CJEU, *Tele2 Sverige and Watson and Others*, judgement of 21 December 2016, Joined Cases C-203/15 and C-698/15, para. 101; CJEU, *Opinion 1/15*, Opinion of the Court (Grand Chamber) of 26 July 2017, para 150.

finding of violation of the essence of the rights to privacy and judicial protection.[61] As a result, the CJEU esteemed that it was not necessary to perform a proportionality test, thus reinforcing the independent conception of the essence of the right in its relationship with proportionality.

Despite the importance attributed to this criterion, the Court has never determined—on a pure theoretical level—*what* the essence of a right actually is. However, there is consensus in the legal doctrine that this is the result of an intentional choice of the CJEU. Even with few opportunities to examine the respect of the rights' essence, the Court seems to suggest that this is necessarily a *contextual* concept and that it can only be determined on a case-by-case basis, in consideration of the factual circumstances of the case.[62] When thinking about the impact of emerging technologies, this vague approach certainly presents its advantages, because it can unfold its potential in ever-new factual and legal situations. In the case of EFR indeed, there are strong reasons to believe that these tools impinge upon the very essence of the rights to privacy, data protection and the freedom of thought, with no further need for performing a proportionality assessment, as it will be shown next.

4.2.1   Privacy and Freedom of Thought

With respect to privacy, for instance, it is well acknowledged that one of the constitutive elements of the right is the protection of one's thoughts and inner states (i.e. so-called mental privacy), which also comprises the freedom *not* to manifest one's thoughts.[63] The protection of the mind and the individual's self-determination serves indeed as the common rationale for privacy and the freedom of thought, which are even jointly conceptualized in some constitutional frameworks.[64]

Also, in the structure of the freedom of thought, people's inner mental space is covered by an absolute protection in Article 9 of the Convention, being only external manifestations subject to possible restrictions.[65] By pretending to capture into datapoints the most intimate aspects of one's life, in absence of any will of the individual to share them, it is possible to argue that EFR technologies engage the very substance of the right to mental privacy and the freedom of thought. Importantly, the outcomes of the processing do not need to be accurate to engender an

---

[61] CJEU, *Maximillian Schrems v Data Protection Commissioner*, judgement of 6 October 2015, Case C-362/14, paras. 94–95. For a thorough analysis, see Ojanen (2016).

[62] Ojanen (2016), p. 326. Christofi and Verdoodt (2019). Tzanou (2017), p. 43. See also Brkan (2018), p. 363 ff.

[63] Koops et al. (2017), pp. 531–532; Mantovani (2013), p. 588, note 6.

[64] Koops et al. (2017), p. 531.

[65] Schabas (2017), p. 420.

interference on the rights at stake.[66] Especially with regards to privacy, but the argument could be extended to the freedom of thought as well, the right may be considered to be violated even if the invasion entails falsely attributing to a person some opinion.[67] In EFR, the contents of the mind are reified and used as basis for decision-making, unbeknownst or against the will of the subject. Being unaware of where this kind of invasive processing may intervene, individuals are also exposed to the chilling effects of surveillance and can be subtly manipulated into avoiding unordinary behavior. Therefore, they may also be restricted in their freedom of self-determination, freedom of expression and assembly in any public place, in such a way that no overriding interest could justify.

Besides, it has also been submitted that the core of fundamental rights is essentially connected to human dignity, which may even work as a grounding basis for an independent conceptualization of their essence.[68] The Explanations to the Charter, indeed, seem to equate the need for respecting human dignity with the core essence of the rights protected.[69] Generally, in the case of AFR, it has been purported that the fact of transforming the human face into an item for objectivization and measurement touches upon the very dignity of the individual.[70] When this biometric processing reaches out to emotions—the most private element of our personal life—it can be argued that people are susceptible of being deprived of their own dignity, provided that this kind of "emotion reading" carried out by the machine is non-consensual or covert.[71]

---

[66] The scientific community is quite divided on whether EFR technologies are accurate and can actually "read our minds". As reported by Murgia (2021), the EFR company 4LittleTrees claims around 85% of accuracy, while Affectiva more than 90%, as indicated by Heaven (2020), p. 504. Nonetheless, these results should be taken with a grain of salt. Indeed, one of the major underlying issues concerning the accuracy of these technologies seems to be data annotation. Before the EFR system is trained, datasets need to be labelled by humans choosing whether a given individual in a picture is expressing feelings of fear, happiness etc., often without any context. Even in this case, experts disagree about whether humans are always able to correctly read other's facial expressions. In this sense, a panel of experts led by psychologist Lisa Feldmann Barrett has recently reviewed more than 1000 contributions on the matter, concluding that there is little to no evidence that people can reliably infer someone else's emotional state from a set of facial movements. See Heaven (2020), p. 503. Cf. also Chen et al. (2018).

[67] Prosser (1984, original work published in 1960), p. 107; Schoeman (1984), p. 16.

[68] Brkan (2018), p. 365.

[69] See Explanation on Article 1. Explanations relating to the Charter of Fundamental Rights OJ C 303, 14.12.2007, pp. 17–35.

[70] McStay (2020), p. 3 (citing Wiewieorowski (2019)).

[71] Different might be the case in which the user voluntarily decides to interact with emotional AI, see McStay (2018).

4.2.2 Data Protection

With regard to the right to data protection, it may be useful to make reference to the *Schrems* case once again. In this decision, the Court considered that the right to judicial protection was compromised in the Safe Harbur regime because any effective remedy to access, erasure or review of individuals' data was lacking. The existence of legal remedies to injustices is the logical premise to the effectivity of any fundamental right, and this need is explicitly recalled in the Charter with special regard to the right to data protection. Article 8(3) provides indeed that compliance with data protection rules should always be subject to the control of an independent authority. Because of the specific features of EFR technologies, it is safe to argue that an effective review of this kind of biometric processing would be impossible or very difficult, thereby making the safeguard of Article 8(3) CFREU practically ineffective.

The difficulties in challenging the decisions of EFR systems stem from doubts concerning the science underlying emotion recognition technologies. From a psychological perspective, these find their roots in the work of Paul Ekmann, who in the 1960' developed a theory according to which all human emotions can be reduced to small number of "micro-expressions".[72] Today, the mistrust towards the scientific foundations of this approach has significantly increased, to the point that emotional AI—and consequently EFR—has often been labelled as a "pseudoscience".[73] Among the most critical arguments against Ekman's work there is the supposedly discriminatory nature of his findings, which would be blatantly ignorant of social, cultural and contextual factors impacting on the display of emotions.[74] Against this background, it could be asked whether any effective remedy against a supposedly arbitrary or highly mistaken profiling of the data subject—possibly involving racial discrimination—is imaginable.

Where the very scientific foundations of the technology are unclear or highly questioned, which criteria should be employed to perform a sound review the data processing? Would it ever be possible to achieve a reasonable outcome in such process? According to which scientific standards should it be determined? In other words, the idea that it would be possible to ensure an effective review of data processing operations carried out by EFR technologies seems to be highly questionable.

As highlighted by Tzanou, the "hard core" of the right to data protection—but the argument could be extended to the right to privacy and the freedom of thought—would be "what needs to be protected", i.e. the final values that are protected by such rights: dignity, informational self-determination and individual autonomy. In light of what mentioned above, these values may be irreparably jeopardized by the use of

---

[72] See Crawford (2021); Thomas (2018); Kelion (2019).

[73] Article 19 (2021), p. 6; McStay (2020), p. 2.

[74] Crawford (2021); Article 19 (2021), pp. 15–16; Sedenberg and Chuang (2017), p. 2; Korte (2020). For empirical evidence, see Chen et al. (2018).

EFR technologies in (urban) public spaces. In other words, there is an *a priori* incompatibility between these tools and the European human rights framework.

As it has been noted, when a shortcoming is detected in assessing one of these first compatibility requirements, there is no need to perform a proportionality test. In the case of EFR, it can be argued here that such technologies should be banned because their use is simply incompatible with the essence of the right to privacy, the freedom of thought and the right to data protection. Nonetheless, it may still be useful to engage in a proportionality assessment of EFR. Considering the significant economic interests behind the development of the emotional biometrics industry and its implicit acknowledgement in the Proposal for the AI Regulation, limiting ourselves to proposing a ban of the technology would not probably bring a great practical contribution to the ongoing debate. Also, if end-users of the technology (e.g. law enforcement agencies) did not consider the essence of the rights at stake to be interfered upon, these would still need to carry out a proportionality assessment of the technology at hand. To this end, the next Section will engage with such test. This analysis will reveal that, even if the use of EFR in law enforcement were compatible with EU human rights standards, its acceptable deployments in real case scenarios would be very limited.

5 Proportionality: Applying AFR Requirements to EFR

5.1 Suitability and Necessity

The proportionality principle is the last requirement listed in Article 52(1) of the Charter. Notably, the CJEU was heavily inspired by the German Federal Constitutional Court in developing the procedural steps of its proportionality test, which first comprises an assessment of the suitability and necessity of the measure. In the specific context of data-driven technologies, the European Data Protection Supervisor (EDPS) has also clarified that the necessity test calls for an "assessment of the effectiveness of the measure for the objective pursued and of whether it is less intrusive compared to other options for achieving the same goal".[75] Thus, the assessment of the strict necessity—but also of the suitability of the technologies— requires a factual evidence basis.

Against this background, it is useful to recall an often-cited initiative, the US Transportation Security Authority's 2003 Screening Passengers by Observation Techniques (SPOT) program. The employed software was directly built on a system set up by Ekman, which could automatically detect at a large scale the six fundamental micro-expressions studied by the psychologist. Ekman's method was then further leveraged to train "behaviour detection officers". During the implementation phase, the program was highly criticized not only for its supposedly embedded racial

---

[75]EDPS (2017), p. 5.

biases, but also for its lack of effectiveness and credibility.[76] Specifically, involved officers reported that passengers were flagged and interviewed more or less randomly, and the scarce number of arrests made was totally unrelated to terrorist offences, which were the main targets of the initiative.[77] Even more worryingly, it was claimed that the program itself was leveraged to cover racial profiling practices.[78] Eventually, the US Transportation Security Authority decided for the future to limit funding for behaviour detection activities, claiming that no evidence could support the suitability and effectiveness of the system which had costed the government 900 million US dollars.[79]

Moreover, the suitability of policing initiatives leveraging EFR could also be called into question from another perspective. When deployed in public spaces, especially those passed through by a significant number of people, AI cameras would presumably collect many different inputs. To review them, police departments in charge would need to allocate a considerable amount of trained personnel in dedicated control rooms. This would be a necessity imposed from both practical and legal requirements. On the one hand, indeed, human review would be essential to exclude from further scrutiny people that have been targeted due to an obvious error of the machine. On the other, Article 11 of the Police Directive would require in any case a human in the loop before any negative decision—like being subject to a search—is taken with regard to the individual. Thus, regardless of the level of accuracy reached by the machine, any effective EFR initiative would have to be supported also by human resources, which are often lacking in under budgeted law enforcement agencies. Hence, one could wonder if deploying EFR in urban policing would be more financially burdensome than directly sending patrolling officers looking in strategic venues. Decisions on the deployment of EFR should consider the financial affordability and sustainability of such programs when compared to traditional stop and frisk practices. In such assessments, it should also be taken under consideration that CCTV cameras in uncontrolled environments may provide lower quality images, which in turn may affect the accuracy of the processing and the effectiveness of these initiatives.[80]

5.2   Proportionality *Stricto Sensu*

The last argumentative passage of the CJEU's test is the proportionality *principle in its strictest application*. Almost indulging on a political task, the Court balances the

---

[76] Schwartz (2019).

[77] *Id.*

[78] Ackerman (2017).

[79] US Government Accountability Office (2013). However, the US government has not completely given up emotional biometrics initiatives in the aviation security field, see Hogdson (2019).

[80] European Union Agency for Fundamental Rights (2019), p. 3.

impinged rights and the pursued values, questioning whether the legislator has made a correct use of its margin of appreciation. When the limitation imposed on the right is considerably serious, it tends to apply a stricter approach,[81] thereby requiring the foreseen restrictions to be outbalanced by strong safeguarding countermeasures.

5.2.1 The Need for a Stricter Scrutiny

In the case of EFR use in public spaces, it should be preliminarily highlighted that a very strict proportionality assessment should be performed in light of the seriousness of the interference at stake. Three elements push us towards this direction: (i) the kind of data and processing involved; (ii) the scope and context of the surveillance measure; (iii) the absence of notification mechanisms for individuals interacting with EFR systems. First of all, EFR technologies imply the automated processing of biometric data. Here, sensitivity invests both the kind of data and means of processing employed, and major safeguards against abuse by public authorities are required.[82]

Secondly, the scope of the envisaged interference should be taken under consideration. The use of EFR in uncontrolled environments can indeed capture the data of any individual passing within the range of the camera indiscriminately.[83] This kind of scheme thus involves the collection of biometric data on a large scale, and the significance of such interference is magnified in public urban spaces where individuals do not often have the chance neither to opt-out nor to control the processing.[84]

Thirdly and finally, the lack of notification obligations for public authorities has been identified in the CJEU's case law as a criterion by which the seriousness of the interference can be assessed. That is because the absence of notification is "likely to generate in the minds of the persons concerned the feeling that their private lives are the subject of constant surveillance".[85] Such danger is very much present for EFR implementations in the security domain. Article 52(2) of the Proposal exempts users of biometric categorization systems from notifying targeted individuals of their *interaction* with an AI system when the technology is used for the detecting, preventing and investigating criminal offences.

---

[81] Cf. CJEU, *Digital Rights*, para. 48. Within the ECtHR's case law see ECtHR, *Segerstedt-Wiberg and Others v Sweden*, judgement of 6 June 2006, Appl. No. 62332/00, para. 88.

[82] *Id.* para. 54. See also Ienca and Malgieri (2021), pp. 9–10.

[83] The notion of uncontrolled environments covers "places freely accessible to individuals, where they can also pass through, including public and quasi-public spaces such as shopping malls, hospitals, or schools". Consultative Committee (2021), p. 5.

[84] Information Commissioner's Office (ICO) (2021), p. 9; see Consultative Committee (2021), p. 6 (discussing the role of consent in the use of AFR by public authorities).

[85] CJEU, *Digital Rights*, para. 37.

While this derogation from the general transparency regime seems coherent with the latest ECtHR's approach to bulk surveillance systems,[86] its compatibility with the CJEU's view is less clear. In *Tele2/Watson* indeed, the Court has considered that when access to retained data is granted to law enforcement, targeted individuals should be notified of such processing and of the right to effective remedy, once such notification is no longer liable to jeopardize the investigations.[87] Translating this condition in the EFR context may not require law enforcement authorities to notify *every* individual of their exposure to an EFR system, but it may impose notification to every subject that has been labelled as dangerous by the technology once this can no longer affect the efficacy of investigations. In absence of any clear indication on this point, however, the absence of notification can certainly be taken into consideration as a factor demanding the application of a stricter proportionality assessment of EFR security deployments.

The need for a close scrutiny of EFR can also be argued from the angle of its fundamental difference with AFR identification. What strikes the most, indeed, is the lack of personal criteria of scope limitation in EFR applications. In these scenarios, law enforcement agencies are not looking for someone that is already known or warranted by the police, and inserted in pre-populated watchlists; they are pursuing the "unknown unknowns", scrutinizing anyone that displays suspicious behavior compatible with her being involved in criminal undertakings. This parameter of "scope-limitation" is thus excluded from the proportionality assessment. Instances of preventive EFR could then be associated with a *hybrid* form of surveillance featuring characteristics of both targeted and unfettered surveillance systems. On the one hand, the EFR surveillance initiatives are susceptible of being circumscribed from a temporal and especially geographical perspective, being deployable in restricted chosen venues for limited periods of time; on the other, EFR cameras can capture anyone within their visual range, even though the people pinpointed may not have any connection whatsoever with the commission of criminal offences.[88]

Overall, two main elements support the application of a very strict proportionality assessment. First, the greater intrusiveness of EFR technologies in the law enforcement domain. Second, in comparison with AFR, the inapplicability of personal limitations to the deployments of these technologies. To exemplify the repercussions of adopting a stricter approach with EFR, it could be useful to look at the

---

[86] While the ECtHR has acknowledged that subsequent notification is a relevant factor when assessing the effectiveness of remedies (see ECtHR, *Roman Zakharov*, para. 234; see also ECtHR, *Klass and Others v Germany*, judgement of 6 September 1978, Appl. No.5029/71, paras. 68–71; ECtHR, *Weber and Saravia*, para. 135), it has also considered that in bulk interception systems remedies that do not depend from previous individual notification may even provide better guarantees (see ECtHR, *Big Brother Watch*, para. 358). On notification in the ECtHR's surveillance case law, see De Hert and Malgieri (2020), pp. 26–29.

[87] CJEU, *Tele2/Watson*, para. 121.

[88] The same happens when social media databases are integrated in AFR software, enabling the identification of people that have not been inserted in watchlists. See Neroni Rezende (2020), p. 385.

proportionality requirements already set out for remote biometric identification in public spaces by the Proposal for the AI Regulation. At the moment of writing, the Proposal is undergoing an ordinary legislative procedure before the competent EU institutions.[89] Being the outcomes of this process unknown at present, the analysis certainly bears some degree of speculative character.[90] This is all the more uncertain considering the joint Opinion of the European Data Protection Board (EDPB) and the EDPS, rejecting the regime laid down at Article 5 of the Proposal and calling for a ban of the AFR technology altogether. With regard to EFR specifically, the EDPB and EDPS have also indicated that "the use of AI to infer emotions of a natural person is *highly undesirable* and should be prohibited".[91]

Regardless of the outcome of the legislative procedure undergone by the Proposal, this analysis may hopefully bring some theoretical and practical contribution to the debate on the regulation of EFR technologies.[92] Indeed, the rules set out in the proposed Article 5 embed certain criteria elaborated, in the last few years, by the European national and supranational Courts in surveillance case law. Certainly, it has been underlined that *not all* EFR applications could automatically fall within the purview of the regime of Article 5 of the Proposal.[93] That is because some of these tools may not be designed to directly perform identification operations, specifically by matching the images of the people labelled as suspicious with a database of pre-stored templates. However, given the specificities of the law enforcement context, it seems pertinent to apply these criteria to EFR tools. Here, as said, public authorities always need to perform identification activities to pursue their primary objectives of preventing, and especially investigating and prosecuting criminal offences. Practically, emotional AI capabilities may be embedded in facial recognition software already designed for the identification of individuals. When such features are not available in the system, identification operations will probably be carried out subsequently by police officers themselves.

5.2.2 Guidelines from the European Surveillance Case Law

Different aspects should be taken into account when assessing fair and balanced implementations of EFR technologies in law enforcement: (i) grounds for authorization; (ii) scope-delimitation criteria; (iii) data storage requirements; (iv) *ex ante* and *ex post* supervision. To begin with the grounds that could legitimize EFR in public places, not all the criminal offences that authorize the use of facial recognition could probably serve the same purpose in this context. For instance, Article 5(1)(d)

---

[89] 2021/0106(COD) Artificial Intelligence Act, Legislative Observatory.

[90] EDPB-EDPS (2021), p. 3.

[91] *Id.* The same opinion is shared by the Consultative Committee (2021), p. 5 [emphasis added].

[92] For instance, it has emerged that controllers often give insufficient consideration to necessity and proportionality issues tied to the deployment of such systems. See ICO (2021), p. 11.

[93] Above, Sect. 2.

(iii) of the Proposal refers to the crimes listed at Article 2(2) of Council Framework Decision 2002/584/JHA and "punishable in the Member State concerned by a custodial sentence or a detention order for a maximum period of at least three years, as determined by the law of that Member State". Although these criminal offences are identified within the EU framework as falling within the category of serious crime,[94] they may not always reach such a level of gravity to justify the deployment of EFR, which implies the setup of an indiscriminate surveillance system (even though in specific locations). EFR, if suitable and effective, could be used only to address the most serious forms of crime which also fall within the State needs of protecting its national security. For example, that would be the case of terrorism, a domain where the overlap between intelligence and law enforcement activities is evident.[95] This argument finds corroboration also in the position recently adopted by the CJEU in *La Quadrature du net*. Here the Court found that only the objectives of safeguarding national security—including tackling terrorist offences—can justify more serious interference with fundamental rights.[96] Considering that the "mental data processing"[97] performed by EFR poses greater dangers than mere AFR identification, this kind of surveillance could be implemented only on the basis of objective evidence establishing a risk of a terrorist attack or of another immediate danger for national security.

Furthermore, Article 5 refers to geographical, temporal and personal limitations to ensure a proportionate use of AFR in public places for law enforcement purposes. Clearly, these criteria are drawn from the approach consistently applied by the CJEU in (mass) data retention cases since *Digital Rights Ireland*. The Court considers indeed that the goal of fighting against serious crime does not allow in itself an indiscriminate surveillance: any monitoring measure needs to be circumscribed by objective criteria presenting an objective link with the stated aims.[98] These criteria can for instance limit data collection measures to particular areas or categories of people presenting—in specific timeframes—objective risks related to the commission of serious criminal offences.[99] In absence of personal criteria of scope

---

[94]The same categories of offences are listed as constituting serious crime in the Annex II of the Directive (EU) 2016/681 of the European Parliament and of the Council of 27 April 2016 on the use of passenger name record (PNR) data for the prevention, detection, investigation and prosecution of terrorist offences and serious crime, OJ L 119, 4.5.2016, p. 132–149.

[95]On the issues that the growing proximity between intelligence and law enforcement has raised, see generally Vervaele (2005); De Hert (2005).

[96]CJEU, *La Quadrature du Net*, paras. 135–137.

[97]Ienca and Malgieri identify "mental data" with emotions or other thoughts that are not "related to health status, sexuality or political/religious beliefs". See Ienca and Malgieri (2021), p. 1.

[98]CJEU, *Digital Rights*, para. 57; CJEU, *Maximilian Schrems v Data Protection Commissioner*, para. 93; *Tele2/Watson*, para. 110; CJEU, *Opinion 1/15*, para. 191; CJEU, *La Quadrature du Net*, para. 133; CJEU, *Privacy International v Secretary of State for Foreign and Commonwealth Affairs and Others*, judgement of 6 October 2020, Case C-623/17, para. 78. With regard to the application of these criteria to the case of the AFR app Clearview, see Neroni Rezende (2020), p. 385 ff.

[99]This approach has also made inroads outside the EU legal system with the recent decision *R (Bridges) v the Chief Constable of South Wales Police* [2020] EWCA CIV 1058. Specifically, the

delimitation, temporal and geographical restrictions in EFR should be interpreted even more strictly than it would be the case for AFR. Quantifying the length and breadth of the surveillance measure remains however difficult at a theoretical level. As provided by Article 5 of the Proposal, decisions authorizing practical implementations of the technology need to be guided by risk-informed criteria, such as the likelihood of the foreseen negative event and the seriousness of its consequences. Only in light of such information, it would be possible to perform a balancing test to decide on the specific timeframe and location of EFR implementations. However, in order to avoid leaving a too wide margin of appreciation to public authorities, the relevant legislation should establish with sufficient clarity maximum delays and procedures for renewal of the measure.

According to the long-standing surveillance case law of the ECtHR and the CJEU,[100] clear and precise rules should also govern the procedures to be followed for subsequent storing of the data. In addition to data security standards, access to stored data shall be granted only to specifically trained officers, who should probably be less in number compared to those authorized to analyze AFR feeds. In this context, precautions to be taken before communicating data are also important. The expertise of the deployed officers has indeed a bearing on the effective application of the right not to be fully subject to an automated decision, foreseen in the EU general data protection framework.[101] In the preventive phase specifically, this right should be triggered automatically, regardless of any request of the data subject who is often unaware of the processing. This means that before taking any further action towards an individual flagged as suspicious, law enforcement agencies should *proprio motu* submit the assessment made by the AI agent to a manual review.[102]

When it comes to storage conditions, also maximum periods of retention play a significant role when assessing the proportionality of the surveillance system. To keep the intrusion within the limits of what strictly necessary, a difference should be made between data relating to individuals identified as potentially dangerous, and those that have not been determined to be so.[103] Similarly to what had been foreseen in the AFR "Locate" regime, data relating to the individuals that have not been

---

Court of Appeal stated that two concerns arose within the legal framework of AFR Locate, namely the "who question" and the "where question". Indeed, in relation to the people that could be inserted in the watchlists and the locations where the technology could be deployed, legal rules were too generic and left an excessive margin of appreciation to public authorities.

[100] Starting from the *Huvig* judgement, the ECtHR elaborated a set of foreseeability criteria against which surveillance laws need to be assessed. These criteria have been later refined in the *Weber and Saravia* case, and have been thus called "Huvig" or "Weber" criteria since then. According to De Hert and Malgieri, these criteria have been implicitly integrated in the CJEU case law since the *Digital Rights Ireland* case. See De Hert and Malgieri (2020), p. 32.

[101] See Art. 11 of the Police Directive and Art. 22 GDPR.

[102] A similar mechanism is already provided in Art. 6(5) of the PNR Directive.

[103] The need for establishing difference in the storing regime according to the specific situation of the data subjects emerges clearly in the case law of the CJEU. See CJEU, *Opinion 1/15*, paras. 196–203.

labelled as dangerous should be immediately erased.[104] Also, retention periods for data relating to people flagged as suspicious should be severely restricted. Two scenarios can be discerned in this regard. If the initial positive match does not overcome the manual review, data shall be immediately erased as in the first case. If, however, the human agent esteems that the pinpointed individual does actually express a suspicious attitude, the data storage should be limited to the time strictly necessary for the authorities to decide whether and how to take action, or for the notified individual to challenge the decision.[105] Especially in real-time EFR scenarios, these decisions should be made in a very short timeframe to satisfy the preventive purposes of the surveillance initiative. In other words, EFR should only function as a tool for highlighting promising targets of intervention, assuming that one considers these systems capable of such a task. Thus, data should be retained for a very limited amount of time. Also, immediate erasure of the data should prevent any further use or "leak" in subsequent criminal proceedings, where these could be used as evidence.

With regard to the nature and organization of *ex ante* and *ex post* supervision of EFR processing, one first concern is the system of authorization of EFR deployments. To ensure that these are circumscribed to what strictly necessary and that competing interests are reasonably balanced, the authorization should be given by an independent authority, in compliance with Article 8(3) of the Charter and the case law of both the CJEU and the ECtHR. Even though the ECtHR has expressed in the past a preference for judicial control, it suffices that the authority in question is capable to freely adjudicate without suffering interference by the government.[106] In the case at stake, this requirement does not seem to pose problems, as it is already foreseen by Article 5(4) of the Proposal.

Instead, a second set of concerns regards notification obligations for surveilled individuals. To ensure a fair balancing of the interests at stake, the interference with the rights to privacy and data protection should be compensated by strong safeguards, among which the right to an effective remedy. Regardless of their being checked by the police, should individuals targeted by EFR be notified that a positive match has occurred in their situation? Different answers may be given depending on how the surveillance scheme put in place by EFR-equipped cameras is qualified. For instance, expressing a difficulty in totally embracing notification requirements,[107] the ECtHR esteems that bulk surveillance systems may not require a regime of bespoke individual notification, if remedies against inaccurate or unlawful processing are granted on a general basis to the population as a whole. According

---

[104] The AFR Locate program, implemented by the Welsh police and censured in the *Bridges* case, provided that when the facial data processing of passers-by did not lead to any positive match, such data should have been immediately erased. See *R (Bridges) v Chief Constable of the South Wales Police* [2019] EWHC 2341, para. 16.

[105] See paragraph below.

[106] De Hert and Malgieri (2020), p. 10. See also Malgieri and De Hert (2017).

[107] See De Hert and Malgieri (2020), pp. 26–29.

to the Court, in some cases this may even be the best solution to provide the highest standards of protection.[108] Nonetheless, when the intrusiveness of the technology is so serious, nothing would prevent legislators from cumulating two systems of remedies: one generalized and independent from the previous notification, and one based on notification for people having been specifically targeted by the system.

Considering the opposing interests at stake, it would indeed seem reasonable to generally exempt law enforcement EFR processing from transparency requirements, as provided by Article 52 of the Proposal. On the other hand, however, this derogation from the general regime does not appear to achieve a fair balance between security and fundamental rights needs when it comes to people singled out as dangerous by the system. In this case, the potential negative consequences for the data subject and the seriousness of the intrusion in her private sphere should outweigh the exigencies of opacity normally underlying law enforcement activities. Therefore, in conclusion, a fair balancing of the needs at stake could probably be obtained only with a bespoke regime of subsequent notification for individuals labelled as dangerous by the EFR system.

6   EFR and the Presumption of Innocence

It is widely acknowledged in the literature that digital technologies are bringing about new challenges for the presumption of innocence.[109] Foreseen in different constitutional traditions,[110] as well as at the international[111] and EU level,[112] this principle is at the core of the notion of fair trial as enshrined in Article 6(1) of the

---

[108] *Big Brother Watch*, para. 358.

[109] See, e.g., Caianiello (2019); Hadjimatheou (2017), p. 40; De Hert (2005), p. 85.

[110] As indicated by Sayers (2014), p. 1305 ff. In 2012, the CJEU recognized the presumption of innocence as "a feature of the constitutional traditions common to the Member States". See CJEU, *Criminal proceedings against Marcello Costa and Ugo Cifone*, judgement of 16 February 2021, Joined Cases C-72/10 and C-77/10, para. 86.

[111] All EU Member States are part to the International Covenant on Civil and Political Rights, whose Art. 14(2) explicitly refers to the accused's right "right to be presumed innocent until proved guilty according to law".

[112] In primary EU law, the presumption of innocence is enshrined in Art. 48 of the Charter, whose explanations equate to the contents of Art. 6(2) of the Convention. Even before the entry into force of the Charter, however, the CJEU had already recognized the presumption of innocence as one of the fundamental rights protected in Union law (see CJEU, *Montecatini S.p.A*, judgement of 8 July 1999, Case C-235/92, para. 175). At the level of secondary law, this right is explicitly recalled at Art. 2 of the Directive (EU) 2016/343 of the European Parliament and of the Council of 9 March 2016 on the strengthening of certain aspects of the presumption of innocence and of the right to be present at the trial in criminal proceedings OJ L 65, 11.3.2016, pp. 1–11. On the protection of the presumption of innocence in the EU legal system, see generally Sayers (2014); Balsamo (2018), pp. 253–255; Manes and Caianiello (2020), pp. 249–255.

Convention.[113] In criminal proceedings, the presumption of innocence functions both as a rule of judgement[114] and as a rule of treatment.[115] While the presumption finds application only in *ongoing* criminal proceedings, it is not specifically devised for the preventive phase.[116] Only persons that have been "charged" with a criminal offence can benefit from this important safeguard.[117] Despite the statutory limits of the principle, surveillance scholarship has raised multiple concerns over a supposedly increasing erosion of the presumption of innocence, weakened by emerging mass surveillance programs.[118]

These positions rely on an extensive interpretation of the principle, which is reworked as a "moral entitlement" based on civic trust. People have a right to be treated as trustworthy and should be presumed as acting in compliance with their main obligations in society, thus making any unfettered monitoring measure implemented by the State unjustified (e.g. mass data retention systems, ANPR, live facial recognition in public places). Where surveillance is not grounded on individual suspicion, the presumption of innocence is subverted by assuming everyone to be guilty of something. In the domain of criminal legal scholarship, Ashworth and Zedner have proposed a similar concept, i.e. the presumption of *harmlessness*. Like the presumption of innocence, this principle is underlined by the respect for each individual's status as a responsible agent in society.[119] This implies that, setting aside high-risk settings (e.g. airport security), people should not be subject to universal risk assessments as they should be "presumed free from harmful intentions".[120] Albeit being suggestive, these attempts to broaden the interpretation of the presumption of innocence have been criticized by some other scholars holding that this safeguard should continue to be understood in strict legal terms, i.e. as a specific fair trial entitlement applicable only within the boundaries of ongoing criminal proceedings.[121]

---

[113] ECtHR, *Konstas v. Greece*, judgement of 24 May 2011, Appl. No.53466/07, para. 29. It is no surprise that the ECtHR frequently examines complaints of violations of the presumption of innocence with joint reference to both the first and second paragraph of Art. 6.

[114] This means that the burden of proof is placed on the prosecution, and any doubt on the criminal responsibility of the accused should profit the latter. Cf. ECtHR, *John Murray v. United Kingdom*, judgement of 8 February 1996, Appl. No.18731/91, paras. 54; ECtHR, *Telfner v. Austria*, judgement of 20 March 2011, Appl. No.33501/96.

[115] This rule prohibits that the accused person is considered or treated as guilty before her responsibility is established by a court of law. Cf. ECtHR, *Shyti v. Romania*, judgement of 19 November 2013, Appl. No. 12042/05.

[116] De Hert (2005), p. 85.

[117] In this regard, it should also be noted that the Charter used a more neutral language compared to the Convention. Indeed, while Art. 6(2) ECHR employs the expression "charged with a criminal offence"—which should be nonetheless interpreted in light of the so-called '*Engel* criteria'—the Charter only uses the term 'charged', avoiding any explicit reference to criminal offences.

[118] Hadjimatheou (2017), pp. 41, 43 ff.

[119] Ashworth and Zedner (2014), p. 66.

[120] *Id.*, p. 130 (citing Floud, Young (1982)).

[121] Hadjimatheou (2017), p. 41.

It can nonetheless be observed that preventive criminal justice cannot avoid all considerations associated to the presumption of innocence. If that were the case, eluding individual fair trial safeguards would be extremely easy for public authorities. Indeed, these would simply have to make recourse to preventive instruments to subtly circumvent the rights that are granted to suspects in the framework of criminal proceedings.

Against this background, there emerges in this case as well the need to pay a closer attention to the scope of the principle, possibly "anticipating" its protective effects also to the preventive phase. In a world where individuals are increasingly singled out thanks to ever more insidious technologies,[122] indeed, the risks for individuals to be wrongfully stigmatized are only destined to grow, dramatically. When it comes to EFR, specifically, potential issues with the presumption of innocence are twofold: (i) the lack of personal limitations in the scope of surveillance operations; (ii) the possibility of drawing adverse inferences against the suspect from inaccurate or unreliable processing carried out by the EFR system. In tackling these gaps, procedural safeguards attached to the rights to privacy and data protection seem to offer comparable standards of protection.

6.1 Absence of Personal Limitations

As said, the first issue with EFR implementations—contrary to remote biometric identification—is the lack personal limitations in scope. People having no connection whatsoever with the commission of criminal offences may in fact suffer the negative consequences of EFR surveillance, and be wrongfully stigmatized because of it.[123] Interestingly, the absence of personal criteria and the resulting risks of undue criminalization seem to generate concerns for both the presumption of innocence and the rights to privacy and data protection. On the one hand, the ECtHR has indeed stated that the presumption of innocence shields the individual from the stigmatizing effect of an allegation of criminal liability, thus preserving her dignity.[124] On the other, the rights to privacy and data protection are—as pointed out above[125]—ultimately aimed at the preservation of human dignity. Their relevance to this end is only increasing with the world's digital transformation, as personal data processing can easily result in discriminatory and otherwise stigmatizing practices.

---

[122] On the preventive turn taken by policing and the role played by digital technologies, see van Brakel and De Hert (2011); Brayne (2017); Ferguson (2017).

[123] Wrongful criminalization can be defined as "treating someone as if they have a particular propensity towards criminality or indeed are already involved in criminal activity, without proper grounds for doing so". See Hadjimatheou (2017), p. 45

[124] Balsamo (2018), p. 116.

[125] Above, Sect. 4.

The conceptual links between these safeguards could be spotted in the case law of the CJEU. While anchoring its considerations to the rights to privacy and data protection—and not specifically the presumption of innocence—the CJEU has raised concerns over the absence of personal limitations with regard to the provision of unfettered surveillance systems in the Union. In *Digital Rights*, for instance, the CJEU stated that the Directive 2006/24/EC (the Data Retention Directive) was susceptible for its indiscriminate scope of creating in the minds of the people concerned a (rather stigmatizing) "feeling that their private lives are the subject of constant surveillance".[126] Since this landmarking judgement, the approach taken by the Court in data retention cases has continued to be consistent. As confirmed in the recent *La Quadrature du Net* judgement, indeed, a data retention system targeting "persons with respect to whom there is no evidence capable of suggesting that their conduct might have a link, even an indirect or remote one, with that objective of combating *serious crime*"[127] is simply not compatible with the principle of proportionality as enshrined in EU law.

In the same line of reasoning, more invasive measures involving the *real-time* collection and analysis of communication metadata directly by law enforcement can only be justified with regard to specific individuals, thus requiring "a valid reason to suspect that they are involved in one way or another in terrorist activities".[128] What emerges from this analysis is that particular serious forms of interference with the rights to privacy and data protection—if not justified by objectives of national security—need to be circumscribed by criteria of a personal nature, may these operate at a group or individual level. Further evidentiary elements need to substantiate a reasonable suspicion that such individuals may be involved in a criminal undertaking of a serious nature. As things stand, EFR seems not to be fit to ensure that such subjective limitations are enforced.

Thus, the use of EFR seems to be at odds with the requirements of the CJEU, and this gap cannot probably be overcome. Overall, if legal theorists are still struggling to stretch the applicability of the presumption of innocence—understood as a component of the fair trial—the rights to privacy and data protection seem to offer an equivalent coverage for individuals in less safeguarding phases of law enforcement activities broadly understood (including preventive ones). It goes outside the scope of this contribution to explore the implications of this argument. Nonetheless, it can be observed here that the link between the presumption of innocence and the rights to privacy and data protection should probably be found in the centrality of the value of fairness in the safeguards they provide. These rights share a common concern for undue stigmatization, and more broadly for any *unfair* adverse treatment against the individual. This underpinning rationale translates into safeguards of a *procedural* nature, aimed at identifying justifications for encroachments on individuals' personal freedoms. This aspect further emerges in the guarantees that the rights

---

[126] CJEU, *Digital Rights*, para. 37.

[127] CJEU, *La Quadrature du Net*, para. 143 [emphasis added].

[128] CJEU, *La Quadrature du Net*, para. 188.

to privacy and data protection can afford with regard to adverse inferences that can be leveraged against the individual based on the processing of her personal data.

6.2   Adverse Inferences

Another way in which the presumption of innocence could negatively be affected by EFR surveillance is the use of adverse inferences against the suspect or accused. In the case of EFR, these may be drawn from the "emotional demeanor" of the individual, caught in situations that the police find to be connected to the commission of a criminal offence. The use of presumptions can raise tensions with the presumption of innocence, as these can subtly reverse the burden of proof that should always weigh on the prosecution. Still, the ECtHR has clarified that the existence of presumptions of fact or law that may operate against the accused does not necessarily violate the presumption of innocence. This only requires such presumptions to be circumscribed within reasonable boundaries, ensuring a fair balancing of the interests at stake and the rights of the defence.[129]

Looking at these requirements, could someone be fairly presumed to be "suspicious" only based on EFR processing? It seems difficult to argue in this direction. At the outset, it could be assumed that the use of such invasive technology may be proportionate in relation to most serious criminal offences and threats to national security. However, several issues would persist so as to the *fairness* of these operations. As argued above,[130] the scientific unsoundness of EFR and its underlying technology makes the decisions of such software opaque and thus difficult to challenge for targeted individuals. If garnered datapoints—even where collected in preventive operations—were introduced in the proceedings, these could hardly be considered rebuttable by the defence,[131] also in light of an aura of objectiveness that often surrounds scientific evidence. Needless to say, this would irremediably impair the individual's rights of defence, her right to the equality of arms, to an effective remedy and the overall fairness of the proceeding.

Once again, similar procedural concerns are also supported in the data protection legislation, applicable to the preventive phase as well. Fairness as a basic tenet of data protection law prevents data controllers from taking any unjustified adverse or

---

[129] ECtHR, 20 October 1998, *Salabiaku v. France*, Appl. No.10519/83, para. 28. More recently, see also ECtHR, 26 January 2016, *Iasir v. Belgium,* Appl. no. 21614/12, para. 30. In EU law, this approach was confirmed in the Directive on the presumption of innocence. Its Recital (22) indicates that the principle is not impinged by the use of presumptions, provided that these are "rebuttable", "used only where the rights of the defence are respected", and "confined within reasonable limits", also considering the proportionate use of means employed in relation to the aims pursued.

[130] Above, Sect. 4.

[131] On the issues brought about the use of AI system with regard to the defence rights, especially in adversarial systems, see Contissa and Lasagni (2020); Quattroccolo (2019).

stigmatizing action towards the data subject based on the processing of its personal data. The right not to be fully subject to an automated decision represents another an important entitlement in this sense, as it ensures that EFR processing is surrounded by adequate safeguards, among which the right to obtain human intervention and—as added by Recital (38) of the Police Directive—the rights to express her point of view, to obtain an explanation for the decision or to challenge it. All in all, whether presumptions based on EFR processing were introduced at trial or taken as bases for preventive and investigative measures, similar safeguards should be available to individuals to defend their presumption of innocence.

7   Conclusions

In this contribution preventive uses of EFR technologies in public places were examined. In light of recent developments suggesting an increasing use of such tools in the law enforcement context, it was considered appropriate to evaluate them in light of the European standards of fundamental rights protection. Specifically, EFR deployments were assessed against four fundamental rights, sharing a common rationale: the rights to privacy and data protection, the freedom of thought and—to some extent—the presumption of innocence.

Ostensibly, a certain degree of speculation could not be avoided in this preliminary assessment of EFR. Indeed, two levels of unpredictability are involved. On the one hand, the legal framework for regulating the use of AI in the EU is still underway and the future work of legal interpreters may further impact on its concrete application. On the other, specific instances of implementation of EFR technologies are still surrounded by many uncertainties and tailored assessments can only be supported by a substantial factual basis. These information gaps can only be tackled in future research.

All in all, the surveillance case law elaborated both by the ECtHR and the CJEU is still under development, but provides by now a comprehensive framework through which new technological advancements can be assessed. While it is acknowledged that such tools may have a beneficial impact on the efficiency of law enforcement activities, their use should also be critically evaluated in democratic societies. This implies that relevant actors should not only be able to determine when and how new technologies can be fairly deployed, but also which uses should simply be rejected in a democratic society. In the case of EFR, the latter seems to be the most obvious conclusion.

Acknowledgement This contribution was written in the framework of the European Union's Horizon 2020 research and innovation programme under the Marie Sklodowska-Curie ITN EJD 'Law, Science and Technology Rights of Internet of Everything' grant agreement no. 814177.

References

2021/0106(COD) Artificial Intelligence Act, Legislative Observatory. https://oeil.secure.europarl. europa.eu/oeil/popups/ficheprocedure.do?reference=2021/0106(COD)&l=en. Accessed 9 July 2021

Ackerman S (2017) TSA screening program risks racial profiling amid shaky science – study. The Guardian. https://www.theguardian.com/us-news/2017/feb/08/tsa-screening-racial-religious-profiling-aclu-study. Accessed 3 July 2021

Adam R, Tizzano A (2014) Manuale di Diritto dell'Unione Europea. Giappichelli Editore, Torino

Albino V et al (2015) Smart cities: definitions, dimensions, performance and initiatives. J Urban Technol 22:1–19

Article 19 (2021) Emotional Entanglement: China's emotion recognition market and its implications for human rights. https://www.article19.org/wp-content/uploads/2021/01/ER-Tech-China-Report.pdf. Accessed 22 June 2020

Article 29 Data Protection Working Party (2012) Opinion 02/2012 on facial recognition in online and mobile services, 00727/12/EN, WP 192, Brussels, 22 March 2012

Ashworth A, Zedner L (2014) Preventive justice. Oxford monographs on criminal law and justice. Oxford University Press

Balsamo A (2018) The content of fundamental rights. In: Kostoris RE (ed) Handbook of European criminal procedure. Springer, pp 99–170

BBC News (2018) 2,000 wrongly matched with possible criminals at Champions League. https://www.bbc.com/news/uk-wales-south-west-wales-44007872. Accessed 11 July 2021

Berle I (2020) Face recognition technology. Springer, Law, Governance and Technology Series

Brayne S (2017) Big data surveillance: the case of policing. Am Sociol Rev 82(5):977–1008

Brkan M (2018) The concept of essence of fundamental rights in the EU legal order: peeling the onion to its Core. Eur Const Law Rev 14:332–368

Caianiello M (2019) Criminal process faced with the challenges of scientific and technological development. Eur J Crime Crim Law Crim Just 27(4):267–291

Caianiello M (2021) Dangerous liaisons. Potentialities and risks deriving from the interaction between artificial intelligence and preventive justice. Eur J Crime Crim Law Crim Just 29(1): 1–23

Castelvecchi D (2020) Is facial recognition too biased to be let loose? Nature 587:347–349. https://www.nature.com/articles/d41586-020-03186-4. Accessed 28 June 2020

Chen C et al (2018) Distinct facial expressions represent pain and pleasure across cultures. Proc Natl Acad Sci U S A 115(43):E10013–E10021. https://www.pnas.org/content/pnas/115/43/E10013.full.pdf. Accessed 2 July 2021

Christofi A, Verdoodt V (2019) Exploring the essence of the right to data protection and smart cities. CiTiP Working Paper. Available at SSRN: https://papers.ssrn.com/sol3/papers.cfm?abstract_id=3483616. Accessed 2 July 2021

Consultative Committee of the Convention for the Protection of Individuals with regard to Automatic Processing of Personal Data (2021) Guidelines on facial recognition. https://rm.coe.int/guidelines-on-facial-recognition/1680a134f3. Accessed 8 July 2021

Contissa G, Lasagni G (2020) When it is (also) algorithms and AI that decide on criminal matters: in search of an effective remedy. Eur J Crime Crim Law Crim Just 28:280–304

Crawford K (2021) Time to regulate AI that interprets human emotions. Nature 592(7853):167. https://www.nature.com/articles/d41586-021-00868-5. Accessed 15 Aug 2022

Daily SB, James MT, Cherry D, Porter JJ, Darnell SS, Isaac J, Roy T (2017) Affective computing: historical foundations, current applications, and future trends. In: Jeon M (ed) Emotions and affect in human factors and human-computer interaction. Associated Press, pp 213–231

De Hert P (2005) Balancing security and liberty within the European human rights framework. A critical regarding of Court's case law in the light of surveillance and criminal law enforcement strategies after 9/11. Utrecht Law Rev 1(1):68–96

De Hert P, Malgieri G (2020) Article 8 ECHR Compliant and Foreseeable Surveillance: the ECtHR's expanded legality requirement copied by the CJEU. A Discussion of European Surveillance Case Law. Brussels Privacy Hub Working Paper 6(1):1–40

EDPB-EDPS (2021) Joint Opinion 5/2021 on the proposal for a Regulation of the European Parliament and of the Council laying down harmonised rules on artificial intelligence (Artificial Intelligence Act). https://edpb.europa.eu/system/files/2021-06/edpb-edps_joint_opinion_ai_reg ulation_en.pdf. Accessed 6 July 2021

EDPS (2017) Assessing the necessity of measures that limit the fundamental right to the protection of personal data: a toolkit. https://edps.europa.eu/sites/default/files/publication/17-06-01_ necessity_toolkit_final_en.pdf. Accessed 16 Aug 2022

European Parliament (2021) Artificial Intelligence in policing: safeguards needed against mass surveillance. Press Release. https://www.europarl.europa.eu/news/en/press-room/20210624 IPR06917/artificial-intelligence-in-policing-safeguards-needed-against-mass-surveillance. Accessed 30 June 2021

European Union Agency for Fundamental Rights (2019) Facial Recognition Technology: Funda-mental Rights Considerations in the Context of Law Enforcement. https://fra.europa.eu/en/ publication/2019/facial-recognition-technology-fundamental-rights-considerations-context-law. Accessed 6 July 2021

Feldman Barrett L (2017) The theory of constructed emotion: an active inference account of interoception and categorization. Soc Cogn Affect Neurosci 12(11):1–23

Ferguson AG (2017) Big data surveillance: the convergence of big data and law enforcement. In: Gray D, Henderson SE (eds) The Cambridge handbook of surveillance law. Cambridge University Press

Gallagher R, Jona L (2019) We Tested Europe's New Lie detector for travelers — and immediately triggered a false positive. The Intercept. https://theintercept.com/2019/07/26/europe-border-control-ai-lie-detector/. Accessed 8 July 2021

Hadjimatheou K (2017) Surveillance technologies, wrongful criminalisation, and the presumption of innocence. Philos Technol 30:39–54

Heaven D (2020) Expression of doubt. Nature 578:502–504

Heilweil R (2020) Big tech companies back away from selling facial recognition to police. That's progress. The Vox. https://www.vox.com/recode/2020/6/10/21287194/amazon-microsoft-ibm-facial-recognition-moratorium-police. Accessed 11 July 2021

Hildebrandt M (2010) Some caveats on profiling. In: Gutwirth S, Poullet Y, de Hert P (eds) Data protection in a profiled world. Springer

Hogdson C (2019) AI lie detector developed for airport security. The Financial Times. https://www. ft.com/content/c9997e24-b211-11e9-bec9-fdcab53d6959. Accessed 8 July 2021

iBorderCrtl (2016) The Project. https://www.iborderctrl.eu/The-project. Accessed 11 July 2021

Ienca M, Malgieri G (2021) Mental Data Protection and the GDPR. Available at SSRN.: https:// papers.ssrn.com/sol3/papers.cfm?abstract_id=3840403. Accessed 8 July 2021

Information Commissioner's Office (ICO) (2021) The use of live facial recognition technology by law enforcement in public places. https://ico.org.uk/media/fororganisations/documents/261 9985/ico-opinion-the-use-of-lfr-in-public-places-20210618.pdf. Accessed 5 July 2021

Kelion L (2019) Emotion-detecting tech should be restricted by law – AI Now. BBC. https://www. bbc.com/news/technology-50761116. Accessed 15 Aug 2022

Kindt EJ (2018) Having yes, using no? About the new legal regime for biometric data. Comput Law Secur Rev 34(3):523–538

Koops BJ, Newell BC, Timan T, Škorvánek I, Chokrevski T, Galič M (2017) A typology of privacy. U Pa J Int Law 38(2):483–575

Korte A (2020) Facial-Recognition Technology Cannot Read Emotions, Scientists Say. American Association for the Advancement of Science. https://www.aaas.org/news/facial-recognition-technology-cannot-read-emotions-scientists-say. Accessed 8 July 2020

Kostoris RE (2018) The protection of fundamental rights. In: Kostoris RE (ed) Handbook of European criminal procedure. Springer

Kotsoglou KN, Oswald M (2020) The long arm of the algorithm? Automated facial recognition as evidence and trigger for police intervention. Forensic Sci Int Synergy 2:86–69

Kummitha RKR, Crutzen N (2017) How do we understand smart cities? An evolutionary perspec-tive. Cities 67:43–52

Lasagni G (2021) La Falsa Confessione come Causa di Errori Giudiziari. In: Lupària Donati L (ed) L'Errore Giudiziario. Giuffrè, pp 189–225

Liao S (2018) Chinese facial recognition system mistakes a face on a bus for a jaywalker. The Verge. https://www.theverge.com/2018/11/22/18107885/china-facial-recognition-mistaken-jay walker. Accessed 11 July 2021

Malgieri G, De Hert P (2017) European human rights, criminal surveillance, and intelligence surveillance: towards "good enough" oversight, preferably but not necessarily by judges. In: Gray DC, Henderson S (eds) The Cambridge handbook on surveillance. Cambridge University Press, New York, pp 509–532

Malgieri G, Ienca M (2021) The EU regulates AI but forgets to protect our mind. European Law Blog. https://europeanlawblog.eu/2021/07/07/the-eu-regulates-ai-but-forgets-to-protect-our-mind/#more-7784. Accessed 7 July 2021

Manes V, Caianiello M (2020) Manuale di Diritto Penale Europeo. Giappichelli

Marat E, Sutton D (2021) Technological solutions for complex problems: emerging electronic surveillance regimes in Eurasian cities. Eur Asia Stud 73(1):243–267

Mantovani F (2013) Diritto Penale: Parte Speciale I. Delitti Contro la Persona, 5th edn. Cedam

McStay A (2018) The Right to Privacy in the Age of Emotional AI. https://www.ohchr.org/Documents/Issues/DigitalAge/ReportPrivacyinDigitalAge/AndrewMcStayProfessor%20of%20Digital%20Life,%20BangorUniversityWalesUK.pdf. Accessed 2 July 2021

McStay A (2020) Emotional AI, soft biometrics and the surveillance of emotional life: an unusual consensus on privacy. Big Data Soc January-June 2020:1–12

Murgia M (2021) Emotion recognition: can AI detect human feelings from a face?. Financial Times. https://www.ft.com/content/c0b03d1d-f72f-48a8-b342-b4a926109452.   Accessed 30 January 2022

Neroni Rezende I (2020) Facial recognition in police hands: assessing the 'Clearview case' from a European perspective. New J Eur Crim Law 11(3):375–389

Neroni Rezende I (2021) Predictive policing: safeguards for the choice of data and automated processing in the preventive context. In: Barona Vilar S (ed) Justicia Algorítmica y Neuroderecho: Una mirada multidisciplinaria. Tirada lo Banch, Valencia, pp 361–387

Nussbaum MC (2001) Upheavels of thought: the intelligence of emotions. Cambridge University Press

O'Flaherty M (2020) Facial recognition technology and fundamental rights. European Data Protection Law Review 6(2):170–173

Ojanen T (2016) Making the essence of fundamental rights real: the court of justice of the European Union clarifies the structure of fundamental rights under the charter. Eur Const Law Rev 12(2): 318–329

Papakostantinou V, De Hert P (2021) EU lawmaking in the Artificial Intelligent Age: Act-ification, GDPR Mimesis, and Regulatory Brutality. European Law Blog. https://europeanlawblog.eu/2021/07/08/eu-lawmaking-in-the-artificial-intelligent-age-act-ification-gdpr-mimesis-and-regulatory-brutality/#more-7788. Accessed 8 July 2021

Peeters B (2020) Facial recognition at Brussels Airport: face down in the mud. CiTiP Blog. https://www.law.kuleuven.be/citip/blog/facial-recognition-at-brussels-airport-face-down-in-the-mud/. Accessed 11 July 2021

Prosser WL (1984, original work published in 1960) Privacy [A legal analysis]. In: Schoeman F (ed) Philosophical dimensions of privacy. An anthology. Cambridge University Press

Quattroccolo S (2019) Equità del processo penale e *automated evidence* alla luce della Convenzione europea dei diritti dell'uomo. Revista Ítalo-Española de Derecho Procesal 2:1–17

Raab T (2019) Germany. Video surveillance and face recognition: current developments. Eur Data Protect Law Rev 5(4):544–547

Rivers J (2006) Proportionality and variable intensity of review. Cambridge Law J 65(1):174–207

Rouvroy A, Poullet Y (2009) The right to informational self-determination and the value of self-developments: reassessing the importance of privacy for democracy. In: Gutwirth S, Poullet Y,

De Hert P, de Terwangne C, Nouwt S (eds) Reinventing data protection? Springer, Dordrecht, pp 45–76

Sánchez-Monedero J, Dencik L (2020) The politics of deceptive borders: 'biomarkers of deceit' and the case of iBorderCtrl. Inf Commun Soc. https://doi.org/10.1080/1369118X.2020.1792530

Sayers D (2014) Article 48 (criminal law). In: Peers S, Hervey T, Kenner J, Ward A (eds) The Eu Charter of fundamental rights. A commentary. Bloomsbury, pp 1305–1350

Schabas WA (2017) The European convention of human rights. A commentary. Oxford University Press

Schoeman F (1984) Privacy. Philosophical dimensions of the literature. In: Schoeman F (ed) Philosophical dimensions of privacy. An anthology. Cambridge University Press

Schwartz O (2019) Don't look now: why you should be worried about machines reading your emotions. The Guardian. https://www.theguardian.com/technology/2019/mar/06/facial-recogni tion-software-emotional-science Accessed 3 July 2021

Science Daily (2017) Emotions are cognitive, not innate, researchers conclude. https://www. sciencedaily.com/releases/2017/02/170215121100.htm. Accessed 12 July 2021

Sedenberg E, Chuang J (2017) Smile for the Camera: Privacy and Policy Implications of Emotion AI. http://arxiv.org/abs/1709.00396. Accessed 3 July 2021

Thomas D (2018) The Cameras that Know if You're Happy – or a Threat. BBC. https://www.bbc. com/news/business-44799239. Accessed 2 July 2021

Tzanou M (2017) Data protection as a fundamental right. In: Tzanou M (ed) The fundamental right to data protection: normative value in the context of counter-terrorism surveillance. Hart Publishing, Oxford

US Government Accountability Office (2013) Aviation Security: TSA Should Limit Future Funding for Behavior Detection Activities. https://www.gao.gov/products/gao-14-159. Accessed 3 July 2021

Vaele M, Borgesius FZ (2021) Demystifying the Draft EU Artificial Intelligence Act. https://osf.io/ preprints/socarxiv/38p5f. Accessed 8 July 2021

van Brakel R, De Hert P (2011) Policing, surveillance and law in a pre-crime society: understanding the consequences of technology based strategies. Cahiers Politiestudies 20:163–192

Vervaele JAE (2005) Terrorism and information sharing between the intelligence and law enforcement communities in the US and the Netherlands: emergency criminal law. Utrecht Law Rev 1(1):1–27

Wiewieorowski W (2019) Facial recognition: A solution in search of a problem? European Data Protection Supervisor. edps.europa.eu/node/5551. Accessed 2 July 2021

Part II
ICT Tools and New Investigative Techniques

The Use of Drones and the New Procedural Safeguards in Crime Control and Criminal Investigation

Claudio Orlando

Abstract Drones have become of enormous practical usefulness for crime prevention and criminal investigation. The use of drones, indeed, contribute to the collection of a wide range of information and data that could convey crucial knowledge for criminal proceedings. However, considering the highly intrusive potential of such tools on people's private lives, serious concerns arise within the perspective of fundamental rights. The purpose of this study is to analyse the potentialities of drones in a modern criminal justice system while examining whether and how their usage is compliant with the rights to privacy and data protection.

1 The Use of Drones for Law Enforcement Purposes: New Challenges and Perspectives

The rapid technological developments we are experiencing day by day in almost all fields of human life have given rise to radical transformations in criminal justice as well.[1] Worldwide we have witnessed the increasing use of ever new technological tools to satisfy the investigative needs of criminal proceedings by way of obtaining data and information which are more and more indispensable for the ascertainment of facts.

Among such tools, 'remotely piloted aircraft systems', also known as 'drones', have become of enormous practical usefulness also for crime prevention and criminal inquiries. Drones have several potentialities and can be employed for different goals beyond the extensive use in war scenarios. Within the crime prevention and

---

[1] On the potentialities of technological tools in law enforcement and criminal proceedings see Czerniawski and Boyack (2021); Camon (2021); Caianiello (2019).

C. Orlando (✉)
Law Department, University of Messina, Messina, Italy
e-mail: claudio.orlando@studenti.unime.it

prosecution field, their use rank from intelligence-led-policing to investigating of serious crimes.

However, the extensive use of drones for law enforcement purposes raises serious concerns regarding the protection of several fundamental rights. Modern drones, indeed, can be equipped with advanced surveillance technologies (*e.g.*, thermal imaging systems, GPS systems, facial recognition software etc.), which allow monitoring and tracking an unprecedented number of spaces and people from a distance.[2] The 'smarter' drones become, the more law enforcements agents are able to observe and record relevant information and data.

The difficult challenges set by such widespread use of drones require an in-depth study on the benefits and the risks for individual freedoms within the two main areas of crime control and criminal investigation. Notwithstanding the clear advantages of these tools, it is necessary to define the limits within which we can justify their usage, as well as the procedural safeguards due to ensure proper compliance especially with the right to privacy and the right to data protection.

2   What Are Drones?

According to the International Civil Aviation Organisation (ICAO), a drone is "a set of configurable elements consisting of a remotely-piloted aircraft, its associated remote pilot station, the required command and control links and any other system elements as may be required, at any point during flight operation".[3] Generally speaking, the word 'drone' refers nowadays to different categories of unmanned aerial vehicles (UAV), such as radio controlled, remotely-piloted, semi-autonomous or fully autonomous aircrafts.[4]

Drones can be used for different purposes. Hobbyists use drones for fun and pay up to $500 for an unmanned aircraft system (UAS), which includes vehicle, batteries, chargers, propellers, electronic sensors, cameras, and flight controller.[5] Commercial users operate them to deliver goods and pay $10,000 or more for "UAVs that will stay airborne longer with an extended range and payload-carrying capability".[6] Judicial police and further law enforcement agencies fly drones to carry out

---

[2] Cf. Tarr et al. (2022); Langham (2021).

[3] See International Civil Aviation Organization (2011), Unmanned Aircraft Systems (UAS), Cir. 328-An 190, Glossary, accessible at https://www.icao.int/meetings/uas/documents/circular%2032 8_en.pdf.

[4] See widely Carr (2021), p. 186 ff.; Carr (2019); Howell (2018); Meola (2017); Takahashi (2012); Ukman (2012).

[5] Cf. Carr (2021), p. 186: the author stresses that "the basic drones can fly for up to 10 min on a battery charge at up to 22 mph, with a range about 150–200 feet"; see also Canis (2015), p. 5; see also Kaminski (2013); Anderson (2012).

[6] Carr (2021), p. 186.

surveillance and investigative activities.[7] The Federal Aviation Administration (FAA) estimates that by 2022 the number of hobbyist drones in use could be as high as 3.17 million and that commercial drones could reach the outstanding number of 717,000.[8] Moreover, it has been forecasted that by 2025 law enforcement and public safety agencies could purchase as many as 20,000 drones annually.[9]

One of the main challenges in regulating the use of drones is to determine the visibility and range restrictions in terms of height levels and horizontal distances allowed in UAV flights.[10] In the United States, the FAA Modernization and Reform Act of 2012 and the Code of Federal Regulations require drones to be flown within the operator's visual line of sight (VLOS)[11] and at a maximum altitude of 400 feet above the ground.[12] VLOS means that the drone operator must be able to see the UAV throughout the entire flight. Thanks to the evolution of technology, operators can today fly drones even beyond a visual line of sight (BVLOS). However, US prohibit the flying of drones BVLOS without a waiver from the FAA regulation.[13] In Europe, the most recent rules classify drones according to risk level criteria, which establish three categories of operations, namely an open, a specific and a certified category.[14] Operations classified in the open category require drones to be flown only VLOS. Therefore, UAV pilots must keep continuous visual contact with drones.[15] Instead, BVLOS drone operations are only allowed in the specific and

---

[7] See widely Engberts and Gillissen (2016), p. 93 ff.

[8] Federal Aviation Administration (2018) FAA AEROSPACE FORECAST: Fiscal Years 2018–2038, pp. 41–43.

[9] Cf. Canis (2015), p. 11; Bond (2015).

[10] See Alamouri et al. (2021), p. 8.

[11] Federal Aviation Administration Modernization and Reform Act of 2012, sec. 336 (c); Code of Federal Regulation, title 14, para. 107.31.

[12] Federal Aviation Administration Modernization and Reform Act of 2012, sec. 334; Code of Federal Regulation, title 14, para. 107.51. Decker (2017), p. 90, pointed out that "beyond this, the FAA has not made any specific attempt to regulate the use of drones by law enforcement, leaving such issues to state and federal legislators".

[13] Federal Aviation Administration, Part 107 Waiver, accessible at https://www.faa.gov/uas/commercial_operators/part_107_waivers/.

[14] See Regulation (EU) 2018/1139, followed by Delegated Regulation (EU) 2019/945 and Implementing Regulation (EU) 2019/947. First, the 'open' category covers operations presenting the lowest risks. The main advantage of this category is that drone operators do not need an operating permit to fly their UAVs. Second, the 'specific' category includes other type of operations presenting a higher risk during the flight in relation to which a thorough risk assessment should be conducted to indicate which requirements are necessary to keep the operation safe. These operations, moreover, necessitate an operating license, based on a performed risk assessment reviewed by the competent authority. Third, the 'certified' category covers cases of high-risk activities, such as flying over assemblies of people, transporting people, and carrying dangerous goods. Cf. Alamouri et al. (2021), p. 4 ff.; Bajáková (2021); Clothier and Walker (2015).

[15] Cf. Alamouri et al. (2021), p. 8: "VLOS is particularly interpreted to mean up to 500 m horizontally and 120 m vertically, but for large and well-visible systems (striking painting, position lights), altitudes up to 1000 or even 1500 m, and a radius of 1.5 km around the operator, have been accepted as VLOS".

certified categories. Nonetheless, EU law requires additional conditions, such as conducting a specific operations risk assessment (SORA).[16] The SORA is of the utmost relevance to create safe flight missions, providing useful guidelines for both the drone operator and the competent authority to determine whether an operation can be conducted as safely as possible.[17] This assessment takes into account several aspects, *i.e.* safety, security, environmental protection, privacy and so on, affording a detailed guide that allows examining risks prior to the use of drones.

3   The Use of Drones for Crime Prevention and Investigation

It the last years, there has been a growing use of drones for purposes of surveillance and criminal investigation. UAVs prove extremely useful to prevent and detect serious forms of crimes, such as terrorism-related crimes, environmental crimes, and further transnational organised crimes.[18] Thus, drones provide investigative authorities with photographs, video footage, data and information regarding people suspected of being involved in criminal activities.[19]

In the field of crime control, drones equipped with high-resolution cameras and modern recording instruments can be used both for citywide and grand scale surveillance as a deterrence factor[20] and for smaller-scale surveillance to prevent potential offences within a confined area characterised by a criminogenic relevance, such as schools, stations, night clubs, and so on.[21] A research paper published in the United States by the Harvard National Security Journal analysed the utility of drones as a means of preventing (or at least containing) the ever-increasing series of homicides in Boston.[22] This research showed that in the period 2015–2020 the number of homicides in Boston tripled and the unsolved crimes rocketed from an already high 53% to nearly 80%.[23] The Boston Police Department (BPD) pointed out that the increase in homicides is closely related to the equally widespread

---

[16] *Id.*, p. 9.

[17] European Union Aviation Safety Agency (2019) Acceptable Means of Compliance (AMC) and Guidance Material (GM) to Commission Implementing Regulation (EU) 2019/947, p. 11, accessible at https://www.easa.europa.eu/downloads/104072/en.

[18] See Bump (2019); Rivello (2018); Bachmaier Winter (2014).

[19] Cf. Engberts, Gillissen (2016), p. 93 ff. Consider, for example, the 2013 Boston Marathon bombing case. McNeal (2014), p. 3, stressed that "a marathon is the type of event where the police would want to use a drone to monitor for unknown attackers, and in the unfortunate event of an attack, use the footage to identify the perpetrators".

[20] See Boštjan (2016), p. 12.

[21] Cf. Quattrocolo (2020), p. 39.

[22] Rosenberg (2020).

[23] *Ibid.*

problem of drug trafficking. In order to drastically reduce the unsolved homicide rate in Boston,

> the BPD wants to use a fleet of up to fifty surveillance drones to fly in public airspace, take twenty-four-hour video footage, and simultaneously follow up to fifty people whom the BPD suspects may be involved in illegal drug sales and responsible for the increased violence.[24]

Against this background, drones entail a radical transformation of law enforcement practices, enabling new preventive activities based on continuous surveillance. Indeed, "the collection of aerial imagery and videos will allow drone operators to know what individuals are doing at different points in time and to build a picture around private detail of a person's life".[25]

Furthermore, drones have become almost indispensable in certain criminal investigations for searching and securing evidence at risk as well. In some cases, investigative bodies must face many difficulties in gathering evidence due to the complexities of the crime scene. Thus, evidence could be located in areas difficult to be reached, such as riverbanks, hilly regions, aircraft crashes in open sea, or dangerous areas in which a fire or toxic elements are present.[26] In such situations, drones enable the collection of evidence without risk of tampering, while preventing the loss of essential information.[27] More specifically, these are the main uses of drones in crime scene investigation:

(a) *Photography and Videotaping.* Modern drones, as noted, can be equipped with high-resolution cameras, which permit taking photos and videos of the area under investigation from different angles and heights, without corrupting the crime scene. Aerial photographs, indeed, provide investigative authorities with a 'bird's eye view'.[28]

(b) *Crime scene management and reconstruction.* Drones equipped with Laser Imaging Detection and Ranging (LiDAR) technology[29] can digitally map and reconstruct the whole crime scene. Such tools allow scanning the scene before investigators examining it in person, and significantly reduce the risks of tampering.

(c) *Searching for evidence and forensic investigation.* Drones can play a key role in searching evidence. Compared to helicopters, drones are cheaper and can fly in narrower spaces and approach the targeted area closer.[30] UAVs are also

---

[24] *Ibid.*

[25] Tarr et al. (2022).

[26] Cf. Mendis et al. (2017); Mishra et al. (2015).

[27] *Ibid.*

[28] Mendis et al. (2017).

[29] According to American Geoscience Institute LiDAR technology uses light in the form of a pulsed laser to measure an object's variable distance from the Earth. These light pulses generate precise, three-dimensional information about the shape of the Earth and the target object. Accessible at https://www.americangeosciences.org/critical-issues/faq/what-lidar-and-what-it-used.

[30] See Boštjan (2016), p. 11.

extremely useful for forensic investigation, creating a real-time connection between crime scene investigators and experts from the laboratory. For instance, a fingerprint found at the crime scene can be scanned and instantly sent to the forensic laboratory by drones to obtain the results within no time while still at the crime scene.[31]

In sum, the benefits of the use of drones are widely acknowledged in crime scene analysis and reconstruction, saving time and human resources in the criminal investigation. Moreover, drones could gain crucial relevance to tackle mafia-type organised crime. The concerns about the negative impact of organised crime on security, stability, the rule of law and sustainable development calls for an equivalent change in investigative strategies. It is worth observing that the 'Falcone Resolution'—adopted by the Conference of the Parties in the event of the twentieth anniversary of the United Nations Convention against Transnational Organized Crime—has recently encouraged the deployment of special investigative techniques and the most advanced technologies in the field of criminal investigations in order to efficiently tackle organised crime.[32] The abovementioned techniques differ from traditional methods of investigation because they require the use of specialised skills and, in some cases, technologically advanced instruments, such as drones.[33] Without a doubt the collection of evidence by means of drones might well be a veritable turning point in the fight against organised crime, as it enables the gathering of enormous amounts of data allowing to piece together habits, lifestyle, and interests of individuals under investigation, all elements that represent extremely important circumstantial evidence for decision-making purposes. Furthermore, drones have given rise to a radical transformation in undercover operations. As Bostjan pointed out "the smaller insect-sized and shaped drones can be easily used to listen to criminal groups, terrorist cells, etc., while larger drones can be used to safely oversee officers involved in undercover operations or to safely follow suspects or persons of interest".[34]

---

[31] Mishra et al. (2015).

[32] Conference of the Parties to the United Nation Convention against Transnational Organized Crime (2020), CTOC/COP/2020/L.7/Rev. 1, Vienna, recital no. 12, in https://www.unodc.org/documents/treaties/UNTOC/COP/SESSION_10/Resolutions/Resolution_10_4_-_English.pdf.

[33] United Nations Office on Drugs and Crime (2012) Digest of organized crime cases. A compilation of cases with commentaries and lessons learned. New York, p. 45, accessible https://www.unodc.org/unodc/en/organized-crime/digest-of-organized-crime-cases.html.

[34] Cf. Boštjan (2016), p. 12.

4 Drones and the Rights to Privacy and Data Protection

Despite the cutting-edge benefits offered by the use of drones, their deployment raises serious concerns about the protection of fundamental rights. In particular, drones have an enormous potential to interfere with the rights to privacy and data protection, as UAVs can collect and store a huge number of data and information regarding people's everyday life. As is well-known, while privacy protects the individuals' claim to shape their personality in private, enabling them to exclude others from some areas of their life, data protection extends the safeguard of the individuals' right to private life, thus guaranteeing control over collection, processing and use of personal data.[35] Yet privacy and data protection are strictly connected to each other, since the protection of personal data is of fundamental relevance for individuals to fully enjoy the right to respect for private and family life.[36] To tackle this problem properly, there is need for a comprehensive approach, aimed at providing an overview of the principal rules that are currently available in Europe and in the United States.

4.1 The European Scenario: The Perspective of ECtHR Case-Law and EU Law

Within the European legal framework, Article 8 of the European Convention of Human Rights, as is well known, provides essential reference points to safeguard the rights to privacy and data protection, which due to their high rank can only be restricted on condition that the principles of legality, necessity and proportionality are fully satisfied.[37] The deployment of technological tools in criminal proceedings, indeed, needs first be sustained by a legitimate legal basis, which lays down the goals and scope of usage.[38] The ECtHR has pointed out that

> the protection afforded by Article 8 ECHR would be unacceptably weakened if the use of modern scientific techniques in the criminal-justice system were allowed at any cost and

---

[35] See widely on this theme Barfield and Pagallo (2020); Raul (2019); Schünemann and Baumann (2017); Tzanou (2017); Pagallo (2014); Belfiore (2013).

[36] Cf. Pollicino (2021), p. 105; Mitsilegas (2009), p. 276; Gutwirth and De Hert (2008), p. 278 ff.

[37] See ECtHR, *Big Brother Watch v. United Kingdom*, judgment of 13 September 2018, Appl. No. 58170/13. On this judgment see Bachmaier Winter (2021). See also, ECtHR, *Zakharov v. Russia*, judgment of 4 December 2015, Appl. No. 47143/06.

[38] See ECtHR, *Siliadin v. France*, judgment of 26 July 2005, Appl. No. 73316/01; ECtHR, *M.C. v. Bulgaria*, judgment of 4 December 2003, Appl. No. 39272/98; ECtHR, *Kokkinakis v. Greece*, judgment of 25 May 1993, Appl. No. 14307/88; ECtHR, *Huvig v. France*, judgement of 24 April 1990, Appl. No. 11105/84. See also De Hert and Malgieri (2020).

without carefully balancing the potential benefits of the extensive use of such techniques against important private-life interests.[39]

Therefore, whatever interference by a public authority with such fundamental rights must be provided by law and can be considered acceptable only if necessary to protect national security, public safety, the economic well-being of the country, the prevention of disorder or crime, the protection of health or morals, or for the protection of the rights and freedoms of others.[40] Hence, an encroachment on privacy and data protection needs to be wisely balanced with the objectives that must be reached in criminal proceedings.[41]

The requirements that Strasbourg case law has traced back to Article 8 ECHR, moreover, show their relevance also for purposes of a proper reading of Articles 7 and 8 of the Charter of Fundamental Rights of the European Union (ChFREU), in the light of the general clause set out by Article 52(3) ChFREU.[42] At the EU level, however, there has never existed a specific regulation regarding the use of drones in the fields of crime prevention and criminal proceedings. Nevertheless, in 2015 Article 29 Data Protection Working Party (hereafter, WP 29), which was later replaced by the European Data Protection Board (EDPB) after General Data Protection Regulation (GDPR) came into force, had drafted an Opinion "on privacy and data protection issues relating to the utilisation of drones".[43] Due to the intrusiveness of drones, the WP 29 stated that

> following Article 52(1) of the Charter and Article 8(2) ECHR, the limitation to the exercise of the rights and freedoms recognised by the Charter must be provided in accordance with the law, made only if it is necessary and genuinely meets objectives of general interest recognised by the Union or the need to protect the rights and freedoms of others.[44]

This confirms that drones can only be used by public authorities on condition of the existence of legitimate legal grounds, and insofar as the principles of necessity and proportionality are pursued. Thus, "the aforementioned authorities shall justify why instruments existing at their disposal and why less intrusive alternatives would not achieve such purpose".[45]

---

[39] ECtHR, *S. and Marper v. The United Kingdom*, judgment of 4 December 2008, Appls. Nos. 30,562/04 and 30,566/04, para. 112.

[40] See Article 8(2) ECHR.

[41] Cf. Barfield and Pagallo (2020); Quattrocolo (2020); Brkan (2018); Belfiore (2013), p. 355 ff.

[42] Article 52(3) ChFREU establishes that "in so far as this Charter contains rights which correspond to rights guaranteed by the Convention for the Protection of Human Rights and Fundamental Freedoms, the meaning and scope of those rights shall be the same as those laid down by the said Convention".

[43] Article 29 Data Protection Working Party (2015) Opinion 01/2015 on "Privacy and Data Protection Issues relating to the Utilisation of Drones", 01673/15/EN, WP 231, Brussels, 16 June 2015, accessible at https://ec.europa.eu/newsroom/article29/items/640602. See also Covino (2018), p. 267 ff.

[44] Article 29 Data Protection Working Party (2015), p. 11.

[45] *Ibid.*

The enactment of the GDPR (EU) 2016/679 has not at all dealt with the effects on the rights to data protection and privacy deriving from the deployment of drones. Therefore, the fundamental principles governing this problem remain those defined by the WP 29 in Opinion n. 01/2015. Moreover, the 2016 GDPR lays down some useful indications. In particular, Article 6(1)(e) GDPR, which expressly refers to the necessity criterion, states that personal data processing shall be lawful only if and to the extent that is necessary for the performance of a task carried out in the public interest or in the exercise of official authority vested in the controller. According to the principle of proportionality, the 'necessity test' requires a combined "assessment of the effectiveness of the measure for the objective pursued and of whether it is less intrusive compared to other options for achieving the same goal".[46] Further, Article 6(3) GDPR stresses the need for the treatment to be appropriately supported by legal grounds, be they in EU legislation or in the Member State law to which the controller is subject. To ensure that personal data collected through such equipment are treated in full respect of the aforementioned criteria, Article 25 GDPR establishes the principles of privacy by design (namely at the time of the determination of the means for processing and at the time of the processing itself) and privacy by default.[47] The formulation of 'data protection by design and by default' refers to a proactive, rather than reactive, approach to the field of data protection.[48] Data protection by design entails that the developer shall adopt appropriate technical and organisational measures (such as pseudonymisation),[49] aimed at effectively implementing data protection principles, *i.e.* minimisation, and to integrate all the necessary safeguards to protect the rights of data subjects into the treatment-process.[50] Otherwise, data protection by default requires that the controller adopt appropriate technical and organisational measures to ensure that only personal data which are necessary for the objectives of the proceedings are processed.[51] Consequently, the default configuration of drones which can process personal data must be designed in such a way that the procedural safeguards established to protect data subjects' guarantees are implemented into the functioning of the system.

---

[46] European Data Protection Supervisor (2017) Assessing the Necessity of Measures That Limit the Fundamental Right to the Protection of Personal Data: A Toolkit, p. 5, accessible at https://edps.europa.eu/sites/edp/files/publication/17-04-11_necessity_toolkit_en_0.pdf.

[47] See Barfield and Pagallo (2020); Ubertis (2020), p. 7; Leenes et al. (2017); Merla (2016); Klitou (2014).

[48] Barfield, Pagallo (2020).

[49] According to Article 4(5) GDPR "pseudonymisation means the processing of personal data in such a manner that the personal data can no longer be attributed to a specific data subject without the use of additional information, provided that such additional information is kept separately and is subject to technical and organisational measures to ensure that the personal data are not attributed to an identified or identifiable natural person".

[50] Adapted from Article 25(1) GDPR.

[51] Cf. Article 25(2) GDPR.

Furthermore, it must be taken into account that the recent EU Proposal for AI Regulation[52] (hereafter, Proposal) highlights the significant impact on fundamental rights by the use of AI systems for law enforcement purposes. While the Proposal does not specifically deal with drones, some AI technologies (*e.g.*, 'real-time' remote biometric identification systems)[53] that could be embedded in UAVs are considered. The Proposal classifies these systems as 'high-risk', outlining that their use in publicly accessible spaces shall comply with the safeguards of necessity and proportionality and shall be subject to a prior authorisation granted by a judicial authority or by an independent administrative authority of the Member State in which the use is to take place.[54] Only in case of a justified situation of urgency, recourse to these systems can be commenced without an authorisation, which may be requested only during or after their usage.[55]

4.2   The United States Perspective: The Use of Drones and the Implications on the Fourth Amendment Rights

Outside Europe, the use of drones in the field of crime control and criminal investigation has had a significant impact on the fundamental rights acknowledged by the Fourth Amendment of the US Constitution.[56] As is well-known, the Fourth Amendment protects "the right of the people to be secure in their persons, houses, papers, and effects, against unreasonable searches and seizures", while requiring a warrant based upon probable cause, and "particularly describing the place to be searched, and the persons or things to be seized".[57] The Fourth Amendment enshrines, therefore, an exclusionary rule, which entails the impossibility to introduce illegally gathered evidence at trial.

Drones equipped with advanced technologies can observe people and places from a vantage point.[58] In the light of this, a relevant question is whether the deployment of modern drones gives rise to an 'unreasonable search'. As technology advances, the US Supreme Court has constantly modified the definition of an 'unreasonable

---

[52] Proposal for a Regulation of the European Parliament and of the Council Laying Down Harmonised Rules on Artificial Intelligence (Artificial Intelligence Act) and Amending Certain Union Legislative Acts, Brussels, COM(2021)206 final.

[53] See widely in this volume Neroni Rezende, para. 2.

[54] Cf. Article 5(2) of the Proposal.

[55] *Ibid.*

[56] See widely Langham (2021); McNeal (2014); Celso (2014); Villasenor (2013); Olivito (2013); Takahashi (2012); Calo (2011).

[57] U.S. Const. Amend. IV.

[58] Langham (2021), p. 71; see also Celso (2014); McNeal (2014); Takahashi (2012).

search',[59] in comparison with the landmark decision *Katz v. United States*.[60] In this case, the federal agents gathered evidence using an electronic listening tool to eavesdrop Mr. Katz's phone conversations. The Court alleged that the police's actions constituted a 'search'.[61] However, the Court held that the governments agents ignored "the procedure of an antecedent justification [...] that is central to the Fourth Amendment".[62] Therefore, the evidence obtained was inadmissible.[63] According to Justice Harlan's concurring opinion in *Katz*, the protection awarded by the Fourth Amendment exists when a person has exhibited a subjective expectation of privacy, which is recognised by the society as 'reasonable'.[64] Even though, the '*Katz* test' is still widely used today to deal with the delicate issue of aerial surveillance.

In the light of this, it is questionable whether a warrantless aerial observation constitutes an illegal search, thus violating the Fourth Amendment. In *California v. Ciraolo*, the Court held that a reasonable expectation of privacy cannot be claimed when the aircraft is used in a navigable airspace, reasoning that the federal agents' naked eye watching of Mr. Ciraolo's backyard was not physically intrusive.[65] The respondent's backyard was enclosed by two fences and shielded from view at ground level.[66] All members of society could have viewed what was inside Mr. Ciraolo's backyard while flying in the airspace. Therefore, according to the *Katz* test, the government agents did not need a warrant to carry out such activity. Indeed, the Court held that the Fourth Amendment did not prohibit a warrantless aerial observation conducted in a navigable airspace.[67] Based on these considerations, we can argue that the use of drones does not inherently clash with the Fourth Amendment.

This conclusion, however, needs further clarifications. Can we assume that every type of UAV technology fits the Fourth Amendment rights? Thus, modern drones can be equipped with high-resolution cameras, thermal imaging systems, LiDAR technology, GPS systems, automated facial recognition technology, acoustical systems, interceptor technology, and so on. This allows law enforcement agents to carry

---

[59] See in this volume Di Nuzzo.

[60] Carrol v. United States, 267 U.S. 132 (1925); Olmstead v. United States, 277 U.S. 438 (1928); Silverman v. United States, 365 U.S. 505 (1961); Hayden v. United States, 387 U.S. 294 (1967); Katz v. United States, 389 U.S. 347 (1967).

[61] Katz v. United States, 389 U.S., para. 359.

[62] *Id.*, para. 359; see also Osborn v. United States, 385 U.S. 323 (1996), para. 330.

[63] Katz v. United States, 389 U.S., para. 359.

[64] *Id.*, para. 361, (Harlan J concurring opinion).

[65] See California v. Ciraolo, 476 U.S. 207 (1986), paras. 208–209.

[66] *Id.*, para. 209.

[67] *Id.*, paras. 211–215; see also Dow Chemical Co. v. United States, 476 U.S. 227 (1986), in which the Court held that "the use of an aerial mapping camera to photograph an industrial manufacturing complex from navigable airspace similarly does not require a warrant under the Fourth Amendment".

out investigative activities that go far beyond the capabilities of human perception. In *Kyllo v. United States*, the US Supreme Court upheld that

> it would be foolish to contend that the degree of privacy secured to citizens by the Fourth Amendment has been entirely unaffected by the advance of technology. The question we confront today is what limits there are upon this power of technology to shrink the realm of guaranteed privacy.[68]

In *Kyllo*, the federal agents suspected that marijuana was growing in Mr. Kyllo's house. The indoor farming of marijuana needs high-intensity lamps. Therefore, the government agents used a thermal-imaging device to detect the amount of heat within the petitioner's home. Consequently, they obtained a search warrant, which allowed them to seize more than one hundred marijuana plants that were growth inside Mr. Kyllo's house. In this case, the Court held that such observation—carried out with a device that was not in public use—was a 'search' and was presumptively unreasonable without a warrant.[69]

A few years later, the Court faced similar problems in *United States v. Jones* and in *Riley v. California*.[70] In *Jones*, law enforcement officers installed without a warrant a GPS tracking system[71] on Mr. Jones's car (who was suspected of trafficking narcotics) and gathered more than 2000 pages of data about the respondent's location and movements over the course of 4 weeks. Justice Sotomayor stressed that "GPS monitoring generates a precise, comprehensive record of a person's public movements that reflects a wealth of detail about her familial, political, professional, religious, and sexual associations".[72] In this light, as Justice Alito pointed out, longer term GPS tracking can be considered acceptable only when most serious offences are suspected.[73] Instead, in *Riley* the Court held that warrantless police searches of smartphone through interceptor technology violated the Fourth Amendment because such activity allowed law enforcement agents to monitor phone calls and text messages remotely.[74]

These cases suggest that only emergency circumstances permit the use of certain types of equipment that impinge upon people's privacy from a distance. Furthermore, as new technologies enable law enforcement officers to carry out investigative activities remotely, a judicial oversight is necessary due to the deep intrusion on the rights to privacy and data protection that such activities entail.[75] Therefore, we can conclude that not every available technology that can be implemented into drones inherently suits the requirements of the Fourth Amendment without a warrant. Only

---

[68] Kyllo v. United States, 533 U.S. 27 (2001), paras. 33–34.

[69] *Id.*, para. 40.

[70] United States v. Jones, 565 U.S. 400 (2012); Riley v. California, 573 U.S. 373 (2014).

[71] See widely Militello in this volume.

[72] United States v. Jones, 565 U.S., paras. 414–415 (Sotomayor J concurring opinion).

[73] *Id.*, paras. 430–431 (Alito J concurring opinion).

[74] Riley v. California, 573 U.S., para. 386.

[75] Langham (2021), p. 92.

emergency situations can justify the use of such tools for law enforcement purposes, provided that a judicial supervision is ensured.

5 Balancing the Protection of Public Health and the Rights to Privacy and Data Protection: The Use of Drones During the Pandemic

In the light of the analysis carried out hitherto, the use of drones needs a fair balancing of the goals pursued for crime prevention and investigation with the protection of fundamental rights, especially privacy and data protection.

However, in the current historical context there is a further aspect which deserves special attention. The progressive spread of the pandemic emergency has made public health the uppermost priority in the hierarchy of values in many areas. In this scenario, drones have played a crucial role in the fight against Covid-19 pandemic. In several countries, UAVs have been deployed to monitor the observance of quarantine measures aimed at reducing the steady increase in coronavirus cases. For instance, in the United States law enforcement officers throughout the country have recently relied on drone technologies—such as night vision and loudspeakers—to patrol and enforce lockdown orders.[76] This aspect takes on relevance for this study insofar as monitoring citizens' movements through drones can also help to detect various criminal offences.

All this enhances the need to balance the protection of public health with the rights to privacy and data protection.[77] In Europe, the "statement on the processing of personal data in the context of the Covid-19 outbreak" released in March 2020 by the EDPB is particularly significant. The EDPB stressed that

> data protection rules (such as the GDPR) do not hinder measures taken in the fight against the coronavirus pandemic. The fight against communicable diseases is a valuable goal shared by all nations and, therefore, should be supported in the best possible way. It is in the interest of humanity to curb the spread of diseases and to use modern techniques in the fight against scourges affecting great parts of the world.[78]

From this it follows that European regulation on data protection cannot clash with the need to adopt measures—including more invasive ones—aimed at countering the coronavirus disease, provided that the proportionality principle is satisfied. Indeed, the EDPB argued that 'emergency' is a legal condition which legitimises restrictions of freedom as long as they are proportionate and limited to the emergency period.[79]

---

[76] Carr (2021), p. 201; McGee, Stacey (2020).

[77] See widely Fardo (2020).

[78] European Data Protection Board (2020) Statement on the processing data in the context of the Covid-19 outbreak. Brussels, accessible at https://edpb.europa.eu/news/news/2020/statement-processing-personal-data-context-covid-19-outbreak_en.

[79] *Ibid.*

Of course, this does not mean that exceptional circumstances allow for restriction of individuals' rights through technological tools for preserving public safety without ensuring full respect for the right to privacy and data protection.

Consequently, the use of drones in running authoritative security checks that restrain individuals' privacy must be justified pursuant to legal grounds as appropriately designed at the national level and based on the indications provided by European institutions.[80] In this respect, it is worth mentioning a recent ruling of the 'Commission nationale de l'informatique et des libertés' (CNIL), which deals with the sensitive issue of the use of drones in the French territory as a means to ensure compliance with Covid-19 containment measures.[81] CNIL has observed that the lack of legislative provisions authorising, on one hand, the processing of personal data gathered through camera-equipped drones and clarifying, on the other hand, how to balance public health protection and citizens' right to privacy results in an excessive risk to fundamental rights and freedoms.[82] All this confirms that public authorities can use drones in carrying out investigative activities only to the extent that such activities are sustained by law.[83]

6   Concluding Remarks: Drones and Techno-Regulation

Without a doubt, drones have changed the way in which crime prevention and criminal inquiries are carried out. As they represent the "technological frontier of remote sensing and data acquisition",[84] judicial police and law enforcement agencies will continue to rely on this technology for preventing and detecting serious forms of crimes. Nonetheless, as has been expressed above, the use of drones raises serious concerns with regard to the protection of the rights to privacy and data protection, which requires also an increased effort in ensuring procedural safeguards.

The analysis of statutory and case-law both in Europe and in the United States shows that the use of drones for law enforcement purposes should be permitted insofar as it is necessary and proportionate to the pursued objective. Only emergency circumstances could justify the deployment of drones equipped with advanced surveillance technologies, on condition that a judicial oversight (*i.e.*, a judicial authority or an independent authority of the State in which the use is to take place) is guaranteed. However, this is not enough.

---

[80]Triggiani (2019), p. 186 ff.

[81]Commission nationale de l'informatique et des libertés (2021) Délibération de la formation restreinte n°SAN-2021-003 du 12 janvier 2021 concernant le ministère de l'intérieur, https://www.legifrance.gouv.fr/cnil/id/CNILTEXT000042960768.

[82]*Id.*, para. 44.

[83]Cf. Iorio (2021); Naddeo (2021).

[84]Takahashi (2012), p. 113.

As a matter of fact, the law is not able to keep pace with the technological progress. Bert-Jaap Koops held that "regulation should not hinder the development of ICT. If a law is too technology-specific, it is not likely to cover future technological developments, and it will therefore have to be adapted sooner rather than later".[85] Consequently, the best solution in this field seems to be encoding legal requirements in the design of drones through techno-regulation.[86] Techno-regulation is "the intentional influencing of individuals behaviour by building norms into technological devices".[87] It has been considered that several legal requirements and safeguards can be implemented in the drone's software (e.g., limiting the duration or resolution of footage; outfitting the device with an auto-erase function to retain only the relevant data for the investigation; automatic scrambling of faces),[88] with a view to prevent an unreasonable infringement of people's privacy. Firstly, drone developers shall determine whether and to what extent the software complies with privacy and data protection regulation.[89] Secondly, the design of the software shall control when and how drones collect and process personal data.[90] Techno-regulation could surely allow for higher privacy and data protection efficiency. Thanks to this type of regulation, any breach of the rules would be impossible or still very hard. Therefore, hardcoded rules will enable the law to cover future technological developments.

Nevertheless, it is still not clear to what extent techno-regulation is feasible. It must be taken into account that embedding extensively legal requirements in system software poses serious challenges because

> some legal rules are intentionally open, vague, overinclusive or underinclusive, and often they are indeterminate and require interpretation. Complying with legal rules that are open to interpretation requires taking into account relevant case-law, legal history, and other relevant sources for assessing the legal status.[91]

In such circumstances, techno-regulation could be almost impossible due to the fuzziness of provisions. This entails that only simple and very detailed rules and

---

[85] Koops (2006), p. 77 ff.

[86] See widely Leenes et al. (2017); Leenes and Lucivero (2014); Koops and Leenes (2014); Leenes (2011); Brownsword (2008); Zaccagnino et al. (2021), p. 15804: "An example of techno-regulation can be seen in Digital Right Management systems, which incorporate copyright law into technological safeguards by limiting the use of copyrighted artifacts".

[87] Van den Berg and Leenes (2013).

[88] Leenes et al. (2017), p. 29; Rosenberg (2020); Koops and Leenes (2006); Robolaw (2014) Guidelines on Regulating Robotics. Regulating Emerging Robotic Technologies in Europe: Robotics Facing Law and Ethics, accessible at http://www.robolaw.eu/RoboLaw_files/documents/robolaw_d6.2_guidelinesregulatingrobotics_20140922.pdf.

[89] Leenes et al. (2017), p. 28: the Authors stress that "this not only implies that designers will have to build technologies capable of operating within these constraints, but also that certain kinds of robots will have to be able to 'reason' explicitly with legal norms or at least to execute particular norms in particular circumstances".

[90] Id., p. 27.

[91] Koops and Leenes (2014), p. 159 ff.

specific safeguards could fit this particular modality of regulation. In order to fill this gap, a synergic work of computer scientists and lawyers needs to be deeply encouraged, especially in an era in which new technologies are increasingly used for preventive and investigative purposes.

References

Alamouri A, Lampert A, Gerke M (2021) An exploratory investigation of UAS regulations in Europe and the impact on effective use and economic potential. Multidisciplinary Digital Publishing Institute, Drones 5(3):1–16

Anderson C (2012) How I Accidentally Kickstarted the Domestic Drone Boom. https://www.wired.com/2012/06/ff-drones/

Bachmaier Winter L (2014) Section III – criminal procedure. Information society and penal law. General report. Revue internationale de droit penal 1(85):75–127

Bachmaier Winter L (2021) Proportionality, mass surveillance and criminal investigation: the Strasbourg court facing big brother. In: Billis E, Knust N, Rui JP (eds) Proportionality in crime control and criminal justice. Hart Publishing, Oxford, pp 317–335

Bajáková EA (2021) The New European Drone Rules. https://www.schoenherr.eu/content/the-new-european-drone-rules/

Barfield W, Pagallo U (2020) Advanced introduction to law and artificial intelligence, Chapter V, issues of data protection. Elgar, Cheltenham

Belfiore R (2013) The protection of personal data processed within the framework of police and judicial cooperation in criminal matters. In: Ruggeri S (ed) Transnational inquiries and the protection of fundamental rights in criminal proceedings. A study in memory of Vittorio Grevi and Giovanni Tranchina. Springer, Berlin, pp 355–370

Bond M (2015) Drones give law enforcement a new edge, but also raise concerns. https://www.inquirer.com/philly/news/20150810_Drones_give_law_enforcement_a_new_edge__but_raise_concerns.html

Boštjan S (2016) Drones in (Slovene) criminal investigation. Kriminalistička teorija i praksa 3:7–25

Brkan M (2018) The concept of essence of fundamental rights in the EU legal order: peeling the onion to its Core. Eur Const Law Rev 14:332–368

Brownsword R (2008) Rights, regulation, and the technological revolution. Oxford University Press, Oxford

Bump P (2019) Law Enforcement Robotics and Drones – 5 Current Applications. https://emerj.com/ai-sector-overviews/law-enforcement-robotics-and-drones/

Caianiello M (2019) Criminal process faced with the challenges of scientific and technological development. Eur J Crime Crim Law Crim Just 27(4):267–291

Calo MR (2011) The drone as privacy catalyst. Stanford Law Rev 64(29):29–33

Camon A (2021) The project devices and digital evidence in Europe. In: Caianiello M, Camon A (eds) Digital forensic evidence. Towards common European standards in antifraud administrative and criminal investigations. Wolters Kluwer, Milan, pp 1–12

Canis B (2015) Unmanned Aircraft Systems (UAS): commercial outlook for a new industry. Congressional Research Service, pp 1–14

Carr NK (2019) Look! It's a bird! It's a plane! No, It's a trespassing drone. J Technol Law Policy 23(2):147–183

Carr NK (2021) Programmed to protect and serve: the Dawn of drones and robots in law enforcement. J Air Law Commer 86(2):183–218

Celso J (2014) Comments: droning on about the fourth amendment: adopting a reasonable fourth amendment jurisprudence to prevent unreasonable searches by unmanned aircraft systems. Univ Baltimore Law Rev 43(3):461–494

Clothier R, Walker R (2015) The safety risk management of unmanned aircraft systems. In: Valavanis KP, Vachtsevanos GJ (eds) Handbook of unmanned aerial vehicles. Springer, Dordrecht, pp 2229–2275

Covino S (2018) L'impiego dei droni con finalità di law enforcement nel contesto normativo italiano ed europeo. In: Biasiotti MA, Palmerini E, Aiello GF (eds) Diritto dei droni: regole, questioni e prassi. Giuffrè, Milan, pp 267–292

Czerniawski J, Boyack C (2021) Reviewing the privacy implications of law enforcement access to and use of digital data. Utah J Crim Law 5(1):73–92

De Hert P, Malgieri G (2020) Article 8 ECHR compliant and foreseeable surveillance: the ECtHR's expanded legality requirement copied by the CJEU. A discussion of European surveillance case law. Brussels Priv Hub Work Pap 6(1):1–40

Decker LK (2017) Droning on: the state and Federal Legal Response to the deregulation of U.S. airspace for small unmanned aircraft systems. J Crim Just Law 2(1):89–110

Engberts B, Gillissen E (2016) Policing from above: drone use by the police. In: Custers B (ed) The future of drone use. Information technology and law series. T.M.C. Asser Press, The Hague, pp 93–113

Fardo M (2020) Utilizzo dei droni nel contrasto al Covid-19. Il complesso bilanciamento tra la salute pubblica e la riservatezza personale. Giurisprudenza Penale Web 3:1–7

Gutwirth S, De Hert P (2008) Regulating profiling in a democratic constitutional state. In: Hildebrandt M, Gutwirth S (eds) Profiling the European citizen. Springer, Cham, pp 271–293

Howell E (2018) What Is a Drone? https://www.space.com/29544-what-is-a-drone.html

Iorio C (2021) Droni e privacy: un rapporto complesso all'esame della Cnil francese ai tempi del Covid. https://dirittodiinternet.it/droni-privacy-un-rapporto-complesso-allesame-della-cnil-francese-ai-tempi-del-covid/

Kaminski ME (2013) Drone federalism: civilian drones and the things they carry. Calif Law Rev Circuit 57(4):57–74

Klitou D (2014) Privacy-invading technologies and privacy by design. Safeguarding privacy, liberty and security in the 21st century. TMC Asser Press, The Hague

Koops BJ (2006) Should ICT regulation be technology-neutral? In: Koops BJ, Lips M, Prins C, Schellekens M (eds) Starting points for ICT regulation. TMC Asser Press, The Hague, pp 77–108

Koops BJ, Leenes RE (2006) "Code" and the slow erosion of privacy. Mich Telecommun Technol Law Rev 12:115–188

Koops BJ, Leenes RE (2014) Privacy regulation cannot be hardcoded. A critical comment on the 'privacy by design' provision in data-protection law. Int Rev Law 28(2):159–171

Langham L (2021) Domestic drones – the rise of the flying machines: is big brother watching you? Western Mich Univ Cooley Law Rev 36(1):69–94

Leenes RE (2011) Framing techno-regulation: an exploration of state and non-state regulation by technology. Legisprudence 5(2):143–169

Leenes RE, Lucivero F (2014) Laws on robots, Laws by robots, laws in robots: regulating robot behaviour by design. Law Innov Technol 6(2):193–220

Leenes RE, Palmerini E, Koops BJ, Bertolini A, Salvini P, Lucivero F (2017) Regulatory challenges of robotics: some guidelines for addressing legal and ethical issues. Law Innov Technol 9(1): 1–44

McGee P, Stacey K (2020) California police to use drones to patrol coronavirus lockdown. https://www.ft.com/content/c7d0dee1-6125-475c-9cc7-78f4671d7cea

McNeal G (2014) Drones and Aerial Surveillance: Considerations For Legislators. https://www.brookings.edu/research/drones-and-aerial-surveillance-considerations-for-legislatures/

Mendis NDNA, Dharmarathne TSS, Wanasinghe NC (2017) Use of unmanned aerial vehicles in crime scene investigations – novel concept of crime scene investigations. Forensic Res Criminol Int J 4(1):1–2

Meola A (2017) The FAA rules and regulations you need to know to keep your drone use legal. Business Insider. https://www.icex.es/icex/wcm/idc/groups/public/documents/documento_anexo/mde4/nzc3/~edisp/dax2018777817.pdf

Merla L (2016) Droni, privacy e tutela dei dati personali. Informatica e diritto 25(1):29–45

Mishra V, Dedhia H, Wavhal S (2015) Application of drones in the investigation and management of a crime scene. Forensic Sci 4(4):1–2

Mitsilegas V (2009) EU criminal law. Hart Publishing, Oxford

Naddeo G (2021) Droni 2021, la nuova normativa europea e il contrasto al Covid-19. https://www.iusinitinere.it/droni-2021-la-nuova-normativa-europea-e-il-contrasto-al-covid-19-36018

Olivito J (2013) Beyond the fourth amendment: limiting drone surveillance through the constitutional right to informational privacy. Ohio State Law J 74(4):670–702

Pagallo U (2014) Il diritto nell'età dell'informazione. Il riposizionamento tecnologico degli ordinamenti giuridici tra complessità sociale, lotta per il potere e tutela dei diritti. Giappichelli, Turin

Pollicino O (2021) Judicial protection of fundamental rights on the internet. A road towards digital constitutionalism? Hart Publishing, Oxford

Quattrocolo S (2020) Artificial intelligence, computational modelling and criminal proceedings. A framework for a European legal discussion. Springer, Cham

Raul AC (2019) The privacy, data protection and cybersecurity law review. Law Business Research, London

Rivello PP (2018) Gli aspetti giuridici connessi all'uso dei droni. https://www.dirittopenaleglobalizzazione.it/wp-content/uploads/2018/05/Gli-aspetti-giuridici-connessi-all'uso-dei-droni.pdf

Rosenberg J (2020) Drones as Crime-Fighting Tools in 2020: Legal and Normative Considerations. https://harvardnsj.org/2018/01/drones-as-crime-fighting-tools-in-2020-legal-and-normative-considerations/

Schünemann WJ, Baumann M (2017) Privacy, data protection and cybersecurity in Europe. Springer, Cham

Takahashi TT (2012) Drones and privacy. Columbia Sci Technol Law Rev 14(1):72–114

Tarr JA, Tarr T, Thompson M, Wilkinson D (2022) Data protection, privacy and drones. https://www.clydeco.com/en/insights/2022/2/data-protection-privacy-and-drones

Triggiani N (2019) Le videoriprese investigative e l'uso dei droni. In: Scalfati A (ed) Le indagini atipiche. Giappichelli, Turin, pp 161–190

Tzanou M (2017) Data protection as a fundamental right. In Tzanou (ed) The fundamental right to data protection: normative value in the context of counter-terrorism surveillance. Hart Publishing, Oxford

Ubertis G (2020) Intelligenza artificiale, giustizia penale, controllo umano significativo. Sistema penale:1–15

Ukman J (2012) Privacy Group seeks to lift on domestic drones. https://www.washingtonpost.com/blogs/checkpoint-washington/post/privacy-group-seeks-to-lift-veil-on-domestic-drones/2012/01/12/gIQABH6OuP_blog.html

Van den Berg B, Leenes RE (2013) Abort, retry, fail: scoping techno-regulation and other techno-effects. In: Hildbrandt M, Gaakeer AMP (eds) Human law and computer law: comparative perspectives. Springer, Cham, pp 67–87

Villasenor J (2013) Observation from above: unmanned aircraft systems and privacy. Harv J Law Public Policy 36(2):458–517

Zaccagnino R, Capo C, Guarino A, Lettieri N, Malandrino D (2021) Techno-regulation and intelligent safeguards. Multimed Tools Appl 80:15803–15824

Search and Seizure of Digital Evidence: Human Rights Concerns and New Safeguards

Viviana Di Nuzzo

Abstract In the last decades, the use of technological tools for investigative purpose has considerably increased, due to the digitalisation of daily activities in any field of private and social life. Search and seizure of digital evidence stand out among the most used means of investigation, being able to find and collect communicative as well as non-communicative data from an electronic device in a short period of time. Since modern technologies allow people to be permanently in contact, recourse to such measures entails significant implications on fundamental rights, affecting the individuals against whom the investigation is addressed as well as third parties.

Online searches, in particular, can severely interfere with the right to privacy, affecting the most intimate sphere of a person's life. Like traditional searches, moreover, online searches are aimed at seizing information stored in the targeted device. But the data collection, which is generally carried out through a *bit-by-bit* copy, entails the need to strike a balance between privacy and the aims of the criminal investigation.

The present study will try to point out the worrisome lack of an adequate legal basis of the measures of digital search and seizure, from different viewpoints: first, the domestic law level; next, at the European level, both EU law and ECtHR case law; and finally, from a comparative law perspective, with particular regard to the United States.

1 Introduction

In the last few decades, technological development has resulted in an unprecedented extension of the use of electronic devices in our day to day lives: smartphones, tablets, personal computers, smartwatches, including the internet of things at home, transportation, work and the increasing development of the smart cities. Information

V. Di Nuzzo (✉)
Law Department, University of Messina, Messina, Italy
e-mail: viviana.dinuzzo@unime.it

and communication technology (ICT) tools have become almost indispensable and by now most people cannot even imagine their daily lives without them.

This generates a massive amount of digital data stored in our devices and in the cloud containing personal and sensitive information, such as the content of communications, GPS localisation, Internet banking services to name only a few.[1] It is no surprise, therefore, that digital data have become a "valuable resource" in the fields of crime prevention and criminal investigation too.[2] Digital investigations, indeed, enable the competent authorities to rapidly collect a huge volume of data, which are very useful to detect the alleged perpetrators and, even more, to prevent criminal offences. In spite of their unquestionable usefulness, however, digital investigative measures may severely encroach our fundamental rights. ICT tools have a strong impact on the private life of the investigated persons, but affecting also individuals unrelated to the criminal activities under investigation.

Against this background, online searches and seizure allow to collect a huge amount of communicative or non-communicative data from computer systems. As it is known, online searches constitute a hybrid means of investigation that allows the remote access to a digital device, where the authority has previously installed a malware (malicious software),[3] also known as "State Trojan",[4] thus creating a link between the controller computer and the targeted one.[5] Whenever the device 'infected' by the backdoor is connected to the Internet, the controller can monitor all the user's activities, search the stored data, collect them, and also activate a camera or a microphone.[6] Online searches, allowing remote access to data, differ from the on-site computer search, which is physically addressed to the computer system and generally leads to the copy of the entire hardware.[7] The controller could also copy all the data stored in the device through online search and this can happen even if the addressed device is far away from it.

---

[1] Persons nowadays express themselves in the digital world. See Rodotà (2014), p. 102.

[2] Camon (2021), p. 1. The author also highlights the digital shift produced by the need to handle the Covid-19 emergency.

[3] A malware is "a simple or self-replicating program, which discreetly installs itself in a data processing system, without the users' knowledge or consent, with a view to either endangering data confidentiality, data integrity and system availability or making sure that the users are framed for a computer crime". See Filiol (2005), p. 86.

[4] More precisely, trojans constitute just one of the various types of malware which may be deployed in a criminal investigation. Other examples are spyware, viruses, or keyloggers ('keystroke logging'). The latter, in particular, can record and send information on the keys pressed by the user of the infected device, in order to monitor the activity and obtain passwords or other relevant information through the keyboard. See Vaciago and Silva Ramalho (2016), pp. 88 ff.

[5] The backdoor created by the trojan allows the controller to access the system, bypassing the existing authentication mechanisms. Vaciago and Silva Ramalho (2016), p. 89.

[6] For in-depth analysis of telecommunication intercepts through spyware see Foti, in this volume. See also Foti (2021), pp. 202 ff.; Iovene (2014), p. 330.

[7] On the differences between traditional searches and digital evidence searches, see Kerr (2005c), pp. 90 ff.

Like traditional searches, moreover, online searches are usually followed by the seizure of information stored in hardware, servers, clouds, mailboxes, etc.[8] The reach of search and seizure of digital evidence[9] in cyberspace and the cloud is enormous, and sensitive problems arise with regard to the identification of the competent jurisdiction when data are in an unknown location.[10] Indeed, internet offers the opportunity to access data through transborder search, which aims at collecting information kept by service providers in third countries.[11]

As is well known, not only has cybercrime expanded, but also traditional criminal activities have changed their shape through the use of ICTs, which confirms the necessity for investigative authorities to develop specific expertise in the digital world.[12] For this reason, digital investigative measures have proven extremely useful in fighting serious crimes. We shall see that restrictions on fundamental rights can only be justified on condition that the essential principles governing a fair trial— particularly those of lawfulness, necessity and proportionality—are fulfilled, as the European Court of Justice has acknowledged in the landmark decision *Digital Rights Ireland and Others*.[13]

---

[8]Italian scholarship has always encouraged recourse to inspection of computer systems, while limiting search and seizure of hardware to cases in which less intrusive investigative measures are unavailable. Vitale (2008), pp. 506 ff.; Costabile (2005), pp. 531 ff.

[9]Digital evidence "encompasses any and all digital data that can establish that a crime has been committed or can provide a link between a crime and its victim or a crime and its perpatrator". Casey (2004), p. 688.

[10]Škrtić et al. (2013), p. 513.

[11]The recourse to remote search and seizure raises also serious concerns related to a possible breach of sovereignty. Thus, investigative authorities could have access to data stored in foreign countries and such possibility entails an extra-borders application of *lex loci*. Until this moment, international law has not made clear whether the remote access to data (without consent by the State where such data are stored) constitutes a breach of sovereignty. See Osula (2017), p. 37. When a NIT (Network Investigative Techniques) search occurs, the risk of conflicts of jurisdictions is real. On this topic, see Bercovitz (2021), who proposes a legislative regulation of the matter in USA, in order to provide a legal definition of which is the situs of NIT searches. See Koops and Goodwin (2014). Cf. also Goldsmith (2001), pp. 103 ff. This author argued that remote cross-border searches were not "prohibited by norms of territorial sovereignty".

[12]In 2020, due to the distancing measures and lockdown in some European countries, cybercriminals took advantage of the emergency and increased their activity. For instance, digital materials and posts related to child abuse increased. Electronic evidence was essential to face this concern. See *SIRIUS EU Digital Evidence Situation Report about Cybercrime – 3rd Annual Report*, 2021, accessible at https://www.europol.europa.eu/cms/sites/default/files/documents/SIRIUS_ DESR_12_2021.pdf; Exploiting Isolation: Offenders and victims of online child sexual abuse during the Covid-19 pandemic, 19 June 2020, accessible at https://www.europol.europa.eu/sites/ default/files/documents/europol_covid_report-cse_jun2020v.3_0.pdf. Cf., among others, Flor and Oh Jang (2012), pp. 13 ff.

[13]CJEU, *Digital Rights Ireland and Others*, judgment of 8 April 2014, C-293/12 and C-594/12, para. 38 ff. Any limitation on the rights to privacy and data protection laid down by the EUChFR must be provided by law and respect their essence. In compliant with the principle of proportionality, limitations on these rights may be made only if they are necessary and genuinely meet the

Most EU Member States share similar concerns arising from the spread of digital search for both intelligence surveillance and criminal investigation.[14] Notwithstanding the great intrusiveness of digital search and seizure, several jurisdictions in the EU area still lack specific or sufficient legislation, on the scope of such measures, on the safeguards due to the person who undergoes them, and on the remedies that can be used against such interference.[15] Certainly, there is an urgent need to identify the qualitative criteria on the use of these measures in the area of crime prevention as well as in criminal investigations in order to balance all the conflicting interests involved, primarily those regarding the need for exhaustive evidence gathering and the protection of the individuals concerned. Moreover, further essential values, such as the integrity and authenticity of the data to be collected, are aimed at satisfying a reliable fact-finding and ensuring the admissibility of evidence at trial, and they also stand out in the interest of the addressed person.[16]

In the light of the complexity of this topic, the present paper aims at reconstructing the problems related to data protection when searches and seizures of digital evidence are carried out to collect electronic data. This study will also deal with international and EU law regarding the deployment of digital measures of investigation, while focusing on the indications provided by ECtHR case law in regard to the right for respect for private and family life. Digital searches and seizures will also be analysed from a domestic viewpoint, in order to detect those jurisdictions which have enacted adequate rules governing the use of such measures, and to identify the safeguards that need to be granted to the involved people.

---

objectives of general interest recognised by the EU or the need to protect the rights and freedoms of other people.

[14] Intelligence services adopt strategic or mass surveillance to detect "unknown threats" and prevent the commission of serious crimes; police officers are the main users of focused surveillance, generally targeted to "known threats", in order to collect evidence related to an already committed crime. DCAF Parliamentary Brief (2017), *Safeguards in Electronic Surveillance*, accessible at https://issat.dcaf.ch/download/111839/2029468/Safeguards%20in%20Electronic%20Surveillance%20-%20DCAF%20Policy%20Brief.pdf, p. 3.

[15] Some years ago, the *Model Rules for the Procedure of the European Public Prosecutor's Office*, accessible at https://orbilu.uni.lu/bitstream/10993/42085/1/Model%20Rules%20and%20explanatory%20notes%20EN.pdf, already highlighted that the only common element among the legislations of Member States was the absence of a precise regulation on surveillance measures. Cf. Allegrezza (2013), pp. 151 ff.

[16] Iovene (2014), p. 330.

2 The International and EU Law Acknowledgment of Digital Searches and Seizure in the Field of Domestic and Transnational Criminal Justice

In the field of crime prevention and criminal proceedings, digital evidence is increasingly gathered through search of computers and other electronic devices to the aim of seizing electronic data. The acknowledgement of these measures in international and European law has been a long and slow process, which is today still far from being completed. The Convention on Cybercrime, signed in Budapest on the 23th November of 2001 at the Council of Europe level,[17] marked a fundamental step. Remarkably, this international law instrument already subjected the collection of evidence in electronic form, in accordance with the legislation of each State Party, to specific conditions and safeguards to "provide for the adequate protection of human rights and liberties" [Art. 15(1)]. Within a general framework of procedural law provisions,[18] the Budapest Convention focused on search and seizure of computer systems to obtain stored data by requiring the contracting States to adopt "legislative or other measures" in order to establish the conditions for lawfully searching or accessing computer systems or a part of them, as well as a computer-data storage medium.[19] In spite of the apparent vagueness of such provisions, the sought legislative intervention had to comply with the general requirements laid down in Articles 14 and 15. It is worth recalling that the Budapest Convention expressly refers to the guarantees acknowledged by international fundamental rights charters, such as the ECHR and the ICCPR, which include—in the light of the general proportionality principle—the existence of grounds justifying the use of computer-related investigations, the provision of judicial oversight or by another independent authority, the establishment of the maximum duration of the remote control and the procedure to preserve the data's integrity in compliance with the rule of law.

It is also interesting to note that the Convention imposes upon the contracting countries the obligation to consider the impact of computer-related on "the rights, responsibilities and legitimate interests of third parties" [Art. 15(3)]. Such provision is of the utmost importance from the perspective of search and seizure of computer-stored data, highlighting the awareness of the potential of digital measures of investigation to interfere with the fundamental rights (especially the right to free communication and data sharing) of individuals other than the targeted person. But that provision sounded like a declaration of principle, as it did not explain how

---

[17] Council of Europe Convention on Cybercrime (CETS No. 185), 23 November 2001, accessible at https://rm.coe.int/1680081561.

[18] Section II (Arts. 14 ff.) of the Budapest Convention deals with procedural law for collection of evidence in electronic form.

[19] See Art. 19 of the Budapest Convention, which deals with search and seizure of stored computer data. The Convention also provides regulation of real-time collection of computer data (Art. 20) and interception of contents (Art. 21).

contracting States concretely ought to protect the interests of third parties, thus leaving an excessively wide discretionary power to national lawmakers.

At the UN level, the 2000 UN Convention on Transnational Organized Crime encourages the use of "special investigative techniques", as has recently been underlined by the Conference of the Parties to the United Nation Convention against Transnational Organized Crime (2020).[20]

Further relevant developments can be observed at the EU law level. In its 2008 Conclusions on a concerted work strategy and practical measures in transnational investigation against cybercrime, the Council encouraged Member States to "facilitate" the use of remote computer searches with the purpose of fighting cyber-criminality.[21] On the basis of this acknowledgment, EU institutions launched several legislative instruments in the field of judicial cooperation in the years ahead, calling for the introduction of domestic rules on remote control operations and electronic surveillance.[22]

In the same year, Framework Decision on the European Evidence Warrant devoted specific attention to search and seizure without further specification.[23] As is well-known, Framework Decision 2008/978/JHA was later repealed, and the 2014 Directive on European Investigation Order (EIO Directive),[24] although pursuing the aim of establishing in the EU area a wide-ranging regime of transnational evidence gathering based on a new logic of mutual recognition, surprisingly set no specific

---

[20] *Conference of the Parties to the United Nation Convention against Transnational Organized Crime* (2020), CTOC/COP/2020/L.7/Rev. 1, Vienna, 12–16 October 2020, recitable No. 12, accessible at https://www.unodc.org/documents/treaties/UNTOC/COP/SESSION_10/REPORT/ctoc_cop_2020_10_E.pdf. See Balsamo (2020); Orlando (2021).

[21] Council Conclusions of 27 November 2008 on a concerted work strategy and practical measures against cybercrime (2009/C62/05), accessible at https://eur-lex.europa.eu/legal-content/EN/TXT/PDF/?uri=CELEX:52009XG0317(01)&qid=1649320371773&from=EN.

[22] In this sense, see also Directive 2011/93/EU of the European Parliament and of the Council of 13 December 2011 on combating the sexual abuse and sexual exploitation of children and child pornography, and replacing Council Framework Decision 2004/68/JHA, accessible at https://eur-lex.europa.eu/legal-content/EN/TXT/?uri=celex%3A32011L0093. More recently, cf. Council Regulation (EU) 2017/1939 of 12 October 2017 implementing cooperation on the establishment of the European Public Prosecutor's Office ('the EPPO'), accessible at https://eur-lex.europa.eu/eli/reg/2017/1939/oj.

[23] Council Framework Decision 2008/978/JHA of 18 December 2008 on the European Evidence Warrant for the purpose of obtaining objects, documents and data for use in proceedings in criminal matters, accessible at https://eur-lex.europa.eu/legal-content/EN/ALL/?uri=CELEX:32008F0978. Search and seizure had to be always available for the executing authority in all the cases of serious crimes listed in Art. 14(2). Even though this legislative instrument did not contain any express reference to digital or electronic evidence, it promoted the use of "special investigative techniques" to enable access to personal data, a sufficiently broad formulation that would allow for the use of digital search and seizure.

[24] Directive 2014/41/EU of the European Parliament and of the Council of 3 April 2014 regarding the European Investigation Order in criminal matters, accessible at https://eur-lex.europa.eu/legal-content/EN/TXT/?uri=celex%3A32014L0041.

rules regarding either digital measures of investigation or electronic evidence.[25] It is interesting to note that EU institutions extended the scope of the EIO Directive by including into its main goals the taking of evidence that was already in the possession of the executing authority.[26] Further, the possibility of ordering measures available in a similar domestic case under the law of the issuing State empowered the issuing authorities to order digital searches.[27] Therefore, the EIO Directive provides an essential legal basis regarding searches of digital evidence in cross-border situations, although such evidence is frequently gathered also through other investigative channels such as the Joint Investigation Teams (JIT).[28]

In 2018, as is well known, the EU Commission presented the proposal for a Regulation on European Production and Preservation Orders to secure and gather electronic evidence for criminal proceedings stored or held by service providers in another jurisdiction.[29] However, this legislative proposal says nothing about remote computer search or online search, because the order is addressed to the data holder.

In sum, the legislative setup at the EU level is still far from having provided a coherent set of rules on remote searches of computers, which can give rise to serious problems of international cooperation among European countries.

3   Digital Evidence in ECtHR Case Law

In the European context, the European Court of Human Rights (ECtHR) has strongly contributed to enhancing the degree of protection of fundamental rights affected by invasive measures of investigation.

It should be noted that Strasbourg case law has not yet been called upon to examine the problems concerned with search and seizure of digital evidence from remote. Nonetheless, The Court has provided some useful principles that provide

---

[25] See, among others, Caianiello (2015).

[26] Art. 13(1) EIO Directive.

[27] Art. 6[1(*b*)] EIO Directive.

[28] Council Framework Decision of 13 June 2002 on joint investigation teams, accessible at https://www.eurojust.europa.eu/sites/default/files/Partners/JITs/CFDonJITs-2002-06-13-EN.pdf. Interestingly, in 2020 online portals dedicated to law enforcement proved being useful to share digital information between law enforcement agencies, scoring higher than other informal channels used before. Online portals for submission of law enforcement requests have been established individually by several Online Service Providers (OSPs). They are more secure and more informative than e-mail, since it is generally possible to check the status of requests, provide supplementary information and obtain records in a secure environment. Cf. *SIRIUS EU Digital Evidence Situation Report*, cit., accessible at https://www.europol.europa.eu/cms/sites/default/files/documents/SIR IUS_DESR_12_2021.pdf.

[29] Proposal for a Regulation of the European Parliament and of the Council on European Production and Preservation Orders for electronic evidence in criminal matters, accessible at https://eur-lex. europa.eu/legal-content/it/txt/?uri=celex%3a52018pc0225.

valid indications even when such measures are enforced in the context of criminal investigations to gather digital evidence.

Like in other fields and in relation to other rights enshrined in the Convention, the Strasbourg Court has on several occasions focused on the 'quality of law',[30] i.e., on the existence of specific qualitative requirements with which every law, regardless of the different types of legal sources, must comply, with regard to measures affecting the right to respect for private and family life, and correspondence as well.[31] Among the various qualitative requirements, 'foreseeability' in particular needs be adapted to the specific features of most digital investigations, mostly because of their covert nature.[32] Thus, it is apparent that what needs to be foreseeable is not the measure itself but the circumstances, conditions and limits which must be established by the law in advance.[33] In addition, the Court requires the law to establish a legitimate scope for investigations conducted through measures encroaching the right to privacy and secrecy of communications. Further, this scope is strictly linked with the requirement that restrictions on such precious rights not only be justified in cases of strict necessity but can also not outweigh this standard. This means that interference can be considered "necessary in a democratic society" for a legitimate purpose[34] only if it can satisfy a pivotal social interest and is proportionate to the scope, and relevant and sufficient reasons exist in the case at stake.[35]

These requirements reflect the general need to respect the proportionality principle, which plays a crucial role in the field of covert investigative measures and can help prevent undue intrusion into the fundamental rights of the involved people.

---

[30] See Neroni Rezende, Sect. 4.1.

[31] See, for instance, with regard to the right to respect for private life and correspondence, ECtHR, *Malone v. United Kingdom*, judgment of 6 August 1984, Appl. No. 8691/79. After almost 40 years, the principles set by the Court in this decision still represent a relevant guideline to assess whether a breach of Art. 8 ECHR has occurred. Cf. ECtHR, *Bykov v. Russia*, GC, judgment of 10 March 2009, Appl. No. 4378/02, para. 76; ECtHR, *Benedik v. Slovenia*, judgment of 24 April 2018, Appl. No. 62357/14, para. 122 ss. The protection of Art. 8 ECHR is granted to "the right to identity and personal development, and the right to establish and develop relationships with other human beings and the outside world"; ECtHR, judgment of 28 January 2003, *Peck v. United Kingdom*, Appl. No. 44647/98, para. 57.

[32] In this field of law, the European Court has always insisted on the quality of law since the landmark decision *Malone v. United Kingdom*.

[33] ECtHR, *Malone v. United Kingdom*, para. 67; ECtHR, GC, *Roman Zakharov v. Russia*, judgment of 4 December 2015, Appl. No. 47143/06, para. 229.

[34] ECtHR, *Segerstedt-Wiberg and Others v. Sweden*, judgment of 6 June 2006, Appl. No. 62332/00, para. 88: "While the Court recognises that intelligence services may legitimately exist in a democratic society, it reiterates that powers of secret surveillance of citizens are tolerable under the Convention only in so far as strictly necessary for safeguarding the democratic institutions"; cf. ECtHR, *Klass and Others v. Germany*, judgment of 6 September 1978, Appl. No. 5029/71, para. 42.

[35] ECtHR, *Roman Zakharov v. Russia*, para. 230; *D'Auria and Balsamo v. Italy*, judgment of 11 June 2013, Appl. No. 11625/07; *Cariello and others v. Italy*, judgment of 30 April 2013, Appl. No. 14064/07; *Capriotti v. Italy*, judgment of 23 February 2016, Appl. No. 28819/12; *Leander v. Sweden*, judgment of 26 March 1987, Appl. No. 9248/81.

It is precisely in light of the principle of proportionality that ECtHR case law emphasises the key relevance of a prior judicial warrant by an independent body,[36] thus specifically justifying the reasons of the recourse to intrusive means of investigation.[37] The fulfilment of this requirement is of the utmost importance to assess whether digital information has been gathered in full respect of the principles of Art. 8 ECHR.[38] This assessment is even more necessary in cases of investigative measures involving third parties, in which the competent authority is called upon to scrutinise whether and under which conditions interference with the right to privacy of persons other than defendants is legitimate and truly necessary, and to establish the duration of interference. As was pointed out by the Court in relation to other fields, European case law always calls for a 'fair balance' between the need to preserve the objectives of criminal proceedings and the interests of formal participants or a third parties in maintaining the confidentiality of personal data.[39] Another sensitive problem, which is partially linked to the protection of third parties, relates to the need to prevent undue interference with privileged information, since remote access allows gathering all the data stored.[40] In all these situations, therefore, the intrusiveness of digital inquiries imposes a restrictive approach on the investigative authorities, who can only resort to them when other less intrusive measures are

---

[36] ECtHR, *Trabajo Rueda v. Spain*, judgment of 30 May 2017, Appl. No. 32600/12. The Court held that the police seizure of the computer and inspection of the stored files without prior judicial authorisation were disproportionate to the legitimate aims pursued and unnecessary in a democratic society.

[37] The margin of appreciation allows national authorities to determine when an investigative measure could interfere with private life, but the final scrutiny about the effective necessity and proportionality of the measures is up to the Strasbourg Court. However, the Court's case law does not allow "building a complete theory or a common European standard on the proportionality principle with respect to the lawfulness of coercive investigative measures nor on the fairness or admissibility of evidence". See Bachmaier Winter (2013), pp. 94–95.

[38] For an interesting comparison between the protection granted by Article 8 ECHR and Fourth Amendment of United States Constitution, see Fura and Klamberg (2012), pp. 463 ff. These authors compare the conditions for the issuing of a judicial warrant, set out by the Fourth Amendment and those prescribed by European case law.

[39] ECtHR, *Z v. Finland*, judgment of 25 February 1997, Appl. No. 22009/93, para. 99. Even though this decision regards the publication of personal data in the context of a criminal trial, some principles are valid also for the field of criminal investigation.

[40] In this respect, see ECtHR, *Smirnov v. Russia*, judgment of 7 June 2007, Appl. No. 71362/01, para. 45 ff., regarding the physical search and seizure of a lawyer's office. The applicant had not been a party to the ongoing criminal investigation but represented some defendants. The Court observed that no arrangement had been made to safeguard the privileged materials protected by professional secrecy. Thus, having "regard to the materials that were inspected and seized, the Court finds that the search impinged on professional secrecy to an extent that was disproportionate to whatever legitimate aim was pursed. The Court reiterates in this connection that, where a lawyer is involved, an encroachment on professional secrecy may have repercussions on the proper administration of justice and hence on the rights guaranteed by Article 6 of the Convention" (para. 48). On similar issues regarding interception of communications of third parties and communications covered by professional confidentiality, see Bachmaier Winter (2004), pp. 41 ff.

unavailable or inadequate, and in any case provided that relevant and sufficient reasons exist.[41]

Upon close examination, however, even compliance with these requirements could however be ineffective to ensure the full protection of the individuals concerned, especially because digital investigative tools, due to their nature, are able to collect the overall information stored in a device. In most cases, therefore, it is almost impossible for the judicial authority to select in advance those data which are specifically related to the ongoing investigation. For this reason, the European Court emphasises the relevance of a judicial authorisation, which must properly address the reasonable suspicion justifying the search and seizure of digital data, and describe which data are necessary for the ongoing investigation.[42] Furthermore, the protection of digital privacy must in any case be enhanced at a later stage, when the data gathering procedure has already been accomplished and the investigative authorities start examining the collected information and separate what is relevant from what is not.[43] Also, the review of the collected material must be led under the supervision of a judicial authority, whose decision shall be reasoned and legally binding with regard to the destruction of the non-relevant data.[44]

---

[41] ECtHR, *Weber and Saravia v. Germany*, judgment of 29 June 2006, Appl. No. 54934/00, paras. 103-104; ECtHR, *Kruslin v. France*, judgment of 24 April 1990, Appl No. 11801/85, para. 35, according to which French legislation at that time did not define "the categories of people liable to have their telephones tapped by judicial order and the nature of the offences which may give rise to such an order".

[42] ECtHR, *Robathin v. Austria*, judgment of 3 July 2012, Appl. No. 30457/06, para. 51. In that case, the judicial warrant "gave details in respect of the alleged acts, the time of their commission and the damage allegedly caused" (para. 45), but it did not give specific reasons for the search, and it did not describe the necessity of copying all the electronic data.

[43] As stated by ECtHR, *Sigurður Einarsson and Others v. Iceland*, judgment of 4 June 2019, Appl. No. 39757/15, para. 90, "The Court accepts that by its nature the 'full collection of data' inevitably included a mass of data which was not *prima facie* relevant to the case. Moreover, it can accept that when the prosecution is in possession of a vast volume of unprocessed material it may be legitimate for it to sift the information in order to identify what is likely to be relevant and thus reduce the file to manageable proportions. It considers nevertheless that in principle an important safeguard in such a process would be to ensure that the defence is provided with an opportunity to be involved in the definition of the criteria for determining what may be relevant".

[44] ECtHR, GC, *Big Brother Watch and Others v. United Kingdom*, judgment of 25 May 2021, Appls. Nos. 58170/13, 62322/14 and 24960/15, para. 359. In the same decision, the Court underlined the need of legal provisions which made sufficiently clear the circumstances in which the collected data had to be erased or destroyed and established short retention period (para. 405). On this judgment, see Bachmaier Winter (2021b), pp. 317 ff.

4 Searches of Digital Evidence in Domestic Law

Even though the gathering of electronic evidence has become indispensable in criminal investigations, only few jurisdictions have enacted specific rules on computer searches, and especially on online searches. In Europe, the Cybercrime Convention Committee has recently held that several countries have simply extended the provisions originally set out for the traditional search and seizure to their new digital versions, without properly considering the peculiarities of high-tech instruments.[45] To a great extent, therefore, "the call for a new criminal procedure with regard to digital evidence has remained unheard".[46]

Italy amended its CPC only in 2008 by transposing the Budapest Convention.[47] In this regard, it is worth noting that this reform stressed on the respect of the integrity of original data, avoiding any alteration or loss during the gathering process of this type of evidence. However, the 2008 reform failed to regulate remote access to computers or other electronic devices, thus leaving a significant legal lacuna,[48] even though online searches were widely conducted in Italy at that time and became even more frequent in the years ahead. The absence of specific regulation until today has impeded the establishment of standard procedures by public prosecutor's offices, and therefore each investigative team still works on its own, without a coordination and using different ICT tools and protocols.[49] Furthermore, there are no uniform best practices and law enforcement officials have not developed a sufficient level of technical preparation.[50]

The failure to introduce *ad hoc* provisions on online searches turns out to be even more problematic, since there are no legal indications establishing the limits of such means of investigation and mostly the safeguards due to the owner or users of the

---

[45] Cybercrime Convention Committee (T-CY), *The Budapest Convention on Cybercrime: benefits and impact in practice*, Strasbourg, 13 July 2020, accessible at https://rm.coe.int/t-cy-2020-16-bc-benefits-rep-provisional/16809ef6ac, pp. 5 ff., according to which only 42% of national Countries in the world have specifically regulated the procedural powers needed to ensure the preservation of digitally stored evidence, while "many States still rely on general procedural law provisions (for search, seizure and so on) to investigate cybercrime and secure electronic evidence". Furthermore, many countries are reluctant to adopt detailed procedures, due to the lack of their authorities' competence to apply them.

[46] As expressed by Camon (2021), p. 8. In this sense, cf. Kerr (2005a), p. 279, who more than 15 years ago, had already called for the adoption of new rules on digital evidence, highlighting the inadequacy of the traditional investigative procedures to take such information.

[47] See Law No. 48/2008. On this reform see Costabile (2010), pp. 465 ff; Pittiruti (2017), p. 11; Lupária (2009).

[48] Nicolicchia (2020), p. 10.

[49] On the absence of standard operating procedures (*S.O.P.*) in Italy and the implications in terms of reduced safeguards, see Giunchedi (2013), p. 826; Mattiucci (2013), p. 715.

[50] See Sabillon et al. (2017), who examined the best practices in digital forensic analysis. The establishment of best practice procedures for the digital evidence gathering "can bring digital and physical crime scenes as closely together as possible, and ensure at least 'for all practical purposes' that the data given to the court is identical to the data generated by the suspect". Abel (2009), p. 105.

addressed device, who is probably fully unaware of the investigation in course.[51] To fill this legal gap, some scholars suggested to consider remote computer searches as measures of a hybrid nature.[52] This classification has often justified the application of the existing rules regarding communication intercepts and especially the interception of communications between computer systems. But difficult problems persist if search aims at collecting non-communicative data or data regarding communication flows that do not take place during the searching activity.[53] Here, recourse to the regulation on telecommunication interceptions appears to be useless by definition.

Both legal scholarship and case law, being well aware of the substantial differences between cyber interception and online search, therefore today tend to consider the latter as means of investigation without a specific legal basis because of the existence of a general clause in the CPC regarding the so-called 'atypical evidence' ('*prova atipica*').[54] Recourse to this general provision is justified by the need to fulfil the requirement of lawfulness provided for by Italian Constitution in relation to various fundamental rights on which online searches can impinge. This interpretative solution, however, clearly satisfies this constitutional law requirement only in a formalistic way, as this clause does not contain any condition or specific limits, which the competent judge shall define in the concrete case after hearing all the parties. These requirements do not therefore fit the characteristics of covert investigations in general, and specifically of remote searches, whose addressee has to be kept in dark of the ongoing procedure. It is therefore more than doubtful that online searches can produce legal effects on the basis of such general clause.[55] Yet there is an urgent need for legislative intervention, as remote searches produce a severe interference on the right to private life.[56]

Unlike Italy, Germany has shown much more attention to the need to provide digital search with a legal basis. In a landmark ruling of 2008, the German Federal Constitutional Court, while underlining the need for a sufficiently determined legislation, justified the use of this investigative measure only in exceptional situations in order to prevent or ascertain the harm to fundamental interests (such as life,

---

[51] Bartoli and Lasagni (2021), p. 92. These authors highlighted that the 2008 reform went almost unnoticed for a decade.

[52] Art. 266-*bis* of Italian CPC. On the hybrid nature of this investigative measure cf. Marcolini (2010), p. 2859.

[53] Communicative data can be related to chat conversations, phone calls and other contacts between users of different devices; non-communicative data, instead, refer to all sorts of information stored in a device, such as photo, videos, browser histories. See Della Monica (2020), pp. 22 ff.

[54] Art. 189 of Italian CPC. See Aterno (2009), p. 213, and more recently, Parlato (2021), pp. 365 ff. See also Italian Court of Cassation, Joint Sections, judgment of 28 marzo 2006, n. 26795, *Prisco*, accessible at http://servizi.ceda.unina.it/PHP/spec/spec/Cass_26795_2006.pdf.

[55] Daniele (2011), p. 297.

[56] Nicolicchia (2020), p. 37.

public safety and security).[57] Moreover, the constitutional judges ruled that restrictions on privacy and secrecy of citizens' communications necessitated a judicial authorisation which ought to respect the proportionality principle. In light of this essential requirement, the Court established further conditions for using such highly intrusive measure: in particular, it was legitimated in the context of criminal inquiries regarding serious offences and provided that investigative alternatives were not sufficient or equally adequate to establish the facts.[58] Furthermore, the software used for online surveillance must ensure some "securing mechanisms", and collected data need to be preserved for their evidentiary value.[59]

The most significant aspect of this judgment is that the *Bundesverfassungsgericht* recognised the existence of a new fundamental right, that is the right to the guarantee of the confidentiality and integrity of ICT systems (*Grundrecht auf Gewährleistung der Vertraulichkeit und Integrität informationstechnischer Systeme*), as an expression of the general principle of respect for human dignity (*Menschenwürde*, established by Article 1 of *Grundgesetz*).[60] This approach was further enhanced by another relevant judgment that the Court issued some years later, remarking the link between the intrusion of digital measures into private life and the existence of investigative purpose that justifies the limitation of constitutional rights.[61]

German lawmakers, however, intervened in 2017 with a controversial reform of the German CPC, which, albeit in terms not entirely consistent with constitutional case law, empowered law enforcement agencies to conduct online searches and source telecommunications surveillance among other digital means. The competent authorities can resort to such spyware-based means when investigating terrorism-related crimes, homicides, drug trafficking, money laundering, and other serious offences.[62] At any rate, online searches, however, generally require a judicial order, except in cases of imminent danger; here, the public prosecutor's office—and even

---

[57] *Bundesverfassungsgericht* (BVerfG), judgment of 27 February 2008, 1 BvR 370/07, 1 BvR 595/07, in *Official Case Reports BVerfGE* 120, 274, in *Neue Juristische Wochenschrift (NJW)*, 2008, p. 822. See Abel and Schafer (2009), pp. 106. Cf., also, Flor (2009), pp. 697 ff.

[58] Similar indications have been delivered by the Polish Supreme Court, judgment of 26 April 2007, *I KZP*, 6/07, in *Orzecznictwo Sądu Najwyższego Izba Karna i Izba Wojskowa (OSNKW)* 2007, No. 5, p. 37. Cf. Böckenförde (2008), pp. 825 ff. For a comparison between the German and the Polish decision, see Kurek (2009), pp. 377 ff.

[59] Nevertheless, online surveillance targeted to specific individuals was not largely widespread in Germany, due to several technical difficulties. See Derin and Golla (2019), p. 1111. But in the last few of years, since government hacking has been intensified, things have changed.

[60] Hornung (2008), pp. 299 ff.

[61] See *Bundesverfassungsgericht* (BVerfG), judgment of 20 April 2016, 1 BvR 966/09, 1 BvR 1140/09, accessible at https://www.bundesverfassungsgericht.de/SharedDocs/Pressemitteilungen/EN/2016/bvg16-019.html.

[62] Some of the offences that allow the use of online search do not entail serious danger for human lives, as prescribed by the Federal Court. See Herpig and Schuetze (2017). These authors analyse the debate arisen after the 2017 legislative reform.

the police, in terrorism-related investigations—can provisionally authorise them, but judicial validation is needed within 3 days.[63]

Under German law, any information concerning private life, which is found during an online search, cannot be used and must be deleted without delay.[64] Thus, such solution is necessary to avoid or reduce the risk of violations concerned with uninvolved third parties, since nowadays the monitoring of mobile devices (smartphones, tablet, and so on) engenders extensive intrusion into the privacy of people.

Compared to the approach promoted by the Federal Constitutional Court, the 2017 legislative reform in Germany seems to have weakened the standards of human rights protection concerning digital searching activities in favour of a stronger government hacking oriented towards security purposes.[65] It is interesting to observe that constitutional case law has attached such relevance to the right of integrity and confidentiality of computer systems that it has recently extended it also to foreign people in other countries.[66]

In other European countries also, courts have played a crucial role by compensating for the lack of a legislative regulation regarding remote computer searches. This is the case for Spain, where the earliest standards in this matter were not set by the legislator but by national courts. Therefore, *Policía Nacional* and *Guardia Civil* developed some best practice codes collecting the principles elaborated by Spanish case law, with the aim of preserving the integrity of the information.[67]

In 2015, Spanish lawmakers launched a wide-ranging legislative reform, which also aimed at regulating the use of technological measures in the criminal investigation, and thus ensuring the lawfulness and proportionality of any interference with the rights to privacy and secrecy of communications.[68] Nevertheless, even this reform provided no difference between the access to communications and the access

---

[63] Sieber and von zur Mühlen (2016).

[64] Sec. 100d(1) German CPC.

[65] Germany participated in two initiatives in order to facilitate lawful access to electronic devices. See *Council Resolution on Encryption. Security through encryption and security despite encryption*, Council of the European Union, 24 November 2020, accessible at https://data.consilium. europa.eu/doc/document/ST-13084-2020-REV-1/en/pdf; *Non-paper on EU Cyber Diplomacy by Estonia, France, Germany, Poland, Portugal and Slovenia*, German Ministry of Foreign Affairs, 2019, accessible at https://www.auswaertiges-amt.de/blob/2418160/206b3bf9aa4ef45a28873 99231840d23/201119-non-paper-pdf-data.pdf; see also Herpig and Schuetze (2021).

[66] For this reason, the Court declared the unconstitutionality of the surveillance regime. *Bundesverfassungsgericht* (BVerfG), judgment of 19 May 2020, 1 BvR 2835/17, accessible at https://www.bundesverfassungsgericht.de/SharedDocs/Entscheidungen/EN/2020/05/rs2020051 9_1bvr283517en.html.

[67] Cf. Bachmaier Winter (2021a), pp. 169 ff., where the main sources of guidelines and good practices can be read.

[68] *Ley Orgánica* No. 13, 5 October 2015, amending the Spanish CPC on the strengthening of procedural safeguards and regulating technological investigative measures. On this reform, see Marchena Gómez and González-Cuéllar (2015), pp. 173 ff; Bachmaier Winter (2021a), p. 178. Also, Bachmaier Winter (2017), p. 4.

to other digital files stored in electronic devices. According to the Supreme Court also, Spanish lawmaker had not distinguished between communicative and non-communicative data but have granted a "unitary treatment" for the protection of "the virtual environment", including all data that show the personal profile of the people who undergo the search.[69]

As to the procedural requirements, Spanish legislation now requires a judicial warrant authorising remote searches, in which the competent authority must also specify the limits of the intrusion to ensure full protection of fundamental rights of the addressed person.[70]

In 2017, a study, commissioned by the European Parliament's Policy Department for Citizens' Rights and Constitutional Affairs at the request of the LIBE Committee, examined and compared legal frameworks in six European countries (France, Germany, Italy, Netherlands, Poland and United Kingdom) and three non-EU countries (Australia, Israel and United States of America).[71] This research, entitled *"Legal Frameworks for Hacking by Law Enforcement: Identification, Evaluation and Comparison of Practices"*, also included some recommendations and policy proposals addressed to EU Parliament and Member States' Governments in order to strengthen the protection of privacy and the security of Internet during lawful investigative activities.[72]

Among the non-EU countries analysed in such survey, the United States represent a really interesting example, because at both local and federal levels hacking tools have been routinely deployed without sufficiently clear legislative indication.[73] The only relevant regulation is established by Rule 41 of the Federal Rules of US CPC, which was amended in 2016 with the aim of providing a procedure for law enforcement agencies to gain remote access to data.[74]

---

[69] Spanish Supreme Court, judgment of 23 October 2018, No. 3754/2018. See also Supreme Court, judgment of 18 July 2014, No. 587/2014, and already judgment of 17 April 2013, No. 342/2013.

[70] Art. 588-*bis(a) LECrim.*

[71] See Policy Department—Citizens' rights and constitutional affairs (2017), accessible at https://www.europarl.europa.eu/RegData/etudes/STUD/2017/583137/IPOL_STU(2017)583137_EN.pdf.

[72] The controls about the lawfulness of the investigative activity can be "*ex ante*" or "*ex post*". In the matter discussed here, the protection instruments that can be activated by interested subjects will be mostly subsequent to such operations, since the searched person is usually unaware of the measures. Prior safeguards are left in the proceeding authorities' discretionary power or legal requirements, when existing.

[73] See Quinlan and Wilson (2016), p. 2. In US, at least since 1999 FBI and other law enforcement agencies have used technological skills to access private digital networks and material in the process of investigating crimes.

[74] Fed. R. Crim. P. 41(e)(2)(B) regulates the warrant for a tracking device. "A tracking-device warrant must identify the person or property to be tracked, designate the magistrate judge to whom it must be returned, and specify a reasonable length of time that the device may be used. The time must not exceed 45 days from the date the warrant was issued. The court may, for good cause, grant one or more extensions for a reasonable period not to exceed 45 days each. The warrant must command the officer to: '(i) complete any installation authorized by the warrant within a specified time no longer than 10 days; (ii) perform any installation authorized by the warrant during the

In accordance with the Fourth Amendment of the US Constitution, which provides the fundamental safeguards by protecting the "right of the people to be secure in their persons, houses, papers, and effects, against unreasonable searches and seizure", the competent judge can only authorise such investigative measures, as is well-known, if two essential requirements co-exist, i.e. 'probable cause' and 'particularity'.[75] This especially entails that a concrete suspicion "exists where the facts and circumstances within the officers' knowledge, and of which they have reasonably trustworthy information, are sufficient in themselves to warrant a belief by a man of reasonable caution that a crime is being committed".[76]

In relation to the traditional search and seizure, US Supreme Court elaborated the 'plain view doctrine',[77] which, in compliance with the Fourth Amendment, requires a judicial warrant specifying the places that the competent authorities are allowed to enter and explore as well as the conditions of seizing relevant items.[78] This doctrine cannot easily be extended to digital search and seizure, since, for the aforementioned arguments, it is almost impossible to issue a sufficiently specific warrant for digital investigation and determine in advance the contents to be opened and examined.[79]

---

daytime, unless the judge for good cause expressly authorizes installation at another time; and (iii) return the warrant to the judge designated in the warrant'".

During an interview, Kevin Bankston of the Open Technology Institute, said: *"Whatever euphemism the FBI uses to describe it – whether they call it a 'remote access search' or a 'network investigative technique' – what we're talking about is government hacking, and this obscure rule change would authorize a whole lot more of it."* See https://thefreethoughtproject.com/supreme-court-law-enforcement-remotely-hack-search-computer/#ROeWvFFKpMhTFrmQ.99.   Cf.   also Delong (2016).

[75] Interestingly, the US Supreme Court extended these safeguards also to search in smartphones, due to the fact that they contain information related to every aspect of private life; therefore, data kept in phones cannot be less protected than data stored in a personal computer. See *Riley v. California*, 573 U.S. 373 (2014). In NIT searches, the place to be searched is considered "the location of the property to be searched, not the location of the property owner or the agent performing the search". Cf. *United States v. Verdugo-Urquidez*, 449 U.S. 259 (1990).

[76] This definition has been first provided by the US Supreme Court, *Brinegar v. United States*, 338 U.S. 160 (1949). However, the concept of 'probable cause' has been explained in many different ways. For example, the *Oxford Companion to American Law* defines probable cause as "information sufficient to warrant a prudent person's belief that the wanted individual had committed a crime (for an arrest warrant) or that evidence of a crime or contraband would be found in a search (for a search warrant)"; Hall (2002), p. 720.

[77] *Coolidge v. New Hampshire*, 403 U.S. 443 (1971); *Horton v. California*, 496 U.S. 128 (1990), in which the Court held that the Fourth Amendment does not prohibit the warrantless seizure of evidence which is in plain view. The discovery of the evidence does not have to be 'inadvertent'.

[78] The 'plain view doctrine' allows the police to seize pieces of evidence discovered during a valid search whenever the incriminating nature of the item to be seized is immediately evident. See *Horton v. California*, para. 136 ff. For in-depth analysis of case law see *Searching and Seizing Computers and Obtaining Electronic Evidence in Criminal Investigation*, published by Office of Legal Education Executive Office for United States Attorneys (2009), accessible at https://www.justice.gov/file/442111/download, pp. 34 ff.

[79] See Kerr (2005b), pp. 566 ff., who analyses the possibilities of narrowing the plain view doctrine for digital evidence searches. "Computer hard drives store a tremendous amount of private

Therefore, several courts have considered individual files as separate closed containers,[80] thus excluding the application of 'plain view doctrine'.[81] Following this jurisprudence, police officers are not allowed to open files that do not fall into the scope of the judicial warrant. Some courts, however, have developed a different approach, according to which the 'plain view doctrine' justifies an extensive search, without any violation of Fourth Amendment rights.[82] But this last conclusion entails the risk that police officers search and seize all the contents of the entire computer system, which hugely endangers individuals' reasonable expectation of privacy.[83]

Like other means of digital investigation, online searches are increasingly used when States consider themselves endangered by national security threats, such as cybercrime or attacks perpetrated by terroristic or criminal organisations.[84] In these cases, lawmakers are keen to subject people, no matter whether citizens or foreigners, to constant and massive monitoring, in order to prevent serious crimes. Yet this result leads to clear breaches of private life that cannot be tolerated in liberal States.

---

information that can be exposed even in a targeted search. If everything comes into plain view, the plain view exception threatens to swallow the rule."

[80] Cf. Brenner (2012), pp. 1241–1242, which underlines that "the computer-container essentially offers officers a direct portal into the data it contains, a point of 'entry' they can exploit without affecting any physical entry into Fourth Amendment-protected premises."

[81] *Guest v. Leis*, 255 F.3d 325, 335 (6th Cir. 2001); *United States v. Carey*, 172F.3d 1268, 1273–75 (10th Cir. 1999).

[82] *United States v. Runyan*, 275 F.3d 449, 464–465 (5th Cir. 2001); *United States v. Slanina*, 283 F.3d 670, 680 (5th Cir. 2002). In those two cases, the Court held that when a warrantless search of a portion of a computer or storage device had been proper, the defendant no longer retained any reasonable expectation of privacy in the remaining contents of the computer or storage device.

[83] An interesting example is helpful to highlight the need of a judicial oversight in order to verify the lawfulness of the investigative activity. In March 2013, the FBI requested a remote search warrant to Magistrate Stephen Smith, Judge of the Southern District of Texas, in order to locate with a software unidentified persons who had hacked into the victim's email account. Moreover, the IP address used for stealing money from the victim's bank account was from a foreign country. Judge Smith rejected the warrant request, since the requested search would violate the Fourth Amendment's protection against unreasonable search and seizure. Furthermore, the judge noted that accidentally hacking innocent people's computers systems would cause a violation of their fundamental rights. See Vijayan (2013).

[84] For instance, The USA Patriot Act of 2001, expired in 2015, instituted a special derogation from this principle, stating that law enforcement officials may access communications records, credit cards, bank numbers and stored emails held by third parties without any probable cause; instead, they just need a reasonable suspicion that such information was related to criminal activities. Such drastic reduction of safeguards, even if it was a consequence of the New York terroristic attack of 11th September 2001, led to strong interference of investigative authorities with right to privacy and secrecy of communication of lots of people. See Doyle (2002).

5 Seizure of Digital Evidence: The USA Experience

It has been noted that the goal of every search has traditionally been to detect the *corpus delicti* or anyway items related to an alleged crime for investigative purposes, which items, once they are found, must be seized. The seizure of digital information, however, differs from traditional seizure, which takes place in the material world and aims at the securing specific goods. This is largely the result of the very characteristics of digital searches, which, as we have seen, have a wide-ranging scope by exploring electronic devices. Consequently, digital seizure can lead to the remote collection of a huge amount of data,[85] which include, *inter alia*, personal files, photos, videos, clouds, and any other data saved in the searched system. The major outcome is that the competent authorities can reconstruct the features of the addressed people, having access to information regarding their tastes, interests, connections, and other valuable elements to picture their personality.

In the field of ICT investigations, seizure is usually carried out through a copy bit-by-bit (the so-called 'bitstream image technique'), which includes all the data stored in electronic devices.[86] Data analysis takes place after collection, since it is impossible, or it would be truly complicated to identify the information that needs to be seized during the searching activity. Indeed, since people collect all sorts of information in electronic devices, a distinction between relevant and irrelevant information would not be feasible in advance.[87]

In this context, two essential interests must be taken into consideration, that is the integrity of data through adequate procedures ("chain of custody"), and the protection due to the individuals concerned. Since seizure of digital evidence also endangers fundamental rights, the data owner needs be granted specific safeguards, starting with the right to an effective remedy to challenge the lawfulness of seizure, and to claim for the erasure of irrelevant or superfluous data. Otherwise, there is a high risk that digital search turns out to be merely explorative and becomes a

---

[85] Legal scholarship has underlined that traditional search and seizure are regulated taking into consideration the characteristics of physical property, which are totally missing in the digital environment. Therefore, it is precisely in this new context that the constitutional protection against the intrusion of public authority must be reconsidered. See Kerr (2005b), p. 535.

[86] Bachmaier Winter (2017), p. 23, has raised some interesting questions: "Once the data stored in the searched computer have been retrieved and copied, how should the IT law enforcement officers discriminate between the relevant and irrelevant files? Can they scrutinize all the data in order to select those that fall within the scope of the warrant? Should forensic tools be used to also limit the computer search only to certain types of files or data? Should the law impose the obligation to use these types of targeted search tools?".

[87] For instance, Spain, which is one of the States with a quite recent modification of the procedural law regarding digital evidence, still misses a regulation about how the proceeding authorities must separate irrelevant data from useful information and how to treat the first ones. Moreover, there was no rule about accidental discoveries of evidence until 2015, when the reform of *LECrim* (Art. 588-*bis*(*i*) referring to Art. 579-*bis*) added a provision: now it is specified that accidentally found evidence of another crime must be submitted to a judge, who must evaluate how the piece of evidence was collected and assess the circumstances. See Bachmaier Winter (2017), pp. 24 and 26.

powerful means of detecting any sort of crime, no matter whether or not connected to the ongoing investigation. Even more worryingly, the bit-by-bit copy undoubtedly overcomes the scope of a single investigation and implies the danger of "an *inquisitio generalis* upon the person under investigation".[88]

Subsequent remedies have, of course, their own limits, and there is a need for preventative solutions. Beforehand, the protection of privacy can be improved if the authorities lead their search activity by using keywords. This procedure allows detecting and selecting only filtered files, thus narrowing down the number of accessible data, and then the information to be copied.[89] Moreover, it seems to be in line with the traditional requirement that the items to be searched be specified in advance. The shortcoming of this method is that even relevant information for the ongoing investigation could be overlooked, since the use of keywords could unproperly restrict the results of the search.[90] Furthermore, such type of search could also end in failure, whenever the used filter cannot find encrypted files or locked information.[91] In these cases, digital search entails sterile interference with the right to data protection, that results in a loss of time and resources. In sum, on one hand, keywords-based search can excessively narrow down the area of the investigation, on the other, it can turn out to be ineffective or not totally successful from the viewpoint of a proper information gathering.

Regardless of the use of keywords or other ways of filtering results, the solution of copying information bit-by-bit also raises concerns. In the recent past, there has been a heated debate about its legal qualification as a seizure. While, for example, Italian lawmakers classified the copy of digital information as a seizure,[92] in the United States this conclusion was reached only after many decades. Indeed, an earlier doctrine of US Supreme Court, which has not yet been completely overcome, did not consider the mere copying of information as a seizure.[93] This approach raised a huge problem, as the police were empowered to operate outside the requirements of the Fourth Amendment. Therefore, entire files could be copied without a judicial warrant fulfilling the requirements of probable cause and particular description of the items.[94] Independently from whether data forensic deals with original or copy data,

---

[88] Bachmaier Winter (2017), p. 25.

[89] See ECtHR, *Sigurður Einarsson and Others v. Iceland*, para. 16 ff. Here, the competent prosecutor conducted a search of electronic data using the e-Discovery system 'Clearwell'. This program works through certain keywords and allows detecting the documents and files related to those words.

[90] *Ibid*. See also *United States v. Adjani*, 452 F.3d 1140, 1150 (9th Cir. 2006), which underlined that computer files "are easy to disguise or rename" and if the warrant limits the search with keywords, "much evidence could escape discovery simply because of the labelling of the files".

[91] The decryption process usually needs an expert analyst to be successfully done and it also requires a large amount of time; see Kerr (2005b), p. 546.

[92] See art. 254-*bis* or art. 354 of Italian CPC.

[93] See, *ex plurimis*, *Arizona v. Hicks*, 480 U.S. 321 (1987). In that case, the police officers wrote down the serial number of some stereo equipment that they suspected it had been stolen.

[94] Kerr (2005b), pp. 560 ff.

truth is that public authorities have access to private information of people, jeopardising their reasonable expectation of privacy regarding the contents of their devices. For this reason, legal scholarship has rightly held that "when a forensic analyst performs the necessary steps to evaluate a hard drive, the exposure of the information from the hard drive to an output device such as a monitor counts as a search regardless of whether the information was most recently stored as a copy or a more direct original".[95]

Similar concerns can largely be extended to the copies obtained through online searches. Some courts and scholars have suggested that data duplication should be treated as seizure, which would activate all the Fourth Amendment safeguards.[96] Even if this approach seems to enhance human rights protection, most courts and commentators in the US are still reluctant to accept it, or they restrict its application to the cases in which the copying of data interferes with the "possessory interests" of the data owner.[97]

This aspect highlights another relevant difference between traditional seizure and digital seizure.[98] Thus, no matter whether the files are obtained after a search of computer systems or remote search, data remain in the possession and under control of their owner, who can access, modify or even delete them at any time. What differs is the right to exclusive control of data, which the addressee of digital seizure inevitably loses.

---

[95] *Id.*, p. 564.

[96] See Taticchi (2010), for whom exact duplicates must be treated as seizure, since the possessory interest of the data's owner imply the exclusive control of the accountant over them. The Author also proposes that the definition of "possessory interest" must be broaden in order to cover also intrusions into someone's digital information. Also, Brenner (2012), p. 1245. Cf. *United States v. Ganias*, 755 F.3d 125 (2nd Cir. 2014).

[97] In this sense, see Ohm (2005), p. 11, who considers the application of "possessory interest" only when involving "the right to delete", which descends from the traditional property right to destroy the own thing. When the police retain the hardware, it is considered as seizure, but not when they just generate data copies. See Kerr (2010), pp. 712 ff. Cf. Ohm (2008), p. 2 ss., for whom "a constitutionally significant 'seizure' occurs whenever the State takes dominion or control of personally owned data or meaningfully interferes with an individual's right to control his data". Cf. Kerr (2010), p. 724, according to which "the basic principles of the Fourth Amendment can be readily translated from the old to the new".

[98] See Brenner (2012), p. 1245.

6 Computer Search and Seizure in Digital Era: Rights and Procedural Safeguards

The increasing recourse to ICT investigations needs new categories to be elaborated, in order to ensure full protection of individual rights by means of procedural safeguards that fit the challenges set by the digital transformation of criminal inquiries.[99]

Despite the fact that investigative measures accessing computer systems harm essential values, it is difficult to find relevant provisions in traditional constitutions. Some countries have recently amended their own constitutions to strengthen privacy protection, as has happened in some US States.[100] For instance, Michigan, following the example set by Missouri and New Hampshire, in 2020 enacted a reform that prohibited unreasonable search and seizure of electronic data and electronic communications.[101] Mexican Constitution, also, today acknowledges the right to access to Internet and to informatic technologies.[102] Outside US borders, Brazilian Constitution already protected the secrecy of correspondence and the obtained data, as well as phone communications, except when a judicial order was required to authorise the access to private information for purposes of criminal inquiries or evidence gathering.[103] More recently, Constitutional Amendment Act No. 115 of 2022 enacted into the Brazilian Constitution a fundamental provision that recognises the right to the protection of one's own personal data, including digital data.[104] It has been noted that German Constitutional Court has long acknowledged the right to be protected in case of online search, namely the right to integrity and confidentiality of computer systems. Despite the merits of this approach, integrity and confidentiality of computer systems, and even the right to data protection, cover only a part of a much more complex value which is digital privacy.[105]

In several jurisdictions, however, the protection of a new generation of fundamental rights—starting with digital privacy—still remains based upon an extensive interpretation of the pre-existing constitutional rules, which have become of the utmost relevance due to the intrusive potentials of criminal investigations. That

---

[99] See Leacock (2008), p. 225. In the opinion of this author, legal reforms about the electronic world should take into consideration to what extent new technologies, especially the search and seizure regime, could be used for effective investigation and prosecution of cyber conduct.

[100] For further details, consult https://www.ncsl.org/research/telecommunications-and-information-technology/privacy-protections-in-state-constitutions.aspx.

[101] See Ebert (2020). According to Merissa Kovach, policy strategist with the American Civil Liberties Union of Michigan, this new protection entailed that "when there is new technology down the road that we cannot even imagine existing, we are not going to have to wait for years and years for a case to work its way through the courts."

[102] Art. 6(III) of the Political Constitution of the United Mexican States.

[103] Art. 5(XII) of the Brazilian Constitution.

[104] Art. 5(LXXII) of the Brazilian Constitution.

[105] Foti, Sect. 2.

people more and more develop a digital life deserves the protection of two implications of digital privacy, i.e. the right to exclude others (including public authorities) from one's own digital data and activities, and the right to have one's own data fairly treated when they are collected in the context of criminal investigations.[106]

In Europe, the evolution of both EU law[107] and ECtHR case law has strongly contributed to the establishment of constitutional standards of protection of digital rights by national countries. Among the major principles set by the ECtHR in the field of the right to respect for private life and correspondence is the requirement of lawfulness, which holds essential relevance to justify the recourse to ICT measures, such as searches of computer systems and seizure of digital evidence. Of course, the requirement of a legal basis cannot be properly satisfied by generic statutory provisions or well-established case law, as such intrusive tools must be specifically regulated by law, which must set proper conditions and limits. Among the above analysed countries, Spain and Germany provide positive examples, since their legislation include specific provisions about online search along with other covert measures of investigation. Another useful indication emerging from the examination of these jurisdictions is that national law should circumscribe the use of digital investigative techniques only to serious crimes, which may prejudice primary interests (life, public security, and so on) as underlined by German Federal Court. In full respect of proportionality principle, furthermore, ICT tools must be deployed when less intrusive measures are unavailable, thus being indispensable for the ongoing investigation.

At the core of procedural safeguards under ECtHR case law is the guarantee of a judicial control over the use of IT tools, which plays a pivotal role to ensure full compliance with the proportionality principle and all the legal requirements at the

---

[106] It should be taken into account that law enforcement bodies and judicial authorities make more and more use of information achieved for different purposes or gathered in the field of non-criminal inquiries. In the last few years, in particular, European countries have undertaken various administrative measures to digitalise public functions and services. For example, some European States have recently adopted a digital certificate (the so-called *Green Pass*, which includes personal data) to verify if a person is allowed to enter in some places, even for work, having a negative *Covid-19* test, antibodies or vaccination. Therefore, if national legislations impose the use of digital instruments on citizens and people submitted to their jurisdiction, they should consequently ensure adequate protection to all those activities carried out through the deployment of ICT tools.

[107] Cf. Regulation (EU) 2016/679 of the European Parliament and of the Council of 27 April 2016 on the protection of natural persons with regard to the processing of personal data and on the free movement of such data, and repealing Directive 95/46/EC (General Data Protection Regulation, GDPR), accessible at https://eur-lex.europa.eu/eli/reg/2016/679/oj, and Directive (EU) 2016/680 on the protection of natural persons regarding processing of personal data connected with criminal offences or the execution of criminal penalties, and on the free movement of such data, and repealing Council Framework Decision 2008/977/JHA, accessible at https://eur-lex.europa.eu/legal-content/EN/TXT/?uri=celex%3A32016L0680. However, the difficult balance between privacy and security still emerges from European legal instruments, since the *favor* for cooperation in criminal inquiries inevitably collides with the protection of individuals' intimacy.

time in which the sought measure is to be enforced.[108] The European Court, although not deeming judicial authorisation to be a necessary requirement,[109] shows a preference for this solution as an important safeguard against arbitrariness.[110] Judicial intervention is particularly relevant in those States (Italy, for example) where public prosecutors and even police authorities are competent to autonomously carry out several intrusive means during the pre-trial phase.[111] Of course, judicial oversight needs some essential conditions to be met. Indeed, it is apparent that investigative judges do not have the same level of functional independence as those judges who are competent for procedural safeguards without any investigative powers. Only an independent judge or administrative body can ensure the fairness of the proceedings and evaluate the necessity and proportionality of the interference with fundamental rights. At any rate, the competent judge for the oversight of ICT investigations needs be ensured full access to the information collected by the investigative agencies to properly fulfil the aforementioned tasks. Whenever the judges are withdrawn relevant information and are called on to intervene on the basis of the evidence selected by law enforcement authorities or the public prosecutor, their impartiality is at risk. Significantly, in the landmark decision *Big Brother Watch v. United Kingdom*, the European Court has highlighted the importance of the information regarding the purpose of the investigation and of the detailed records of all the operations, which enables the independent authorising body to assess the necessity and proportionality of the bulk interception operations which interfere with Art. 8 ECHR.[112]

Maybe time has come for a reconsideration of this problematic field with a view to a stronger protection of human rights in light of a recent judgment of the CJEU in the case *H.K.*, according to which the access to phone traffic data of a suspected person must be authorised solely after an accurate preventive scrutiny by a court or an independent administrative body. Furthermore, this ruling recognised that the collected information can define the identity of the addressed subject.[113] Even in urgent cases, the intervention of a judge is indispensable, but it must occur in a short span of time. This jurisprudence is extremely relevant for a proper understanding of the problems dealt with in this paper. To start with, if the oversight of an independent body is necessary to obtain phone traffic data, we can argue that it should *a fortiori* apply when access materialises through a backdoor which can carry out a massive

---

[108] Some jurisdictions have reduced the decision-making powers of judges in the pre-trial phase, while strengthening the role of public prosecutors, in relation to European Investigation Order procedures. See Ruggeri (2020), p. 325.

[109] ECtHR, *Big Brother Watch and Others v. United Kingdom*, para. 197.

[110] ECtHR, *Big Brother Watch and Others v. United Kingdom*, para. 351.

[111] In some European judicial systems, the Public Prosecutor's Office presents a lack of independence from the Governments. On this topic in the field of judicial cooperation among Member States, see Falcone (2021), pp. 59 ff.

[112] ECtHR, *Big Brother Watch and Others v. United Kingdom*, para. 352.

[113] CJEU, GC, *H.K.*, judgment of 2 March 2021, C-746/18, para. 51. For more information on this case, see Rovelli (2021). Also, see Foti, in this volume.

intrusion in the private sphere and digital identity.[114] Impartiality and independence of judicial authority represent the hard-core of fair trial safeguards and they must be ensured at any stage of criminal proceedings.[115]

Moreover, it has been noted that any form of preventive independent control has its unavoidable limits. Therefore, once access to data has occurred, the targeted person should be granted the possibility to challenge the lawfulness of the intrusion and to request erasure of those sensitive data which are not relevant for the investigation. EU Directive 2016/680 goes in this direction by imposing upon Member States the obligation to provide the data owner with adequate instruments in order to demand and eventually obtain the erasure of such data.[116] When the data are needed for evidentiary purposes, however, the competent authority shall restrict the processing.[117]

In the light of the principle of fair treatment, the retention of data obtained through online search must be accompanied by the granting of proper information to all the individuals concerned, above all the accused person, so that they might exercise the right to defence.[118] The essential requirement of information was emphasised by the ECtHR in the judgment *Big Brother Watch v. United Kingdom*, which pointed out that, after surveillance has been concluded, the question of subsequent notification of surveillance measures is inextricably linked to the effectiveness of remedies before the courts and hence to the existence of effective safeguards against the abuse of monitoring powers. Specific problems however arise when third parties are involved in digital investigations, especially if domestic law does not acknowledge any right to receive information at all.[119] In this regard, the Court considered two effective remedies: (*a*) the recourse to courts by the individual concerned and notified of the investigative measure taken without its knowledge; (*b*) the access to courts, without any prior notification, granted to any person who suspects that he or she has been subject to surveillance.[120]

---

[114]In 2016, UK introduced the Investigatory Powers Act to regulate the appointment and the oversight functions of the Investigatory Powers Commissioner. For instance, the Commissioner must keep under review the acquisition, retention, use or disclosure of bulk personal datasets, and, in particular, the operation of safeguards to protect privacy.

[115]Cf. ECtHR, *Harju v. Finland*, judgment of 15 February 2011, Appl. No. 56716/09, para. 39 ff.

[116]Directive (EU) 2016/680 of the European Parliament and of the Council of 27 April 2016 on the protection of natural persons with regard to the processing of personal data by competent authorities for the purposes of the prevention, investigation, detection or prosecution of criminal offences or the execution of criminal penalties, and on the free movement of such data, and repealing Council Framework Decision 2008/977/JHA, Art. 16(2), accessible at https://eur-lex.europa.eu/legal-content/EN/TXT/PDF/?uri=CELEX:32016L0680&from=EN.

[117]Art. 16(4) Directive 2016/680.

[118]ECtHR, *Big Brother Watch v. United Kingdom*, para. 310.

[119]Nicolicchia (2020), pp. 156–157.

[120]See ECtHR, *Big Brother Watch v. United Kingdom*, para. 337. In the same sense ECtHR, *Roman Zakharov v. Russia*, para. 234.

The most baffling aspect of search and seizure of digital evidence, as has been observed, is however the risk of disproportionate intrusiveness into the private sphere of people other than the accused people. This explains why several European countries, notwithstanding the absence of specific indications, grant also third parties the right to challenge the lawfulness of (digital) searches and to ask for the restitution or the erasing of the irrelevant seized data.[121] The Netherlands are an exception, as here third parties have no possibility of activating subsequent remedies, but the protection of their privacy is anyway ensured at an earlier stage by the requirement of a judicial authorisation of the collection of data regarding people other than the accused or the addressee of a search.[122] Similarly, Swiss CPC ensures some safeguards to third parties, as a court can authorise covert surveillance measures towards them only if there is reason to believe that the person to be monitored is receiving or passing communications on behalf of the accused.[123]

However, it is often very difficult for data owners to effectively check the way public authorities detain and disseminate their personal data, even if they surely have a legitimate expectation to exclude other parties.[124] It is noteworthy that Brazilian Constitution provided a specific judicial review called '*habeas data*' in order to ensure the possibility for the data owner to know which personal information is detained by public agencies and to claim for their rectification.[125]

To ensure the minimum sacrifice of individuals' rights, adequate communication should also be granted to people against whom no suspicion of guilt has arisen. Of course, this solution requires that third parties be provided with a specific instrument to challenge before a judicial authority the lawfulness of the data collection and to request the erasure of their own data. To be sure, even the requirement of a specific request is more than questionable. Thus, the irrelevant data should be erased or destroyed *ex officio*, in order to avoid the undue dissemination of private information with no evidentiary usefulness.[126] But taking into account all the limits of judicial controls, *quis custodiet ipsos custodes*?

---

[121] Bartoli and Lasagni (2021), pp. 231 ff.

[122] Cf. Sec. 125la Dutch CPC.

[123] Art. 270(b) Swiss CPC. The Swiss procedure law dedicates all the Chapter 8 to covert surveillance measures.

[124] "The mere retention and storing of personal data by public authorities, however obtained, are to be regarded as having direct impact on the private-life interest of an individual concerned of whether subsequent use is made of the data". See ECtHR, *S. and Marper v. United Kingdom*, judgment of 4 December 2008, Appls. Nos. 30562/04 and 30566/04, par. 121.

[125] Art. 5(LXII) Brazilian Constitution.

[126] ECtHR, *Zakharov v. Russia*, para. 231; ECtHR, *Big Brother Watch v. United Kingdom*, para. 226. The Court stressed on the possibility for an individual to pursue legal remedies in order to have access to personal data relating to him, or to obtain the rectification or erasure of such data. These safeguards contribute to grant an effective judicial protection. Also, German *Bundesverfassunsgericht* listed the requirements to obtain the erasing of information among the necessary safeguards descending from the proportionality principle. See *Bundesverfassungsgericht* (BVerfG), 2016.

7 Concluding Remarks

This research has highlighted that search and seizure of digital evidence set very delicate challenges, which neither domestic lawmakers nor supranational or international law have yet properly addressed. The procedural safeguards often prove insufficient to protect people from undue intrusion or accidental access to personal data, also because of the constant evolution of digital measures of investigation.

Albeit originally developed to defend computer systems from cyber offenders, cybersecurity consists of strategies to protect computers, networks, devices, programs, and data from unauthorised access and information disclosure,[127] all activities that nowadays can also be carried out by law enforcement agencies.

Therefore, the protection of privacy is a highly problematic matter, which every digital device user must take seriously into account, by way of adopting all the necessary measures to enhance the inaccessibility of personal information. Even with a simple research on the Internet, everyone can learn some practices for keeping sensitive data hidden from government or law enforcement agencies. In this sense, the term 'cyber-hygiene practices' refers to those lawful measures that allow people to build or enhance their own defence in the digital realm.[128]

Not only people but also companies, which largely use ICT tools, cannot rely on the design of their electronic devices,[129] which should undoubtedly be produced in order to be sufficiently secure. Furthermore, they also need to strengthen the existing protection from both criminal cyberattacks and data access carried out by investigative authorities.[130]

---

[127] Peterson (2021). See Papakonstantinou (2022), which underlines the difficult to achieve a precise definition of 'cybersecurity'. Also Art. 2(1) of Regulation (EU) 2019/881 of the European Parliament and of the Council of 17 April 2019 on ENISA (the European Union Agency for Cybersecurity) and on information and communications technology cybersecurity certification and repealing Regulation (EU) No. 526/2013 (Cybersecurity Act), accessible at https://eur-lex.europa.eu/legal-content/EN/TXT/PDF/?uri=CELEX:32019R0881&from=EN, provides a definition of cybersecurity, which means "the activities necessary to protect network and information systems, the users of such systems, and other persons affected by cyber threats".

[128] Papakonstantinou (2022), p. 12.

[129] *Id.*, p. 5: "Under a participatory approach everybody would somehow need to act or carry out measures: individuals and legal persons would have to take action, as prescribed by law or other regulations, in order for each to contribute proportionately to achieving the cybersecurity aims. For example, organisations would need to implement technical and organisational measures and individuals would have to apply so-called 'cyber hygiene' practices. Altogether, these collective measures would be aimed to serve the cybersecurity aims".

[130] Personal information may be abused "not just by cybercriminals seeking to develop correlations that can be used in fraud", but also by companies or government services, whether intentionally or unintentionally. See Australian Computer Society (ACS), *Cybersecurity. Threats. Challenges. Opportunities*, November 2016, accessible at https://ia.acs.org.au/article/2016/acs-launches-cybersecurity-guide.html.

Moreover, the design of software used for remote search of computer systems in criminal investigation is not different than any other piece of malware.[131] This means that commercial antivirus products may detect even *Trojan Horse* programs and other software deployed by competent authorities for the ongoing investigation. Antivirus programs installed on the target computer "could therefore interfere with, or even block, the law enforcement *Trojan Horse*'s ability to conduct the search (and seizure) authorised by the warrant".[132] Another protective measure to be adopted is the use of a virtual private network (VPN), which creates a secure tunnel between browsers and web servers, aiming at impeding the access to malicious intruders. Encryption and multi-factor authentication also prove extremely helpful in preventing or complicating the access to sensitive information.

Computer companies also provide some interesting indications to reduce online risks:[133] *e.g.* browsing the web safely by way of avoiding the use of public Wi-Fi; using a firewall, which provides protection against outside cyber attackers by shielding your computer or network from malicious or unnecessary network traffic;[134] keeping all your devices and software updated; preventing from the not reading spam emails or emails from unknown or suspicious senders; not downloading applications or programs developed by unknown sources.

Recourse to all these means allows natural and legal persons to build a safe digital environment, in which they have a reasonable expectation of cybersecurity. The very true goal of cybersecurity, indeed, is to protect individuals which are digitally active.[135] To achieve this aim, all the actors need to take some steps to protect the digital realm in which they work. In the light of this, citizens, companies and governments must cooperate and use precautions to build a safe space.[136] For instance, the European Cybersecurity Act expressly acknowledges the need to develop and implement means that protect the digital security of individuals (Recital No. 21). But in doing so, this Regulation also reaffirms the importance of accessing data "in a lawful and targeted manner, in full respect of fundamental rights and the relevant data protection laws, while upholding cybersecurity", while emphasising the need to respect the principle of necessity and proportionality (Recital No. 22).

While protecting individuals from criminal attacks to their data, law enforcement bodies however need to collect digital information of evidentiary relevance for investigative purposes. Therefore, when measures such as search and seizure of digital evidence are necessary, the individuals against who undergo them must be

---

[131] Brenner (2012), p. 1250.

[132] *Ibid.* The risk is that law enforcement agencies persuade antivirus producer to design programs which do not detect government malware or autonomously stop working when a digital search needs to be performed.

[133] See, for example, the advice given by *Microsoft*, accessible at https://support.microsoft.com/en-us/windows/keep-your-computer-secure-at-home-c348f24f-a4f0-de5d-9e4a-e0fc156ab221.

[134] Cybersecurity & Infrastructure Security Agency (CISA), *Understanding Firewalls for Home and Small Office Use* (2009), accessible at https://www.cisa.gov/uscert/ncas/tips/ST04-004.

[135] Papakonstantinou (2022), p. 5.

[136] Redins (2021).

granted all the procedural safeguards in order to reduce the risk of intrusion into their private sphere to the minimum extent.

References

Abel W (2009) Agents, Trojans and tags: the next generation of investigators. Int Rev Law Comput Technol 1-2(23):99–108

Abel W, Schafer B (2009) The German Constitutional Court on the right in confidentiality and integrity of information technology systems – a case report on BVerfG, NJW 2008, 822. SCRIPTed 6:106–123

Allegrezza S (2013) Le misure coercitive nelle "Model Rules for the Procedure of the European Public Prosecutor's Office". In: Ruggieri F, Rafaraci T, Di Paolo G, Marcoli S, Belfiore R (eds) Processo penale, lingua e Unione Europea. Cedam, Padua, pp 151–173

Aterno S (2009) Art. 8. In: Corasaniti G, Corrias Lucente G (eds) Cybercrime, responsabilità degli enti, prova digitale. Commento alla Legge 18 marzo 2008, n. 48. Cedam, Padova, pp 193–219

Bachmaier Winter L (2021a) The handle of digital evidence in Spain. In: Caianiello M, Camon A (eds) Digital forensic evidence. Towards common European standards in antifraud administrative and criminal investigations. Cedam, Milan, pp 165–205

Bachmaier Winter L (2021b) Proportionality, mass surveillance and criminal investigation: The Strasbourg Court facing Big Brother. In: Billis E, Knust N, Rui JP (eds) The principle of proportionality in crime control and criminal justice. Hart Publishing, Oxford, pp 317–335

Bachmaier Winter L (2017) Remote computer searches under the new Spanish Law of 2015: the proportionality principle and the protection of privacy. Zeitschrift für die gesamte Strafwissenschaft (ZStW) 129:2–27

Bachmaier Winter L (2013) The role of proportionality principle in cross-border investigations involving fundamental rights. In: Ruggeri S (ed) Transnational inquiries and the protection of fundamental rights in criminal proceedings. A study in memory of Vittorio Grevi and Giovanni Tranchina. Springer, Heidelberg, pp 85–110

Bachmaier Winter L (2004) Intervenciones telefónicas y derechos de terceros en el proceso penal. La necesidadde una regulación legal del secreto profesional y de otras relacione de confiancia. Revista de Derecho Procesal 1-3:41–82

Balsamo A (2020) Le tecniche investigative speciali e le loro potenzialità sul piano internazionale. In: Balsamo A, Mattarella A, Tartaglia R (eds) La Convezione di Palermo: il futuro della lotta alla criminalità organizzata transnazionale. Giappichelli, Turin, pp 289–313

Bartoli L, Lasagni G (2021) The handling of digital evidence in Italy. In: Caianiello M, Camon A (eds) Digital forensic evidence. Towards common European standards in antifraud administrative and criminal investigations. Cedam, Milan, pp 87–121

Bercovitz R (2021) Law enforcement hacking: defining jurisdiction. Columbia Law Rev 121(4): 1251–1288

Brenner SW (2012) Fourth amendment future: remote computer searches and the use of virtual force. Mississippi Law J 81(5):1229–1262

Böckenförde T (2008) Auf dem Weg zur elektronischen Privatsphäre. Zugleich Besprechung von BVerfG, Urteil v. 27. 2. 2008 – "Online-Durchsuchung". JuristenZeitung (JZ) 19:925–939

Caianiello M (2015) The new directive on the European Investigation Order between mutual recognition and mutual admissibility of evidence. Processo penale e giustizia 3:1–11

Camon A (2021) The project devices and digital evidence in Europe. In: Caianiello M, Camon A (eds) Digital forensic evidence. Towards common European standards in antifraud administrative and criminal investigations. Cedam, Milan, pp 1–12

Casey E (2004) Digital evidence and computer crime, 2nd edn. Academic Press

Costabile G (2005) *Scena criminis*, documento informatico e formazione della prova penale. Diritto dell'informazione e dell'informatica 21(3):531–538

Costabile G (2010) Computer forensic e informatica investigativa alla luce della Legge n. 48 del 2008. Cyberspazio e diritto 11(3):465–508

Daniele M (2011) La prova digitale nel processo penale. Rivista di Diritto Processuale 2:283–298

Della Monica G (2020) Intercettazioni e acquisizioni di dati informatici nella prospettiva del difensore. Incontro di studi "Intercettazioni e acquisizioni di dati in sistemi informatici". Report, pp 22–25. https://www.cortedicassazione.it/cassazione-resources/resources/cms/documents/REPORT_27_ottobre_2020_Anna_Mauro.pdf

Delong K (2016) Big changes in law enforcement remote computer searches. https://accessdata.com/blog/big-changes-in-law-enforcement-remote-computer-searches

Derin B, Golla SJ (2019) Der Staat als Manipulant und Saboteur der IT-Sicherheit. Neue Juristische Wochenschrift (NJW): 1111–1116

Doyle C (2002) The USA Patriot Act: a legal analysis. https://web.archive.org/web/20141206041849/http://assets.opencrs.com/rpts/RL31377_20020415.pdf

Ebert A (2020) Michigan passes warrant requirement for electronic data searches. Bloomberg Government. https://about.bgov.com/news/michigan-passes-warrant-requirement-for-electronic-data-searches/

Falcone A (2021) Indipendenza del Pubblico Ministero e cooperazione internazionale in materia penale nello scenario giudico europeo. Eurojus 3:59–80 http://rivista.eurojus.it/wp-content/uploads/pdf/Qui12.pdf

Filiol E (2005) Computer viruses: from theory to application. Springer, Paris

Flor R, Oh Jang J (2012) Introduction. In: Manacorda S, Flor R, Oh Jang J (eds) Cyber-criminality: finding a balance between freedom and security. Ispac, Milan, pp 13–20

Flor R (2009) Brevi riflessioni a margine della sentenza del *Bundesverfassungsgericht* sulla cd. *Online Durchsuchung*. Aspetti di diritto penale sostanziale. Rivista Trimestrale di diritto penale dell'economia 3:695–716

Foti D (2021) La nuova disciplina del captatore informatico. Un disfunzionale equilibrio? Processo Penale e Giustizia 1:202–214

Fura E, Klamberg M (2012) The chilling effect of counter-terrorism measures: a comparative analysis of electronic surveillance laws in Europe and the USA. In: Casadevall J, Myjer E, O'Boyle M (eds) Freedom of expression. Essays in honour of Nicolas Bratza, President of the European Court of Human Rights. Wolf Legal Publishers, Oisterwijk, pp 463–481

Giunchedi F (2013) Le *malpractices* nella *digital forensics*. Quali conseguenze sull'inutilizzabilità del dato informatico? Archivio Penale 3:821–836

Goldsmith JL (2001) The Internet and the legitimacy of remote cross-border searches. Univ Chic Leg Forum: 103–118

Hall KL (2002) The Oxford companion to American law. Oxford University Press, New York

Herpig S, Schuetze J (2017) Intensification of targeted surveillance of suspect via so called "State Trojan" Software. Stiftung Neue Verantwortung. https://www.stiftung-nv.de/de/publikation/transatlantic-cyber-forum-policy-debates#collapse-newsletter_banner_bottom

Herpig S, Schuetze J (2021) The encryption debate in Germany: 2021 update. Carnegie Endowment for International Peace, pp 1–8. https://carnegieendowment.org/2021/03/31/encryption-debate-in-germany-2021-update-pub-84216

Hornung G (2008) Ein neues Grundrecht. Der verfassungsrechtliche Schutz der "Vertraulichkeit und Integrität informationstechnischer Systeme". Computer und Rechte 5:299–306

Iovene F (2014) Le cd. perquisizioni online tra nuovi diritti fondamentali ed esigenze di accertamento penale. Diritto Penale Contemporaneo 3-4:329–342

Kerr OS (2005a) Digital evidence and the new criminal procedure. Columbia Law Rev 105(1): 279–318

Kerr OS (2005b) Search and seizures in a digital world. Harv Law Rev 11:531–585

Kerr OS (2005c) Search warrants in an era of digital evidence. Mississippi Law J 75:85–138

Kerr OS (2010) Fourth amendment seizures of computer data. Yale Law J 199:700–724

Koops B-J, Goodwin M (2014) Cyberspace, the cloud and cross-border criminal investigation. The limits and possibilities of international law. TILT – Tilburg Institute for Law, Technology, and Society. Tilburg

Kurek J (2009) How to achieve a balance between effective preventing crime and protecting privacy of citizens online search - as a new challenge for Ejustice. Masaryk Univ J Law Technol 3(3): 377–386

Leacock C (2008) Search and seizure of digital evidence in criminal proceedings. Digit Evid Electr Signature Law Rev 5:221–225

Lupária L (ed) (2009) Sistema penale e criminalità informatica. Profili sostanziali e processuali della Legge attuativa della Convenzione di Budapest sul cybercrime (L. 18 marzo 2008, n. 48). Giuffrè, Milan

Marchena Gómez M, González-Cuéllar N (2015) La reforma de la Ley de Enjuiciamiento Criminal en 2015. Madrid

Marcolini S (2010) Le cosiddette perquisizioni *on line* (o perquisizioni elettroniche). Cassazione Penale 7-8:2855–2868

Mattiucci M (2013) Le indagini sui reperti invisibili. High tech crime. In: Curtotti D, Saravo L (eds) Manuale delle investigazioni sulla scena del crimine. Norme, tecniche, scienze. Giappichelli, Turin, pp 707–718

Nicolicchia F (2020) I controlli occulti e continuativi come categoria probatoria. Una sistematizzazione dei nuovi mezzi di ricerca della prova tra fonti europee e ordinamenti nazionali. Cedam, Milan

Ohm P (2005) The fourth amendment right to delete. Harv Law Rev 119:10–18

Ohm P (2008) The Olmsteadian seizure clause: the fourth amendment and the seizure of intangible property. Stanf Technol Law Rev 2:2–59

Orlando C (2021) Crimine organizzato e pandemia: l'intervento programmatico della Risoluzione Falcone. http://www.lalegislazionepenale.eu/crimine-organizzato-e-pandemia-l-intervento-programmatico-della-risoluzione-falcone-claudio-orlando/

Osula A (2017) Remote search and seizure of extraterritorial data. University of Tartu Press, Tartu, pp 1–87. https://dspace.ut.ee/bitstream/handle/10062/55683/osula_anna_maria.pdf? sequence=1&isAllowed=y

Papakonstantinou V (2022) Cybersecurity as *pr5axis* and as a *state*: the EU law path towards acknowledgement of a new right to cybersecurity? Comput Law Secur Rev 44:1–15

Parlato L (2021) Le perquisizioni *on-line*: un tema che resta un tabù. In: Giostra G, Orlandi R (eds) Revisioni normative in tema di intercettazioni, Riservatezza, garanzie difensive e nuove tecnologie informatiche. Giappichelli, Turin, pp 337–388

Peterson T (2021) 7 Quick ways you can improve your IT security. https://www.wearedevelopers.com/magazine/7-quick-ways-you-can-improve-your-it-security

Pittiruti M (2017) Digital evidence e procedimento penale. Giappichelli, Turin

Quinlan S, Wilson A (2016) A brief history of law enforcement hacking in the United States. https://na-production.s3.amazonaws.com/documents/History_Hacking.pdf

Redins L (2021) Cybersecurity: who is responsible? Cybersecurity guide. https://cybersecurityguide.org/resources/cybersecurity-responsibility/

Rodotà S (2014) Il mondo nella rete. Quali vincoli, quali diritti? Laterza Editors, Rome

Rovelli S (2021) Case *Prokuratuur*: proportionality and the independence of authorities in data retention, pp 199–210. https://www.europeanpapers.eu/en/europeanforum/case-prokuratuur-proportionality-and-independence

Ruggeri S (2020) *Nulla coactio sine lege* in transnational evidence law. In: Darázs L, Herger EC, Jakab È, Karsai K, Komlósi LI (eds) Neue Grenzen. Humboldt Kolleg, Pécs, pp 312–329

Sabillon R, Serra-Ruiz J, Cavaller V, Cano JJ (2017) Digital forensic analysis of cybercrimes: best practices and methodologies. Int J Inf Secur Privacy 11(2):25–37

Škrtić D, Kralj D, Švegar M (2013) Search and seizure data in cyberspace – mechanisms to preserve and reproduce data in a non-volatile format. In: Meško G, Sotlar A, Green JR (eds) Proceedings of the biennial international conference "Criminal justice and Security – Contemporary Criminal

Justice Practice and Research". Faculty of Criminal Justice and Security, Ljubljana, pp 509–521.

Sieber U, von zur Mühlen N (eds) (2016) Access to telecommunication data in criminal justice. Duncker & Humblot, Berlin

Taticchi M (2010) Note. Redefining possessory interests: perfect copies of information as fourth amendment seizures. George Wash Law Rev 78:476–511

Vaciago G, Silva Ramalho D (2016) Online searches and online surveillance: the use of trojans and other types of malware as means of obtaining evidence in criminal proceedings. Digit Evid Electr Signature Rev 13:88–96

Vijayan J (2013) Judge rejects FBI's bid to hack computer of suspect in attempted cyberheist. https://www.computerworld.com/article/2496543/judge-rejects-fbi-s-bid-to-hack-computer-of-suspect-in-attempted-cyberheist.html

Vitale A (2008) La nuova disciplina delle ispezioni e delle perquisizioni in ambiente informatico o telematico. Diritto dell'Internet 5:506–511

Digital Privacy and Cyber-Interception of Communications

A New Scenario Needs New Concept

Diego Foti

Abstract Criminal proceedings need continuous updating due to the historical and sociological context in which they operate. The technological innovations impacting in all fields has led legal practitioners to question also its impact on the criminal justice.

In recent decades, technological devices have become not only means for committing offences, but also an efficient tool for the crime investigation, allowing to obtain investigative results faster and with less effort.

The use of a malware to carry out interception of communications provide access to information of great value for the prosecution, but they also increase the risk of breaching the fundamental rights of the persons subjected to such measures, in particular, the right to secrecy of communications which represents a serious encroachment in the right to privacy.

Rethinking the traditional rules becomes necessary, also from the point of view of protected legal values, in order to control the adequacy of the current legal framework, both in Italy as well as in the other European countries.

1 Introduction

Historically, continuous needs for reform have influenced the evolution of criminal justice systems. In modern times especially, international arrangements have played an essential role to this end, contributing to the transformation of legal cultures and justice systems, favouring the enactment into domestic law of new standards aimed at balancing conflicting values, in the sensitive fields of crime prevention and criminal prosecution.

The main factor that has brought about reforms in these areas has always been the emergence of new sensitivities aimed either at strengthening the pursuance of

D. Foti (✉)
Messina University, Messina, Italy
e-mail: dfoti@unime.it

© The Author(s), under exclusive license to Springer Nature Switzerland AG 2022
L. Bachmaier Winter, S. Ruggeri (eds.), *Investigating and Preventing Crime in the Digital Era*, Legal Studies in International, European and Comparative Criminal Law 7, https://doi.org/10.1007/978-3-031-13952-9_7

state-related interests or at protecting individual rights. The challenges that national law makers must face today highlight a real revolution,[1] which is mainly due to the unbelievably rapid changes occurred in preventive and criminal investigation because of technological innovation of criminal inquiries,[2] and the enormous potential of investigative tools to collect evidentiary data and their strong mimetic capacity.[3]

Criminal procedure must, inevitably handle the consequences of digital progress, thus adapting its dynamics to the incredibly rapid evolution of contemporary crime, and resorting to sophisticated IT tools.

However, legislative intervention aimed at regulating the effects of the technological revolution have been up to now very slow in the field of criminal justice, not always being able to keep pace with phenomena that are already at the centre of acting and common feeling.[4]

These preliminary considerations gain specific relevance in relation to investigative activities involving the use of Trojan horse, spyware, and further malware.[5] Certainly these tools have an enormous investigative potential, enabling the obtaining of information, communications, fundamental traits of the private life of a person, through the use of the simple connection of a computer system to any Wi-Fi network.[6] Therefore, such computer agents allow carrying out controls directly affecting the virtual spheres within which each person develops his or her personality.

These unprecedented investigative activities have radically new characteristics which not only rule out any comparison with already existing tools,[7] but also call for distinctions among the new tools, because of the difficulties to handle realities that are still largely unknown and due to their covert nature. Furthermore, the intrusiveness of new investigation tools is due to the capability of modern digital systems to determine a real 'overexposure' of the freedom of the person, which require enhanced protection.[8] In this context, this paper focuses on cyber interception of communication by analyzing the impact of digital covert investigations from the

---

[1] Floridi (2017).

[2] See Czerniawski and Boyack (2021).

[3] Conti (2018), p. 1210.

[4] Quattrocolo (2020).

[5] Cf. Balsamo (2016), p. 2275; Barroccu (2017), p. 379; Bene (2018), p. 23; Brighi (2018), p. 212; Bronzo (2018), p. 235; Camon (2017), p. 91; Lorenzetto (2016), p. 359; Signorato (2018), p. 263; Tonini (2017), p. 373; Torre (2017).

[6] The computer receiver is a software made by two principal modules: the first is a program able to infect a target device, the second is a system able to control from remote the device. A malware like that, can be used to execute any operation and to record any activity performed on a keyboard, to obtain any file on the telephone's memory (such as like photo, videos, date base), to turn on the microphone and the camera to realize an environmental interception and, finally, to receive GPS data. (On the latter issue see Czerniak (2021)).

[7] Caprioli (2017), p. 483; Parlato (2020), p. 291; Camon (2017), p. 91; Giordano (2017), p. 176.

[8] Parlato (2020), p. 292.

viewpoint of fundamental rights, the evolution of domestic legislation, and the perspectives of reform that the development of such phenomena open for future reforms in terms of strengthening individual safeguards. As a matter of fact, indeed, it is apparent that access to the web by anyone cannot imply a simple loss of rights, transforming the user of the network into a "conscious victim" operating in a less safeguarded environment.[9]

Certainly, there are today no "tyrant-rights",[10] that is, rights with such absolute relevance that they cannot be balanced with conflicting interests. Thus, lawmakers are called upon to enact rules that carefully balance even fundamental freedoms, such as the right to free and secret communication, with other state-related needs, in accordance with the principles of reasonableness and proportionality.[11]

This task is of extraordinary complexity in the contemporary world, where the conflict between prosecutorial needs and individual safeguards shows a more hidden and insidious form than in the traditional investigation tools.[12] The spread of new communication channels has in fact changed usual habits and behaviours creating "new scenarios", in which the dynamics of human relations take place. However, "virtual people" are not different from the real individuals, as they are "real individuals" expressing, in an unprecedented way, their "way of being".[13]

In such context, there is a need to verify whether in the light of the distinctive peculiarities of digital tools, the safeguards regarding traditional procedural instruments interfering with the right to free communication and the protection of domicile can be simply extended to them. Indeed, the direct impact of IT tools on the most intime dimension of people requires investigative action to be proportionate and necessary, and a systematic consideration of individual freedoms as a whole. The question is how to ensure the adequate balance in this field.

2 Digital Privacy in Criminal Proceedings

Criminal procedure has always been a crucial testing ground for assessing the extent to which the right to privacy is effectively protected.[14] Criminal proceedings, indeed, are a formidable container of sensitive information that can play a key role to ascertain the criminal responsibility of the individuals charged. Whereas the use of IT tools appears to be indispensable today,[15] attention must be paid to the rights

---

[9]Rodotà (2014), p. 102.

[10]Italian Constitutional Court, judgment of 9 April 2013, n. 85.

[11]Leo (2021), p. 1.

[12]Parlato (2020), p. 292.

[13]Ruggieri (2004), p. 162.

[14]Schünemann and Baumann (2017) and Barfield and Pagallo (2020).

[15]Carnevale (2007), p. 6.

affected by new digital instruments, in order to both avoid undue infringements and achieve better trade-offs of all the conflicting interests.[16]

This is a very complex task, at least on two main levels: first, at the legal level, taking into account the existence of heterogeneous sources in domestic and international jurisdictions; second, in a naturalistic dimension, due to the changing social context, the consequent technological evolution and the growing intrusiveness of the tools used.[17] One of the main transformations brought about by the era of digital investigation has been the overcoming of the notion of privacy in its nuclear negative connotation, as the right to be left alone.[18] This entails the abandonment of any reference to physical reality, as well as the need to focus on the positive side of privacy in terms of self-determination, information, right to control information about oneself, like the right to control the data packets travelling on the web.

Although the above concepts continue to highlight fundamental aspects of the problem, there is a clear need to reshape the notion of confidentiality, where classic boundaries, linked to physical space and the type of information that anybody wishes to withhold from others, fade and dissolve. This determines the urgency of adequate forms of protection for a new "external identity" in which others play a fundamental role in processing and controlling the information contained in different databases.[19]

Computer data, indeed, refer to an incredibly high quantity of information of a very different nature that are able to circulate very rapidly, not only because of the lack of materiality but also due to their duplicability.[20] Furthermore, the distinction between intimate and social data, or between secret and confidential information, can no longer play a crucial role. The promiscuity of such data and the high degree of intrusiveness of the new investigative measures adopted by public authorities entail a serious risk of violation of the digital sphere of the person concerned, which goes far beyond the infringement of the sole right to data protection.

It then becomes necessary to identify rules aimed at governing the interference by law enforcement bodies with private sphere, which calls for proper protection of the IT space managed by individuals, regardless of the nature of the stored data, and with a view to reaching the essential core of the human being who undergoes a digital investigation.

German Federal Constitutional Court has followed a similar approach by dealing with the characteristics of the so-called *Online-Durchsuchung*, thus giving rise to a modern view of the fundamental interests involved.[21] For the first time, a new

---

[16] Quattrocolo (2020) and Brkan (2018).

[17] Torre (2020).

[18] Warren and Braneis (1980).

[19] Rodotà (2012), p. 319.

[20] Iovene (2011), p. 334.

[21] *Bunderveffassungsgericht*, (BVerfG), judgment of 27 February 2008, 1 BvR 370/07, 1 BvR 595/07, in *Official Case Reports BVerfGE* 120, 274, in *Neue Juristische Wochenschrift (NJW)*, 2008, *Bundesverfassungsgericht* (BVerfG), judgment of 20 April 2016, 1 BvR 966/09, 1 BvR 1140/09, in www.bundesverfassungsgericht.de. See Abel and Schafer (2009)

interest was acknowledged in Europe at the constitutional law level, namely the 'guarantee of the integrity and confidentiality of computer systems', as an expression of the essential right to dignity of the individual/user.[22] According to the German judges, this new notion

> protects the personal and private life of right holders from state access to information technology devices, in particular from access by the State to information technology systems as a whole, not only therefore for individual communication events or data storage.[23]

Thus, the use of new investigative channels offered by technology implies a necessary balance between the legitimate expectation of confidentiality and any opposing interests that can only be accomplished at the legislative level.[24]

Based on this reasoning, the German Constitutional Court identified a series of safeguards that can be plastically represented through the logic of concentric circles.[25] First, a broader sphere is represented by the informational right to self-determination, in the abovesaid terms. Second, in an intermediate position is there the fundamental right to the integrity and confidentiality of the ICT systems in respect of intrusive activities aimed at obtaining personal data contained in the violated computer systems. Third, the maximum level of protection is attributed to the so-called "essential nucleus of private life", in relation to which the German Constitutional Court allowed for investigative interference only to protect legal interests of the utmost importance, such as life, physical integrity and individual freedom.

Altogether these areas contribute to creating a sort of virtual extension of the individual safeguards, which are necessary by the widespread tendency to express one's personality through the computer system.[26]

This approach—although being able to enhance the relationship between the virtual space connected to a computer system, its private use and the user's personality—is based on a somewhat outdated concept. Certainly, interference in the digital private sphere often entails the risk of infringement of different interests, such as the right to protection of personal data and the so-called 'digital domicile'.[27] However, this outcome covers only a part of the complex repercussions of the deployment of IT systems, which endanger another fundamental right of new generation, that is, digital privacy. According to a widely accepted definition, digital privacy is an

> interest in the enjoyment and exclusive control of both certain data and information, and of the related IT and telematic means and processing procedures; that while always taking the form of the right to exclude unauthorized third parties from the corresponding access and use, it is wholly or partially regardless of the traditional limits and assumptions of the civil

---

[22] Di Nuzzo, below.

[23] Flor (2009), p. 679.

[24] Torre (2015), p. 168.

[25] On the concentric circles see Hubmann (1957).

[26] Parlato (2020), p. 303.

[27] This notion has long been recognized in countries like Italy, as a virtual projection of physical domicile. Cf. among others Pica (1999), p. 62.

concepts of ownership and possession, or of the conditions that underpin the legal significance of secrecy or personal confidentiality in general.[28]

In light of this, serious concerns can be raised against the doctrine of 'concentric
circles'. As has been noted, this is above all due to the manifest impossibility of
distinguishing between sensitive and social data, which in turn makes it difficult to
differentiate secrecy and confidentiality.[29] From this it follows that we have to face
phenomena concerned with the existence of new virtual spaces in which personality
is more and more developed, and the substantial interest arises to achieve full
protection of confidential information and its control in carrying out legal and
personal relationships online[30] or in other IT spaces.

Based on these considerations, digital privacy finds its protection in Article 7 EUCFR, dealing with family life, home and communication. As is well-
known, this complex right, regardless of some interesting language differences
that are due to scientific and technological progress, is largely inspired by Article 8 ECHR, and therefore must be interpreted in the light of this provision pursuant
to the Explanations to the EUCFR.

3 The Challenges of Communication Intercepts Through Spyware

It has been observed that the omnivorous capacity of computer agents causes
problems that only 20 years ago could hardly be imagined, and at present these
devices set new challenges precisely because of the level of the intrusiveness.

The evolution of technology, moreover, renders the sea of the network increasingly "fishy", enabling the collection of all kinds of conversations, as well as
communication and information flows. All this confirms the difficulties of using
obsolete categories, which no longer seem to satisfy the needs that criminal investigation must fulfill today before the digital revolution, especially in terms of a better
human rights protection.

Consequently, old classifications, which, if followed uncritically, would lead to
the unacceptable weakening of the fundamental rights protection. Trojan horses,
spywares, and further malwares owe their current success to their ability to intercept
communications made through computer or telematic technologies, such as Chat or
Voip (Voice Over Internet Protocol) connections, and created through widespread
applications,[31] which cannot be intercepted using traditional investigative tools.

---

[28] Picotti (2000), p. 20.

[29] Flor (2007), p. 899; Henkel (1957, 1958).

[30] Iovene (2011), p. 335; Flor (2009), p. 705.

[31] For example, WhatsApp, Instagram, Telegram, Facebook Messenger etc. With reference to the
problems relating to investigations in social networks or through social networks see O'Floinn and

While telephone conversations in the analogic era could only be intercepted with the support of telephone companies, these new channels of communication no longer need *ad hoc* infrastructures, as they use the Internet network without hardly any control by a service provider.[32]

Without such advanced tools, the investigative authorities could only ascertain whether the device under control was actually used by the suspect, without any possibility of accessing the data exchanged. Yet new technologies allow capturing the sought data either before their encryption, or just after decryption, directly within the device. This activity is therefore correctly defined as 'active interception', which consists of capturing data inside the device rather than intercepting the telephone line.

In legal terms, the aforementioned peculiarities do not hinder the possibility of classifying the intrusion achieved by means of malwares into the category of interception, provided however that such digital interception only deals with communication flows, rather than with data stored in the targeted device, or communicative information, which can be obtained through different investigative tools such as search and seizure of digital evidence.[33]

Thus, cyber interception raises a number of relevant questions.

A first delicate issue is the possibility of interpreting the dialogue with one's own computer system in terms of 'communication'. A relevant example concerns the activities carried out through search engines, by virtue of which information flows are exchanged between peripherals of the same system[34] that provide responses to specific queries with a huge amount of information.

A second issue refers to the difference between interception and seizure in the case of forwarding e-mails. Here, various criteria have been proposed. Sometimes, a chronological criterion has been deemed crucial to differentiate those measures: interception would aim to capture emails in real time, while emails that have been already stored in the addressee's box could only be seized.[35] This approach, however, does not help to solve some problematic instances, *e.g.* when the email is temporarily stored by the Internet Service Provider, without having yet reached the destination box. In this case, the lack of an ongoing communication makes difficult to classify it as an interception in a strict sense.

Similar problems arise when a communication has not been completed during interception, so that the collection of the sought information is solely possible through a seizure.[36] The Italian Court of Cassation has advocated this approach

---

Ormerod (2011). Roggan (2017) points out that the higher intrusiveness of the computer detector lies in its ability to control more information. See also Singelnstein (2012).

[32] Torre (2017), pp. 22–23.

[33] See extensively Di Nuzzo.

[34] Balsamo (2016), p. 2275.

[35] Luparia (2011), p. 387.

[36] Orlandi (2009), p. 135.

with a new judgment[37] overturning the well-established case law according to which interception is a measure that necessarily aims at capturing communications *in itinere*, that is, communications which run simultaneously with the intercepting activity. Consequently, emails just sent or received constitute an 'IT flow', which as such can be captured pursuant to the rules of the Italian CPC regarding interceptions of computer or telematic communications.[38] Thus, according to the Supreme Court, the peculiarity of an IT flow should be identified in the forwarding of communication by the sender. Furthermore, there could be an even more extreme case, i.e. where different people, sharing the access credentials of a common email account, write various messages then saved as drafts instead of being sent. Here, even though there is formally no communication in a strict sense, such messages flow to another device of the system, where the contents are read by other individuals who in turn replies with new messages not. The main merit of the new Italian case-law has been to promote a different approach to the classic category of 'communication intercepts' based on technological innovation.

A further relevant question is how to identify and delimit the range of the persons involved in the targeted communication. Here also, technology raises unprecedented question. Can we consider as 'communication' a talk that takes place, even remotely and by telephone, with the home automation systems used every day to manage home activities and habits? There are good reasons for overturning the traditional approach that requires a human intersubjectivity, i.e. communications only between individuals.[39] Doubtless, the existence of virtual spaces characterized by a relevant need for confidentiality requires adapting the notion of 'communication' in this respect too. Indeed, virtual spaces, even if belonging or available to the same person, remain separate computer domiciles.[40]

As already pointed out, a traditional interception cannot capture such communications, also because of the use of various shielding systems aimed at countering hacking attacks.[41] This is why investigative authorities today resort to a new generation of active interceptions, availing themselves of computer viruses to obtain and decrypt contents protected by cryptography systems.[42] Moreover, malwares, instead of capturing data immediately, enable the creation of copies saved in the

---

[37] Italian Court of Cassation, 4th Section, judgement of 28 June 2016, n. 40903, commented by Giordano (2017)

[38] Art. 266-*bis* of the Italian CPC.

[39] Moreover, communication (from Latin *cum* + *munire*) means the process and methods of transmitting information from one person to another or from one place to another, through the exchange of a message processed according to the rules of a given code.

[40] See Vele (2011). In this author's opinion, technology changed the way of communicating, but not the concept of communication, which remained the same one. The outcome is that the communication being intercepted still had to involve different persons, as "the expression of the idea and the news must be formulated by a sender in order to reach the cognitive sphere of more or more recipients".

[41] A concrete example is represented by the cryptography end-to-end, used by the social network.

[42] Aterno (2013), p. 958.

device memory and later transmitted at regular intervals to the investigative authority, or once the device is connected to a Wi-Fi network.[43] Therefore, it is nowadays
almost impossible to distinguish between searching activities and surveillance operations within the scope of communication intercepts. This assumption in turn calls
for a re-definition of the very notion of 'contextuality' of communication and
interception. Since the sought data are first copied and later examined, cyber
interception materializes in a time frame that overcomes the period in which
violation has occurred.

In light of the above, the recordings of movements on the web (*i.e.,* the periodic
collection of data from the information system used by the target device) is in turn
totally different from a search. While the latter is instrumentally oriented to find the
body of evidence or items pertaining to the alleged offence, which can be seized, the
operations mentioned above tend to the acquisition of any useful element for
investigative purposes in an indefinite period of time and in full secrecy. In such
instances, suspects have no chance to have the measure supervised by a judicial
authority, nor can they appoint a defense counsel in order to be assisted during the
operations.[44] To be sure, the solution of classifying this case into the category of
interception would enhance individual rights protection, mostly because of the strict
legal requirements and the judicial competence provided for in relation to
intercepting activities.

These few examples highlight the enormous potentialities of ICT technologies
which may seem to know no effective borders and boundaries. At the same time,
these technological tools must be analyzed for their potentially harmful effect on a
fundamental interest like digital privacy.

4   A Look into European Jurisdictions

4.1   The German Approach

Germany stands out among other countries in Europe for specifically addressing the
possibility of framing the 'dialogue' with one's own computer system as a communication. In 2016, the Federal Constitutional Court had already dealt with the
problems concerning the so-called "source telecommunication surveillance"
(*Quellen-Telekommunikationsüberwachung*).[45]

---

[43]Parlato (2020), p. 293; Bartoli (2018), p. 8. Outside the European Union, see the American
experience, characterized by intense debate which is still open. Some courts and scholars have
suggested that data's duplication should be treated as seizure, with all the safeguards that the Fourth
Amendment provides for it. See Ohm (2005), paras. 62–63; Kerr (2010), pp. 712 ff.

[44]Torre (2017), p. 60.

[45]*Bundesverfassungsgericht* (BVerfG), judgment of 20 April 2016, 1 BvR 966/09, 1 BvR 1140/09,
in www.bundesverfassungsgericht.de.

Following this landmark decision, Germany enacted a legislative reform[46] which has recently come into force, concerning—in light of the constitutional case-law— the protection in the field of computer searches compared to traditional interception of communications. This classification therefore implies, for those using the search engine, site visits and image views, a protection that is grounded on the right of communication, pursuant to Article 1(1) GG, which protects the person and their dignity from undue interference.

The German model, implying a lower level of protection than surveillance activities, is also important in countries not yet equipped with rules on these investigative tools. Their qualification as interception of communications would allow effective protection of the interests concretely at stake. In some legal systems, impulses coming from technology are often addressed by the case-law, while in other cases analogy is used, applying provisions covering different measures, as well as the category of atypical evidence. Hence the need to evolve the concept of communication to include in the IT and telematic context any flow that moves from one system to another even if belonging to the same individual, as in the further example of emails sent to oneself or to e-mail addresses that can always be traced back to the same sender.

4.2 The Italian Experience

The critical issues mentioned above should not be more deeply analyzed in relation to the recent reform of Italian legislation on the use of malwares for investigative activities.[47]

Italian lawmakers, indeed, have shown a full awareness of the investigative potential of such IT tools and, at the same time, the relevant impact that they have on the constitutional rights involved in practically feasible activities. The problem regarding the deployment of computer agents, however, was addressed in an incomplete and limited way, as the new regulation dealt with the use of malwares installed in mobile devices exclusively with regard to the interception of communications.[48]

In this way, a new generation of cyber interceptions can be activated on a legal basis, which made it possible to capturing communications in very different physical places. This gives rise to potentially ubiquitous interceptions. In order to avoid these risks, lawmakers delimited the scope of application of the new digital interceptions,

---

[46] Parlato (2020), p. 304; Blechschnitt (2017); Leopold and Beukelmann (2017); Roggan (2017); Singelnstein and Derin (2017).

[47] Legislative Decree of 29 December of 2017, No. 216 and Law Decree of 30 December 2019, No. 161, converted into Law of 28 February 2020, No. 7. Nocerino (2020), Pretti (2020) and Foti (2021)

[48] Parlato (2020), p. 291.

while establishing a complex legal set-up with different approaches tailored to different criminal offences, in line with the principle of proportionality.[49]

In cases of organized crime offences and the most serious crimes committed by public officials against the public administration, computer agents can generally be used regardless of the physical location in which the target system is located. Furthermore, public prosecutors can order interception through an urgent procedure, indicating however the reasons that do not allow a previous authorization by the judicial authority, which must anyway subsequently validate the prosecutorial order.

A different regulation was instead enacted in relation to common crimes. Here, the admissibility of digital interception through spyware is subjected to particular precautions, which have been established to overcome the problems arisen in case-law because of the impossibility of distinguishing interception of conversations in a private domicile and in a public place.[50]

In these cases, in addition to the standard requirements for interception, the reform specifically required the judicial authority to justify the use of the spyware, in the light of the impossibility or at least the particular difficulty of resorting to other means.[51] Furthermore, the authorization must, albeit indirectly, indicate the place and time in relation to which eventually a microphone or a video camera can be switched on, if the spyware aims at capturing conversations between people who are present in a real place. Moreover, any microphone or video camera must be turned off when the intercepted individuals enter their private domicile, as here cyber interception is only allowed where the competent authorities can demonstrate that a criminal activity is ongoing.

It is therefore essential that any microphone or video camera is activated by virtue of a special command sent remotely, not just as a result of the installation of the malware, as it is necessary to avoid continuous listening.[52]

The above-mentioned provisions reveal how Italian lawmakers are aware of the highly intrusive potential of the most modern IT tools. Notwithstanding this, it has been noted that Italian lawmakers have failed to regulate the use of malwares in relation to further investigative activities,[53] thus leaving room for case-law

---

[49] Nicolicchia (2018), Huscroft et al. (2014) and McBride (1999).

[50] Italian Court of Cassation, judgment of 28 April 2016, Scurato, n. 26889. The Court affirms the impossibility of limiting the operation of the sensor in space and time and this implies an *ex post* protection of rights protected by articles 2, 14, 15 of the Italian Constitution. In fact, the protection is realized through the selection of the collected material and the elimination of the injurious recording. The decision is noted by Giordano (2017); Camon (2017), p. 9; Picotti (2016), p. 354.

[51] We can consider, for example, an interception of a conversation between two moving subjects in a public street or in a public place unknown to law enforcement authorities, where the placement of traditional bugs is difficult because of the presence of surveillance cameras.

[52] See Art. 266(2) of the Italian CPC. This provision raises delicate problems in the light of the principle of proportionality, because pursuant to the current legislation computer agents are allowed in all criminal proceedings for which interception is permitted, regardless of the type of crime, provided that the judicial authorization is ensured. Cf. Zampaglione (2019).

[53] Barroccu (2017), p. 386; Orlandi (2016).

interpretations which in recent years have been characterized by uneven and highly disputable outcomes. As has been observed, this has led to investigative practices based upon the general clause regarding the so-called 'atypical evidence', which has often been accompanied by a questionable weakening of fundamental rights under the standards established by the Constitution.[54] From the perspective of professional practice, the problem is further aggravated by the fact that there are still today no remedies to avoid undue interference by way of challenging the judicial authorization of communication intercepts through spyware once the addressees find out that intrusion into their private sphere has been carried out against them.

5 Conclusions

This chapter has highlighted the challenges cyber interception of communication through spyware sets, increased by the continuous and rapid evolution of the technological progress. Indeed, neither national lawmakers nor supranational or international law have up to now addressed them properly. This outcome has led to enormous legal gaps regarding the limits of investigative intervention by law enforcement bodies.[55]

Apart from Germany, Spain also has through Organic Law 13/2015 adopted specific rules which have provided a legal basis for new digital means of investigation, *i.e.* not only online searches but also communication intercepts by means of computer agents.[56] In this sense, only consistent approaches can achieve acceptable standards of guarantees with respect to the IT phenomenon that has been taken into account.

This legal lacuna increases the need for protecting fundamental rights and ensuring procedural safeguards. The analysis conducted in this chapter shows that such activities should be allowed insofar as the requirement of lawfulness and a judicial oversight (*i.e.*, the judicial authority or an independent administrative authority of the State in which such investigative activity must be carried out) are upheld.

This outcome is confirmed by a recent decision of the European Court of Justice (hereafter, CJEU). In *HK v. Estonia*, the CJEU held that

> it is essential that access of the competent national authorities to retained data be subject to a prior review carried out either by a court or by an independent administrative body, and that the decision of that court or body be made following a reasoned request by those authorities submitted, inter alia, within the framework of procedures for the prevention, detection or

---

[54] Maggio (2019), p. 111.

[55] Allegrezza (2013), p. 151.

[56] *Ley Organica* 13/2015, of 5 October 2015, amending the CPC (*Ley de Enjuiciamiento Criminal*) on the strengthening of procedural safeguards and regulating technological investigative measures. See, Bachmaier Winter (2021), pp. 170 ff. On this legal reform, see widely Gómez and Serrano (2015).

prosecution of crime. In cases of duly justified urgency, the review must take place within a short time.[57]

Although this decision expressly refers to the access of the competent authorities to retained traffic and location data, it is then apparent that such conclusions could also be applied in the field of cyber interception of communications, because this type of activity is even more able to interfere with people's privacy. Indeed, the need for a judicial oversight becomes all the more imperative[58] because of the amount and nature of the data and information obtained through cyber interception, which can generate a precise and comprehensive overview of the targeted individual's private life.[59]

Consequently, the use of computer sensors should only be justified on condition that a judicial authorization can be issued in compliance with the proportionality principle, regardless of the type of information collected or the collection itself.

To ensure an effective control, the judicial authority should however be put in a position to access all the necessary information gathered during the investigation, which is an essential condition for a proper assessment of the lawfulness of the interception. The aforementioned ruling of the CJEU may seem to follow this approach. The existing legal lacunas in domestic jurisdictions should thus be filled along the lines provided by Luxembourg judges. Otherwise, somewhat contradictory results would be produced; in particular, the individuals subjected to investigative measures aimed at accessing traffic and location data would have stronger protection than that granted in cases of interception of communication through spyware.

References

Abel W, Schafer B (2009) The German Constitutional Court on the right in confidentiality and integrity of information technology systems – a case report on BVerfG. Neue Juristische Wochenschrift: 106–123

Allegrezza S (2013) Le misure coercitive nelle "Model Rules for the Procedure of the European Public Prosecutor's Office". In: Ruggieri F, Rafaraci T, Di Paolo G, Marcolini S, Belfiore R (eds) Processo penale, lingua e Unione Europea. Cedam, Padova, pp 151–173

Aterno S (2013) Le investigazioni informatiche e l'acquisizione della prova digitale. Giurisprudenza di merito: 955–967

Bachmaier Winter L (2021) The handling of digital evidence in Spain. In: Caianiello M, Camon A (eds) Digital forensic evidence. Towards common European standards in antifraud administrative and criminal investigations. Wolters Kluwer-Cedam, Milán, pp 163–200

Balsamo A (2016) Le intercettazioni mediante virus informatico tra processo penale italiano e Corte europea. Cassazione Penale: 2275–2288

---

[57] CJEU, GC, judgment of 2 March 2021, *Prokuratuur*, C-746/18, para. 51.

[58] *Id.*, para. 39.

[59] *Id.*, para. 36: "such as the habits of everyday life, permanent or temporary places of residence, daily or other movements, the activities carried out, the social relationships of those persons and the social environments frequented by them".

Barfield W, Pagallo U (2020) Advanced introduction to law and artificial intelligence, Chapter V, Issues of data protection. Elgar, Cheltenham

Barroccu G (2017) Il captatore informatico: un virus per tutte le stagioni. Diritto Penale e Processo 3:379–390

Bartoli L (2018) Sequestro di dati a fini probatori: soluzioni provvisorie a incomprensioni durature. www.archiviopenale.it

Bene T (2018) La riforma parziale e il gorilla invisibile. In: Bene T (ed) L'intercettazione di comunicazioni. Cacucci, Bari, pp 15–24

Blechschnitt L (2017) Zur Einführung von Quellen-TKÜ und Online Durchsuchung. Strafverteidiger Forum: 361–365

Brighi R (2018) Funzionamento e potenzialità investigative del malware. In: Giostra G, Orlandi R (eds) Nuove norme in tema di intercettazioni. Giappichelli, Torino, pp 212–235

Brkan M (2018) The concept of essence of fundamental rights in the EU legal order: peeling the onion to its core. Eur Constitutional Law Rev 14:332–368

Bronzo P (2018) Intercettazione ambientale tramite captatore informatico: Limiti di ammissibilità, uso in altri processi e divieti probatori. In: Giostra G, Orlandi R (eds) Nuove norma in tema di intercettazioni. Giappichelli, Torino, pp 235–262

Camon A (2017) Cavalli di Troia in Cassazione. Archivio della nuova procedura penale: 91–100

Caprioli F (2017) Il "captatore informatico" come strumento di ricerca della prova in Italia. Revista Brasileira de Dereito Processual Penal 3(2):483–510

Carnevale S (2007) Autodeterminazione informativa e processo penale: le coordinate costituzionali. In: Negri D (ed) Protezione dei dati personali e accertamento penale. Verso la creazione di un nuovo diritto fondamentale? Aracne, Roma, pp 3–26

Conti C (2018) Prova informatica e diritti fondamentali: a proposito di captatore e non solo. Diritto penale e procedura 9:1210–1221

Czerniak D (2021) Collection of location data in criminal proceedings – European (the EU and Strasbourg) standards. Revista Brasileira de Direito Processual Penal 7(1):123–159

Czerniawski J, Boyack C (2021) Reviewing the privacy implications of law enforcement access to and use of digital data. Utah J Crim Law 5(1):73–92

Flor R (2007) Phishing, identity, theft, and identity abuse. Le prospettive applicative del diritto penale vigente. Rivista italiana diritto e procedura penale 50:889–946

Flor R (2009) Brevi riflessioni a margine della sentenza del Bundesverfassungsgericht sulla cd. Online Durchsuchung. Aspetti di diritto penale sostanziale. Rivista Trimestrale di diritto penale dell'economia 3:695–716

Floridi L (2017) The fourth revolution. Oxford

Foti D (2021) New rules on "trojan horse" software: a dysfunctional equilibrium? Processo Penale e Giustizia 1:202–214

Giordano L (2017) Dopo le Sezioni unite sul "captatore informatico": avanzano nuove questioni, ritorna il tema della funzione di garanzia del decreto autorizzativo. Diritto penale contemporaneo 3:176–195

Gómez M, Serrano G-C (2015) La reforma de la ley de enjuiciamiento criminal en 2015. Castillo de Luna Ediciones Jurídicas, Madrid

Henkel H (1957) Der Strafschutz des Privatlebens gegen Indiskretion, Verhandlungen des 42. Deutschen Juristentages, Düsseldorf

Henkel H (1958) Recht und Individualität. Berlin

Hubmann H (1957) Der zivilrechtliche Schutz der Persönlichkeit gegen Indiskretion. JuristenZeitung 17:521–528

Huscroft G, Miller BW, Webber G (2014) Introduction. In: Huscroft G, Miller BW, Webber G (eds) Proportionality and the rule of law. Rights, justification, reasoning. Cambridge University Press, pp 1–21

Iovene F (2011) Le C. D. perquisizioni on line tra nuovi diritti fondamentali ed esigenze di accertamento penale. Diritto Penale contemporaneo 3–4:330–338

Kerr OS (2010) Fourth amendment seizures of computer data. Yale Law J 199:700, 700–724. https://papers.ssrn.com/sol3/papers.cfm?abstract_id=1378402:

Leo G (2021) Le indagini sulle comunicazioni e sugli spostamenti delle persone: prime riflessioni riguardo alla recente giurisprudenza europea su geolocalizzazione e tabulati telefonici. www. sistema penale.it

Leopold K, Beukelmann S (2017) Online-Durchsuchung und Quellen-TKÜ. Neue Juristische Wochenschrift, p 440

Lorenzetto E (2016) Il perimetro delle intercettazioni ambientali eseguite mediante "captatore informatico". Diritto penale contemporaneo. www.archiviodpc.dirittopenaleuomo.org

Luparia L (2011) Computer crimes e procedimento penale. In: Garuti G (ed) Trattato di procedura penale, VII, Modelli differenziati di accertamento I. Spangher, Torino, pp 309–390

Maggio P (2019) La registrazione occulta curata da una persona presente al colloquio presenti. In: Scalfati A (ed) Le indagini atipiche. Giappichelli, Torino, pp 61–100

McBride J (1999) Proportionality and the European Convention on Human Rights. In: Ellis E (ed) Proportionality and the laws of Europe. Oxford, pp 23–37

Nicolicchia F (2018) Il principio di proporzionalità nell'era del controllo tecnologico e le sue implicazioni processuali rispetto ai nuovi mezzi di ricerca della prova. Diritto Penale Contemporaneo: 176–189

Nocerino W (2020) Prime riflessioni a margine del nuovo decreto legge in materia di intercettazioni. www.sistemapenale.it

O'Floinn M, Ormerod D (2011) Social networking sites, RIPA and criminal investigations. Crim Law Rev 10:766–789

Ohm P (2005) The fourth amendment right to delete. Harv Law Rev: 10–18

Orlandi R (2009) Questioni attuali in tema di processo ed informatica. Rivista di diritto processuale 1:129–137

Orlandi R (2016) Osservazioni sul documento redatto dai docenti torinesi di procedura penale sul problema dei captatori informatici. www.archiviopenale.it

Parlato L (2020) Libertà della persona nell'uso delle tecnologie digitali: verso nuovi orizzonti di tutela nell'accertamento penale. Processo penale e giustizia 2:291–307

Pica G (1999) Diritto penale delle tecnologie informatiche. Utet, Torino

Picotti L (2000) Reati informatici (voce). In: Enciclopedia giuridica Treccani, aggiornamento. VIII, Roma

Picotti L (2016) Spunti di riflessioni per il penalista dalla sentenza delle Sezioni Unite relativa alle intercettazioni mediante captatore informatico. www.archiviopenale.it

Pretti D (2020) La metamorfosi delle intercettazioni, ultimo atto? La legge n. 7/2020 di conversione del d. l. n. 161/2019. www.sistemapenale.it

Quattrocolo S (2020) Processo penale e rivoluzione digitale: da ossimoro a endiadi? www. medialaws.eu

Rodotà S (2012) Il diritto di avere diritti. Editori Laterza, Roma

Rodotà S (2014) Il mondo della rete. Quali vincoli, quali diritti. Editori Laterza, Roma

Roggan F (2017) Die strafprozessuale Quellen-TKÜ und Online-Durchsuchung: Elektronische Überwachungsmaßnahmen mit Risiken für Beschuldigte und die Allgemeinheit. Strafverteidiger 37(12):821–829

Ruggieri F (2004) Profili processuali delle investigazioni informatiche. In: Picotti L (ed) Il diritto dell'informatica nell'epoca di internet. Cedam, Padova

Schünemann WJ, Baumann M (2017) Privacy, data protection and cybersecurity in Europe. Springer, Cham

Signorato S (2018) Modalità procedimentali dell'intercettazione tramite captatore informatico. In: Giostra G, Orlandi R (eds) Nuove norme in tema di intercettazioni. Giuffrè, Milano, pp 263–276

Singelnstein T (2012) Möglichkeiten und Grenzen neuerer strafprozessualer Ermittlungsmabnahmen - Telekommunikation, Web 2.0, Datenbeschlagnahme, polizeiliche Datenverarbeitung & Co. Neue Zeitschrift für Strafrecht 11:593–606

Singelnstein T, Derin B (2017) Das Gesetz zur effektiveren und praxistauglicheren Ausgestaltung des Strafverfahrens. Was aus der StPO-Reform geworden ist. Neue Juristische Wochenschrift:2646–2652

Tonini P (2017) I captatori informatici. JusOnline 3:373–382

Torre M (2015) Il virus di stato nel diritto vivente tra esigenze investigative e tutela dei diritti fondamentali. Diritto penale e processo 21:1163–1172

Torre M (2017) Il captatore informatico. Nuove tecnologie investigative e rispetto delle regole processuali. Giuffrè, Milano

Torre M (2020) Privacy e indagini penali. Giuffrè, Milano

Vele A (2011) Le intercettazioni nel sistema processuale: tra garanzie e prospettive di riforma. Cedam, Milano

Warren SD, Braneis LD (1980) The right to privacy. Harv Law Rev 4:193–220

Zampaglione A (2019) Il recupero della funzione di garanzia del decreto autorizzativo quale "strada maestra" per arginare le potenzialità invasive del trojan e salvaguardare valori di rilievo costituzionale. www.dirittifondamentali.it

Part III
Fact-Finding and Human Rights Challenges in the Digital Era

AI-Powered Investigations: From Data Analysis to an Automated Approach Toward Investigative Uncertainty

Giulia Lasagni

Abstract Criminal law might sometimes be perceived to be at the margins of the automation process that involves increasing sectors of our society. While the expansion of automated-driven cars is by now an established fact, the technological upgrade of criminal justice mechanisms still tends to evocate sci-fi images and Minority-report-style dystopian scenarios to the non-specialists.

However, the high variety of applications that can already be counted in this domain, and the acceleration of this process in the last few years, clearly speaks for a tangible expansion of AI technology also in the field. In particular, against some more-established scenarios, especially related to phenomena of so-called predictive policing, Multi-Agent Systems (MAS) open today the perspective of a much deeper involvement of automated technologies in the very shaping of investigative proceedings.

The chapter offers an analysis of such potential, both with respect to their possible contribution to the efficiency of investigations (in their preventive and repressive dimension), and to avoid or reduce certain negative biases typical of "purely human" investigation processes, first of all, the tunnel vision effect.

1 Challenging Traditional Models of Decision-Making in Criminal Justice

It is difficult to measure the width of a change while you are right in the midst of it, and the advent of AI surely is one that might take more than a lifetime to get used to.

G. Lasagni (✉)
Department of Legal Studies, University of Bologna, Bologna, Italy
e-mail: giulia.lasagni6@unibo.it

© The Author(s), under exclusive license to Springer Nature Switzerland AG 2022
L. Bachmaier Winter, S. Ruggeri (eds.), *Investigating and Preventing Crime in the Digital Era*, Legal Studies in International, European and Comparative Criminal Law 7, https://doi.org/10.1007/978-3-031-13952-9_8

Thanks to an ability to record and process information that yet finds no terms of comparison, and a capillarity similar to that of law itself,[1] AI and algorithms are today transforming most human activities, and in particular decision-making processes. Renown is the statement by Balkin, according to whom we are rapidly moving towards

> the Algorithmic Society [...] organized around social and economic decision-making by algorithms, robots, and AI agents, who not only make the decisions but also, in some cases, carry them out.[2]

Along the same line, other authors talk about a 'transition from history to hyperhistory', a change implying that

> "our current life world can no longer be described by dichotomizing online and offline, which suggests that we require a new term to more adequately depict our current predicament" and partake "in a new kind of world that we are still discovering".[3]

It is worth mentioning that one of the latest paradigm-shifts in AI development led to the adoption of data analysis-induced knowledge methods, which largely set aside traditional approaches based on symbolic representations of human specialist expertise. The fact that most successful AI systems are currently based on Machine Learning (ML) techniques, applied to large masses of (big) data, has indeed become common knowledge.[4]

Equally well known, especially among criminal law scholars, is one of the main technical limitations of ML systems: As much as they are capable of high performances in terms of result accuracy, their functioning, as well as the reasons underlying their outcome, are still not fully explainable. Such technologies are thus also known as 'black boxes', *i.e.*, systems in which input and output are observable, while their internal functioning remains obscure even to their own programmers.[5]

---

[1] As highlighted by Ubertis (2020), pp. 76–77.

[2] Balkin (2017), p. 1219.

[3] Cf. Floridi (2014), pp. 1–24; Hildebrandt (2015), p. 42. See also European Commission, *Explanatory Memorandum to the Proposal for a Regulation of the European Parliament and of the Council Laying Down Harmonized Rules on Artificial Intelligence (Artificial Intelligence Act)* {SEC(2021) 167 final}—{SWD(2021) 84 final}—{SWD(2021) 85 final}, Bruxelles, 21.4.2021, COM(2021) 206 final, pp. 1 ff, highlighting the need to make AI "a tool for people" and "a force for good in society". For some aspects of this proposal see also in this volume Neroni Rezende, Sect. 2.

[4] One of the most remarkable features of such technology, especially from a legal perspective, precisely concerns the decision-making approach: Instead of carrying out its assessments following a set of rules (algorithm) predefined by the programmer, ML systems build their own model of the domain, applying a learning algorithm to analysis of the training data, cf., for all, O'Neil (2016); Russell and Norvig (2010), pp. 525 ff; Ferguson (2018), pp. 504 ff; Henderson (2018), pp. 527 ff.; Lagioia and Sartor (2020), pp. 280 ff; Goodfellow et al. (2018), p. 56 ff.

[5] For all, cf. Pasquale (2015).

As largely observed, the resemblance with an 'oracle'—though gifted with great statistical accuracy—makes it especially critical to deploy such systems in the criminal justice domain.[6]

Indeed, the duty to state reasons, especially in case of decisions affecting core values, like personal freedom, lays at the roots of democratic models of modern justice delivery.[7] It is thus apparent, that without a satisfactory explanation on how and why the decision-maker has assessed the elements at its disposal in a certain way, challenging a decision with reasonable chances of success becomes virtually impossible.[8]

The conclusion, however, does not suggest an ontological incompatibility between AI systems and criminal justice.[9] Actually, the potential of such systems in the field, for instance to improve consistency and predictability of legal interpretation,[10] is rather widely accepted.

Deployment of AI and algorithmic technology is then especially common in the preventive and investigative phases, with various levels of success around the world. This seems to largely depend on the fact that defence rights are considered to be more freely constrainable in the preliminary phases of criminal proceedings, not to mention during intelligence activities. The use of promising technology, though 'inexplicable', is thus regarded as relatively unproblematic in numerous jurisdictions.

Naturally, practice had already shown how illusory such an impression is, especially where, due to copyright protection or excessive privatisation, AI tools are applied without any effective control by public authorities. Several of the tools raising such substantial critical concerns (well-known, but not isolated, the case of COMPAS) have incidentally been largely discussed in literature; hence, they will be mentioned here only to provide the necessary context to the main argument of the contribution.

---

[6]See, *ex multis*, Balkin (2015), pp. 54 ff; Quattrocolo (2020a), pp. 94 ff; Contissa and Lasagni (2020), p. 282. The issue is however relevant also in other fields, see for instance Lagioia and Contissa (2020), pp. 1 ff, with regard to the health care system.

[7]Cf. ECtHR, *Moreira Ferreira v. Portugal* (no. 2), App. no. 19867/12, 11 July 2017, §84; *Papon v. France* (dec.), App. no. 54210/00, 15 November 2001.

[8]For a specific analysis on the profile of the right to an effective remedy in this context, and some constructive proposal, see Contissa and Lasagni (2020), pp. 288 ff.

[9]Firstly, because "inexplicable" decisions are far from unknown, and even accepted to a certain extent also in "purely human" proceedings (Caianiello 2019, pp. 267 ff); Moreover, computer scientists are currently working on the AI technical limitations concerning explainability, and thus might soon produce satisfactory explicable models (Guidotti et al. 2018, pp. 1 ff). In any case, proposals have already been launched, to achieve legal and technical solutions that ensure compliance with fair trial rights, even with the current state of technical development (cf. Kroll et al. 2017, pp. 633 ff and, with specific reference to criminal proceedings, Contissa and Lasagni 2020, pp. 300 ff).

[10]Especially in multilevel legal orders; in this sense, see Caianiello (2021), p. 4, according to which "legality constitutes [...] a promise never fully kept", against which "AI and ML systems could satisfy, in the end, that relentless quest".

Its starting point is that AI and algorithms can be deployed in preventive and criminal investigations also with perspectives different from those experienced in predictive policing.

Certain AI systems, known as *Multi-Agent Systems* (MAS), for instance, point to a much deeper involvement of AI technology in the very shaping of the investigative proceeding. These tools have already proven to be an essential support in certain stages of the investigations, especially in the digital forensics' analysis of big data.

This study argues that MAS technology and in particular some of their specific application, like *MultiAgent Digital Investigation Toolkits*, could actually make a significant contribution also in a different and potentially groundbreaking direction: That of supporting fairness during investigations, by intervening in the formulation, assessment and selection of investigative hypotheses.

To this end, the chapter first offers a brief recollection of the most common criminal justice applications of AI and algorithmic systems, mostly of 'predictive' nature (Sect. 2). Second, the main traits of MAS technology will be introduced, to highlight what makes these tools especially valuable for investigative and preventive purposes (Sect. 3).

Finally, an analysis of the potential of MAS tools will follow, to shed light on how a mindful application of such systems could actually contribute to avoiding or at least reducing some typically human mistakes in investigation processes, capable to generate substantial miscarriages of justice, like the so-called *tunnel vision effect* (Sect. 4).

2 AI and Algorithms for Criminal Justice "Predictive" Purposes: State of Play

Although criminal law is sometimes perceived to be at the margins of the automation process that involves increasing sectors of our society, the high variety of applications that can already be counted in this domain, and the acceleration of this process in the last few years, show quite a different reality.

The deployment of AI and algorithms in criminal justice is often associated to so-called 'predictive' goals. As highlighted by legal scholars, however, the notion of 'prediction', when referred to such technology, needs be cautiously used. AI and algorithmic systems, indeed, can at their best 'only' produce highly accurate statistical analysis, which—as such—does not necessarily have a projection into future behaviours.[11] Hence, the decision to attribute a certain binding value to the assessment produced by these tools entirely relies on the discretionary policy choice of the legal system at stake.

Understood in these terms the general potential of 'predictive' systems, it is worth briefly recalling two main directions towards which they are mostly oriented,

---

[11] Cf. Quattrocolo (2020b), pp. 17–18; see also Caianiello (2021), p. 8, highlighting how statistics "cannot tell us with precision anything that concerns the position of a single individual".

namely: (1) supporting law enforcement in certain phases of the investigations (*predictive policing*); (2) support courts in judicial decision (*predictive justice*).

2.1 Predictive Policing

Predictive policing is today a very operational reality in several countries worldwide. In this regard, AI and above all algorithmic systems may be used for different purposes, mostly either to 'predict' some objective element of criminal activities (*e.g.* time and place of possible offences; potential victims), or to 'predict' the occurrence of individual behaviours with potential criminal relevance.[12]

Critical implications for the protection of fundamental rights however significantly vary in the two cases.

The first approach reflects traditional investigative techniques to map criminal activities in a given area, by analysing data on social, demographic, economic, environmental, and criminal background.

Its deployment mainly aims at optimising the allocation of human resources and equipment, channelling forces to areas where criminogenic risk is higher.[13] Examples of such tools, largely examined by legal scholars and mostly directed at predicting where street offenses are likely to occur, are, for instance, *PredPol,*[14] *XLaw,*[15] *Delia,*[16] *CAS,*[17] *PreCobs,*[18] *CAPP-PGH,*[19] or *KLB-Operativ.*[20]

---

[12] For a comprehensive overview, see Perry et al. (2013), pp. 8 ff; cf. also Isaac (2018), pp. 543 ff; Joh (2018), pp. 559 ff.

[13] The use of such systems is so common, that online databases have been created to check which software finds deployment in a certain local district, cf. https://atlasofsurveillance.org/search?utf8=%E2%9C%93&location=&technologies%5B86%5D=on.

[14] Developed by the police and the University of California, Los Angeles, the system makes forecasts based on three classes of data (type of offence, place where the offence was committed, and the date/time of its commission), that allow to identify, on a Web interface based on Google Maps, the high-risk areas in certain time periods, cfr. https://www.predpol.com/law-enforcement/#predPolicing; cf. also Huq (2019), p. 1070; Joh (2014), pp. 44–45.

[15] Designed by the Questura of Napoli, to predict the geographical and temporal occurrence of thefts and robberies, cf. https://www.xlaw.it/presentazione/index_eng.asp.

[16] Developed by the company *KeyCrime*, created by a former police officer and currently in use by the Milano police department, cf. https://www.keycrime.com/, on which see also Parodi and Sellaroli (2019), pp. 56 ff.

[17] *Crime Anticipation System*, created by the Amsterdam police (https://documen.site/download/crime-anticipation-system_pdf), on which see Mutsaers and van Nuenen (2020), pp. 1 ff.

[18] *Pre Crime Observation System*, http://www.ifmpt.de/, cf., *e.g.*, Bayerisches Landeskriminalamt (2015).

[19] *Coalition against Predictive Policing*, cf. https://capp-pgh.com/files/CPP%20Teach-in%2007-1 6-2020.pdf.

[20] *Kriminalitätslagebild*, https://atlas.algorithmwatch.org/datenbank/klb-operativ/, on which see Seidensticker et al. (2018), pp. 1 ff.

These systems can be appreciated, for their potential in contributing to a better management of law enforcement personnel and know-how, improving investigative performances at the local level in conditions of limited resources. Yet, their deployment has been long criticized in literature,[21] although in recent times such tools started to be considered relatively less problematic, at least in comparison with individual risk assessment technology.

This is not tantamount to say that they are devoid of critical aspects. Nonetheless, these systems seem to 'merely' perpetuate criticalities that already characterize the same activities when they are carried out by human beings, rather than being strictly related to the functioning of AI or algorithmic technology.

Moreover, although even severe discrimination cannot be excluded, these preventive systems are usually applied to guide the action of law enforcement, and not to directly issue decisions with binding legal effects.

Definitely more problematic are the instruments designed to issue individual assessments.

To put it simply, such systems—thanks to mathematical models and ML techniques, and by accessing huge amounts of data, otherwise often not available to law enforcement agencies—correlate statistical risk factors with specific individuals.

In many countries, case law has in the last few years started to attach legal value to such score risks, for instance by making the granting of probation or of alternative measures dependent upon a low-risk result. This phenomenon raises a number of concerns about the protection of fundamental rights, which have been repeatedly flagged by legal scholars and specialized working groups on both sides of the Atlantic.[22] In this sense, notorious is the case of COMPAS,[23] and of its judicial aftermaths in the *Loomis* case.[24] However, there are several more examples of tools

---

[21] For instance, by incorporating human bias, *e.g.* encouraging law enforcement to oversee certain neighbourhoods (not unfrequently, characterized by non-white communities) and thus making it more likely that the people living there will be subject to stop-and-frisk practices, cf. Huq (2019), p. 1109; Brayne (2017), pp. 977 ff; Epp et al. (2014), pp. 117–119. As it will be discussed below, however, once aware of such biases, AI can also be used to correct them (cf. n 55).

[22] Among which, as widely discussed, many of the USA national jurisdictions, and, to a lower extent, the United Kingdom; for a reference to the vast literature on the matter, see Garapon and Lassègue (2018); Huq (2019), pp. 1043 ff, Council of Europe (2017), pp. 10 ff.

[23] Developed by Equivant, a private company based in California (https://www.equivant.com/practitioners-guide-to-compas-core/), and currently adopted in several US states to calculate the rate of recidivism, as when issuing decisions on alternative measures or suspended sentences. The data used by COMPAS to issue its predictions are only partially known to the public, due to intellectual property rights on the software, and have already been strongly accused of creating discriminatory effects by non profit organizations, cfr. *ProPublica* Reports: Angwin et al. (2016) and Larson et al. (2016). See also Huq (2019), pp. 1047 ff.

[24] *State of Wisconsin v. Loomis*, 881 N. W.2d 749 (Wis. 2016), 36. Among the vast literature commenting the case in a critical perspective, see, *ex multis*, Lightbourne (2017), pp. 327 ff; Recent cases (2017), pp. 1530 ff; De Miguel Beriain (2018), pp. 45 ff; Quattrocolo (2020a), pp. 166 ff; Gialuz (2019), pp. 1 ff; Caianiello (2021), p. 16; Freeman (2016), pp. 75 ff. An unpublished case, similar to *Loomis* and issued by the Supreme Court of the District of Columbia, is reported by Quattrocolo (2020a), pp. 161 ff.

deployed worldwide to issue individual risk assessment, in the US (SASSI, LSI-R,[25] or PSA,[26] just to mention a few), as well as elsewhere (*e.g.* the British *HART*[27]).

Also, goal pursued by individual assessment risk tools can vary. For instance, in certain legal frameworks, they are reportedly used to perform like a polygraph (and with the same controversial implications[28]). This is, for instance, the case of the Spanish *Veripol*, used to 'measure' the truth of statements released by witnesses in car insurance proceedings, with the goal of avoiding insurance fraud.[29]

2.2 Predictive Justice

In contrast to the relatively consolidated application of predictive policing tools, instruments of predictive justice are still sensibly underdeveloped.

A comparison with civil proceedings especially reveals a significant gap in the field of criminal justice. In the civil law domain, indeed, AI and algorithms are increasingly deployed not only to support human decision-making, but also to directly substitute it, at least for cases with limited monetary value.[30] In criminal law, on the contrary, predictive justice is, at most, in a testing phase.

Examples of such projects may be found in several jurisdictions, although especially renown are the attempts to predict the behaviour of the United States Supreme Court Justices,[31] or the decisions of the Court in Strasbourg.[32] Regardless for the progressive improvement of their accuracy,[33] similar systems are still

---

[25] Level of Service Inventory-Revised (LSI-R) and Substance Abuse Substance Subtle Screening Inventory (SASSI), on which cf. *Malenchik v. State*, 928 N. E. 2d 564, 574 (Ind. 2010).

[26] The *Public Safety Assessment* is an individual risk assessment tool developed especially for the pretrial phase by the Laura and John Arnold Foundation and currently used in dozens of jurisdictions in the United States and in some of the largest cities in the country, such as Phoenix, Chicago Houston. To distance PSA from the numerous criticisms moved to *Compas*, the creators of this system decided to make information about its functioning public and to reveal the different weight of each of main nine factors used in the risk assessment calculation, cf. https://www.psapretrial.org/about.

[27] The Harm Assessment Risk Tool has been developed by the Durham Police and the University of Cambridge. It makes predictions based on 33 different metrics, including the offender's criminal record, age, and postcode. The parameters used by HART have been made at least partly accessible to the public, allowing to identify a number of relevant criticalities (*e.g.* that the tool is designed to promote false positives over false negatives, which means that it is more likely that a low-risk individual is wrongly classified as a high-risk person rather than the other way around, see Oswald et al. (2018), p. 236).

[28] See, for all, Steinbrook (1992), pp. 122 ff.; Brett et al. (1986), pp. 544 ff.

[29] https://www.rtve.es/noticias/20180918/inteligencia-artificial-para-detectar-denuncias-falsas-policia/1801640.shtml, on which see Liberatore et al. (2019), pp. 89 ff.

[30] See for instance the Estonian example, cf. Niller (2019).

[31] Cf. Katz et al. (2017) and Guimerà and Sales-Pardo (2011).

[32] Cf. Altreas et al. (2016), pp. 2 ff.

[33] Average accuracy could be estimated around 80%, or—at least—most renown studies are within that range, cf. Katz et al. (2017), p. 14: "over nearly two centuries, we achieve 70.2% accuracy at the

generally deemed too low performers to play a significant role in the resolution of criminal cases.[34]

Perhaps because of their reference to the trial phase, rather than to the less defence-oriented investigative stage, accuracy seems indeed to be examined in this context through much narrower lenses than in their predictive policing correspondents.[35]

At least for the time being, hence, these instruments continue to retain no legal binding value and are widely regarded as mere scientific experiments.

3 Much More than Predictions: Exploring New(er) Frontiers for AI-Powered Investigations

'Prediction', however, represents only a fraction of the AI and algorithmic potential in criminal proceedings, and perhaps not even the most groundbreaking one.[36]

Data analysis carried out through AI tools, for instance, although less cinematographic, has drastically changed both the way evidence search is pursued by law enforcement, and the realistic expectations of privacy in most of our daily activities.

In truth, against a massive and constant production of digital data in every field of private and professional life, relying on AI seems an increasingly appealing option for the law enforcement, struggling to find a sustainable way to select relevant information.

This is a task for which a specific form of this technology, namely Multi-Agent Systems (MAS), seems to offer a particularly promising contribution.

---

case outcome level and 71.9% at the justice vote level. More recently, over the past century, we outperform an *in-sample optimized* null model by nearly 5%"; Guimerà and Sales-Pardo (2011), p. 4: "For these artificially–generated ideal courts, we find that both the majority rule and the stochastic block model algorithms correctly predict 71% of individual justices votes [...] For real courts, on the other hand, the block model algorithm correctly predicts 83% of the individual justices' decisions"; Altreas et al. (2016), p. 2: "Our models can reliably predict ECtHR decisions with high accuracy, i.e., 79% on average".

[34] In this sense also the Council of Europe (2017), p. 11, according to which the low level of accuracy "is therefore considered premature at the current time to imagine such systems replacing judges".

[35] Garapon and Lassègue (2018); Manes (2020), pp. 551 ff.

[36] Other relevant applications of AI technology in this domain, just to mention a few, concern facial recognition (specifically dealt with in this volume by Neroni Rezende). Although this specific sector has somehow long received less attention by legal scholars (see, however, Susskind (2017), pp. 11 ff; Caianiello (2021), pp. 2 and 5, also with regard to the advantages for legal entities), extremely relevant is also the deployment of AI technology in providing support to the defence counsels' activity, today addressed by several dedicated platforms, see, *e.g.*, CrossJustice (*Knowledge, Advisory and Capacity Building Information Tool for Criminal Procedural Rights in Judicial Cooperation*) developed within the EU Justice Programme (GA no. 847346), available at: https://crossjustice.eu/en/index.html.

As it will be argued further below, though, the potential of MAS technology could actually be even greater, bringing to an util now unprecedented level of integration between human and machine skills in carrying out investigations.

Before moving to this analysis, however, a brief clarification on MAS functioning is in order.

Multi-Agent Systems are a development of AI technology, characterized by a set of specific features.

The main idea behind its development is that there are problems too complex to be solved with predefined reasoning settings.[37] Such problems hence call for different approaches: structured and, at the same time, granted with a certain versatility.

MAS present a number of characteristics that made this technology particularly suitable to address these challenges, especially where solutions do not appear easily pre-definable—as it could well be a criminal case scenario.

As the term reveals, Multi-Agent Systems are based on the coordinated action of several 'agents', that cooperate with each other to deliver a result. Such agents may be defined as *autonomous*, *reactive*, and *interactive*. The action of each agent is indeed shaped by *intention*, in other words, by the goal that the agent aims to achieve through its assigned task in a rational and not-predefined way.[38]

Another fundamental element of MAS technology is that agents "should be somehow *organized*".[39] To this end, norms must be established, that agents should obey or comply with. It follows that agents could be structured in a hierarchical framework, under the supervision of an operational or strategic manager,[40] which could, for instance, take care of task allocation.[41]

---

[37] Hindriks (2014), p. 4; Wooldridge (2009), p. 19 ff.

[38] Cf. Hindriks (2014), p. 2; Wooldridge and Jennings (1995), pp. 115 ff; Rao and Georgeff (1991), pp. 473 ff.

[39] Hindriks (2014), p. 4.

[40] Hoelz et al. (2009), p. 884.

[41] Different organization models can actually be designed, whose complexity depends on the system and the needs emerging from the case at stake. For a quite structured organizational system, see *e.g.* Ganesch (2018), p. 97: The "strategic manager receives different cases to perform the forensic analysis. According to the organization's priorities, the strategic manager defines the order of execution and amount of resources (number of computers) for each case. A tactical manager is the[n] assigned to one specific case which can contain several evidences, like a number of hard drives. The tactical manager defines the priority of its evidences and distributes them to the available operational managers, which are limited by the resources available to that case. The operational manager will employ the necessary specialized agents to perform the different tasks it deems important to examine a piece of evidence".

4   MAS: Shaping a New Way to Carry Out Investigations

As anticipated, MAS technology has proven a very valuable tool for digital investigations.[42]

This is indeed one of the contexts where, *par excellence*, investigators must struggle not only in identifying the potential solution of a case, but, preliminarily, in determining which elements are potentially relevant to that end.[43] Given the vast amount of information that might be present on a device, or on the cloud, this step is inherently challenging, especially if similar activities need to be carried out in almost every criminal case.

It is therefore not surprising that several tools have been developed, in the last decades, precisely to support human investigators in such tasks.[44] Examples in this regard are, for instance, the *Open Computer Forensics Architecture* (OCFA),[45] the *Digital Forensics Framework* (DFF),[46] *Fiwalk*,[47] the *Advanced Automated Disk Investigation Toolkit* (AUDIT).[48] Among the vast range of MAS technology deployed in this field, particularly interesting for this contribution is then the *MultiAgent Digital Investigation toolKit* (MADIK).

MADIK systems are composed of a set of intelligent software agents, set to perform different analysis on pieces of digital evidence. The rationale behind the use of such technology is to facilitate the classification of digital information, through a score system that differentiates from "Absolutely Irrelevant" to "Probably Case-Relevant".[49]

To do so, each agent contains a set of rules and knowledge base, derived from human expertise (*e.g.* from law enforcement officers). Thanks to it, agents are enabled to examine the elements at their disposal and determine which piece(s) of information are most pertinent to the case.

Such tools can be applied within criminal investigations, as well as, actually, to any other forms of digital investigations in other sectors (for example, labor law disputes).

At the same time, MAS systems may also be usefully deployed in preventive investigations.

---

[42] Cf., *e.g.*, Beebe and Clark (2005), pp. 147 ff; Karabiyik and Aggarwal (2016), pp. 379 ff.

[43] Cf. Brighi and Ferrazzano (2021), pp. 43 ff.

[44] Among the first to propose such deployment, Stallard and Levitt (2003), pp. 160 ff. See also the further proposals by Liao et al. (2009), pp. 1881 ff; Fizaine and Clarke (2013), p. 73.

[45] Vermaas et al. (2010), pp. 45 ff.

[46] www.digital-forensic.org, France, 2016.

[47] Garfinkel (2009), pp. 73 ff

[48] Karabiyik and Aggarwal (2016), pp. 381 ff.

[49] Hoelz et al. (2009), pp. 883 ff; Ganesch (2018), pp. 96 ff.

Perhaps the most immediate reference in this sense goes to inquiries carried out on social media, to identify potential offenders or crime patterns and reduce victimisation.[50] Concrete applications can hence vary enormously, from anti-hate speech control to terrorism or organized crime.

The use of MAS alike technology is also increasingly appealing in the fight against financing of terrorism and money laundering. As Suspicious Activity Reports by financial institutions are steadily increasing, Financial Intelligence Units throughout the world struggle to keep up with a preventive action that has already gone way beyond human-only capacities.[51] Deployment of AI technology hence more and more appears as a compulsory choice, to trace back the 'digital trail' of suspicious financial flows in a globalized and hyperconnected world.[52]

4.1 Not Only Digital Forensics: An AI Approach to Investigative Uncertainty

The potential of MAS systems, however, could extend also to goals which go far beyond digital data analysis.

Particularly interesting, in this regard, is the aforementioned MADIK system and its so-called 'distributed nature'. The idea behind this feature refers to the fact that a task (*e.g.* identifying relevant information on a device) can best be carried out not only by one single agent at the time, but, simultaneously, by several agents.

Each of them is thus performing its own assessment of the given problem. This profile has a direct impact on the way in which decision-making is shaped within these tools. Since different agents can produce diverging results, it is indeed for the system operational manager to solve divergences. Several rules can be established in this regard.

For instance, Hoelz et al. describe a system where the manager decides to rely on those agents which—due to their specific training—have better performed in the past with regard to similar tasks.[53] If the results provided by a specific agent are deemed to be inaccurate, the 'confidence' of the manager on its ability to answer to the given

---

[50] As supported by several political instances, cf. Rifkind (2014), pp. 143 ff; Toor (2016). For some examples of technical implementations, see Gonçalves Evangelista et al. (2020), pp. 1 ff.; Scrivens et al. (2019), pp. 179 ff; Panagiotou et al. (2019), pp. 1 ff; Ball (2016), pp. 147 ff.

[51] For an in-depth comparative examination of AML/CFT regimes, cf. Vogel and Maillart (2020); for a recognition of Financial Intelligence Units' structure and powers, see Lasagni (2019), pp. 93 ff.

[52] IBM (2019), pp. 1 ff; Deloitte (2018), pp. 1 ff; on the compatibility of such systems with fundamental rights in the EU, see Maxwell et al. (2020), pp. 5 ff.

[53] Similarly to the machine learning procedure, the correctness of the agents' results relies—at least at first—on a review interface used by the human experts, cf. Hoelz et al. (2009), p. 886; Ganesch (2018), p. 97: "MADIK uses case-based reasoning (CBR) to determine which agents are better employed in which kind of investigation. This also allows the agents to reason about the evidences in a way that is more adequate to the special case in question".

problem will diminish. Its performances will thus likely bear less weight in future queries of the same sort. On the contrary, where the performance of the agent is deemed positive, the manager's confidence increases, and this 'appreciation' will be recalled also in future investigations.[54]

This, however, does not represent a fixed rule. Different rule models could be developed, for example by diminishing the role of precedents, in order to reduce potential investigative blind spots caused by overreliance on past assessments.

Against this background, MAS show a broad range of potential for AI technologies in criminal justice.

Indeed, those who promote the recourse to AI and algorithmic systems often do so with the aim (or the hope) of objectivizing or standardizing the human based criminal justice system towards more accurate outcomes. In other words, to obtain a fairer justice by making it less subject to variable, subjective and potentially discriminatory influences.[55] Making it simpler for human beings to assess a complex and uncertain situation is certainly a positive and desirable goal that poses in favour of a mindful deployment of AI technology to the criminal matter. This aim, however, is not the only goal that can be pursued thanks to Multi-Agent Systems.

MAS, and especially MADIK systems, open also to a different perspective, that is a use of AI technology not to pursue (legal) certainty, but to rationally manage (legal) uncertainty. Indeed, these AI systems seem already capable of living with a certain degree of complexity and unpredictability, typical of human vicissitudes. Due to their characteristics, MAS show us that machines can today be deployed for tasks other than simplifying the performance of complex human activities, requiring a certain predictive reasoning or high statistical calculating skills.

Said otherwise, the AI potential to "reduce the noise"[56] in criminal proceedings— for instance, by selecting *the* relevant information in digital investigations among a bulk of available data—is only one of its possible applications.

Especially in the early stages of the proceedings, also a different skill does reveal its crucial importance, *i.e.* the capacity to leverage the notion of conflict, instead of avoiding it, thus ensuring fairness to the whole procedure.

Building on the illustrated features, a further use for MADIK technology (or alike) could hence be foreseen, namely a deployment aiming *precisely to preserve the necessary degree of uncertainty* that is typical of the investigative phases.

As is well-known, one of the features that makes initial stages of criminal proceedings so sensitive to potential miscarriages is the difficulty of detecting the best investigative hypothesis among the different possible ones.

---

[54] Cf. Hoelz et al. (2009), p. 886.

[55] Cf. Sunstein (2019), pp. 499 ff; illustrative in this sense also the expression by Deskus (2018), p. 243: "A judge's bad day or heavy docket does not affect the algorithm". Highlighting the influence of daily activities (such as breakfast or lunch time schedules) on the harshness of human sentencing, Eagleman (2015), p. 266; see also Sartor and Lagioia (2020), pp. 63 ff.

[56] This is often the desired outcome: cf. famously Kahneman et al. (2021).

Philosophers and social scientists have long recognized how human understanding is usually quite struggling in dealing with multiple-option contexts, observing that, once we have

> adopted an opinion, [it] draws all things else to support and agree with it. And though there be a greater number and weight of instances to be found on the other side, yet these it either neglects and despises, or else by some distinction sets aside and rejects; in order that by this great and pernicious predetermination the authority of its former conclusions may remain inviolate.[57]

This almost involuntary tendency towards simplification has significant repercussions for criminal investigations. This is the reason why forensic psychologists identify a substantial safeguard against miscarriages of justice in the capacity of investigators not to pre-determine their minds.[58]

The reference, in particular, goes here to the so-called *tunnel vision effect*, according to which criminal justice actors tend relatively early to focus on a specific suspect or investigative trail. The significance of evidence and clues that could 'build a case' supporting the adopted insight gets thus elevated, while elements which appear inconsistent with it are overlooked or dismissed as irrelevant, incredible, or unreliable.[59]

Tunnel vision effect, however, "is more often the product of the human condition as well as institutional and cultural pressures, than of maliciousness or indifference".[60] To this regard, social scientists highlighted that the human tendency to "typically consider only one hypothesis at a time and often make the assumption at the outset that that hypothesis is true" does not exclude a potential for improvement, achievable by "training people to think of alternative hypotheses early in the hypothesis-evaluation process".[61]

4.2   MAS as a Tool to Ensure Fairness in Criminal Investigations?

Against this background, MAS technology could be a way to make those aspirations viable. To this end, it is argued here that the same approach developed for digital

---

[57] Cf. Bacon (1939), original work published in 1620, p. 36; more recently, see *e.g.* Nickerson (1998), pp. 176 ff.

[58] See, among others, Wason (1960), pp. 129 ff; Lange (1975), pp. 311 ff; Nickerson (1998), p. 193, inquiring also on the potential causes that lead to this confirmation bias tendency (pp. 197 ff); Meissner and Kassin (2004), pp. 85 ff; Findley and Scott (2006), pp. 291 ff; Dror et al. (2006), pp. 74 ff; Forza (2018), pp. 395 ff.

[59] Cf. Martin (2002), pp. 847–848; Raeder (2003), pp. 1327–1328.

[60] Findley and Scott (2006), p. 292.

[61] Nickerson (1998), p. 211, according to whom "evidence provides reason for optimism that the approach can work".

evidence could be applied by Multi-Agent Systems also with regard to investigative hypothesis.

The idea is, that AI might be usefully deployed to support human investigative decision-making *by guaranteeing that divergent reconstructions within criminal investigations remains unsolved, at least to a certain stage.*

Multi-Agent Systems can support human law enforcement in the selection process of investigative insights, at the same time maintaining a certain degree of openness to the material examined. This is so, because the different reconstructions produced by the autonomous 'agents' are brought back to (a certain) unity only with the intervention of the operating manager.

Until then, MAS distributed nature could be exploited to ensure that agents composing the investigative team are sufficiently diversified, so as to be able to spot, and develop, as many investigative hypotheses as possible.

Naturally, the identification of a precise timeline (until when shall the uncertainty of investigations be preserved?) is far from being a straightforward task. The demand not to preclude any potential investigative lead, to ensure a more comprehensive examination, shall indeed also be balanced with the necessity of safeguarding the rights of the individuals that might become involved in the investigations (defendants or other third parties). Needless to say, the use of AI in this domain should be carried out carefully.

It should be considered, however, that the risk to either close too early or broaden too much the investigations already exists in purely 'human' scenarios. As it is the case for all AI applications, MAS or MADIK technology do not contain a predefined magic formula that suddenly erases all human biases, although they can make them more visible.

Thus, a crucial role will continue to be played by the principle of proportionality and by the supervisory mechanisms already in place to oversee on the correct performance of criminal investigations (first of all, judicial review).

Also, the capacity of such systems to operate as a 'mind-openers' clearly depends on how much human experts carried out a diversified training of automated agents. Machine training is however an 'old' issue, which risks undermining the effectiveness (and fairness) of all Machine Learning technology, and not of MAS exclusively.[62]

If proper training is ensured, the potential of MAS technology could be groundbreaking. The analysis carried out by automated agents could help testing the soundness of diverging investigative hypotheses or identifying reconstructions of the event difficult to spot.

AI expertise might be used, for instance, in contexts where it is not possible to deploy enough human agents to ensure an adequate variety of investigative perspectives since the beginning of the proceeding, due to limited human resources. MAS

---

[62] Cf., *e.g.*, Miller (2014), pp. 106 ff; Quattrocolo (2020a), p. 67; Roberts et al. (2021), pp. 199 ff, highlighting the limits of ML technology with regard to the Covid-19 pandemic.

technology could also help deciphering unintelligible crime scenes, where clues or relevant material is scarce or hard to interpret.

Regardless of the subject matter, the reasoning model of Multi-Agent Systems could indeed be deployed to prevent relevant investigative insights be lost at an early stage of the proceeding, due to time or resources constraints.

Lastly, it is worth recalling that MAS technology could be successfully exploited also by actors other than law enforcement and prosecutors.

Such tools could actually be used also by the counsellors representing the defendant or the victim, to check whether all potential investigative leads had been duly pursued. In this regard too, therefore, AI technology could find so far unexplored, but potentially revolutionary areas of applications within the criminal justice system.

5   Conclusion

This contribution aimed at lifting the veil on a new possible deployment of AI technology within preventive and criminal investigation.

To do so, an inventive effort is requested to lawyers, legal informatics and computer scientists, with a view to trying to walk unexplored paths for criminal justice principles to find effective implementation in the 'hyperhistory' time that we are living.[63]

Obviously, mistakes are in order in this quest, and options that seem easy to realise on paper do not necessarily share the same fate in practice. This awareness should not however discourage from insisting on trying.

Multi-Agent Systems, for once, seem to open interesting and innovative perspectives over an AI-enabled version of the ancient Socratic method. Falsification[64] as a way to achieve procedural fairness is an essential feature of modern criminal justice systems. In most legal orders, however, fair trial principles find only a partial application in the investigative phase.

Here it is argued that MAS technology could help extend their safeguarding value also to the very beginning of the proceeding, giving new tools to law enforcement, as well as to defence lawyers, to better perform in their respective roles.

Of course, the limited remit of this contribution only allowed to begin shedding light on a new potential for AI in criminal investigation.

Its provisional conclusion will need to be further substantiated, also to face the many questions that arise any time AI technologies are at stake. Actual technical capacities of MAS tools in this domain, for once, will have to be specifically tested, and highly specialized investigative training shall be carefully designed to transform the illustrated potential into operational reality.

---

[63] For the term, see again Floridi (2014), p. 24.

[64] On which, see, famously, Popper (2002), original work published in 1934.

Who worries that investigative procedures may be "dumbed down"[65] by excessive human reliance on automation, however, should feel reassured: Human skills are far from becoming irrelevant in the process. Training, in particular, clearly draws a dividing line between a true empowerment of human investigative skills and a mere digital re-proposition of old biases and prejudices.

AI technology is here to stay; as famously stated, all we have to decide is what to do with the time that is given to us, and, of course, with its challenges.

Finding new ways to put automated technology at the service of fairness in criminal justice, and not just of its (supposed) efficiency, might be a good idea. In other words, the question is not whether humans are still making a difference, we do. Point is: We have to make it an encouraging thought.[66]

References

Altreas N, Tsarapatsanis D, Preoţiuc-Pietro D, Lampos V (2016) Predicting judicial decisions of the European Court of Human Rights: a Natural Language Processing perspective. PeerJ Comput Sci (Open Access). https://peerj.com/articles/cs-93.pdf

Angwin J, Larson J, Mattu S, Kirchner L (2016) Machine bias: there's software used across the country to predict future criminals. And it's biased against blacks, 23.05.2016. https://www.propublica.org/article/machine-bias-risk-assessments-in-criminal-sentencing

Bacon F (1939) Novum organum. In Burtt EA (ed) The English philosophers from Bacon to Mill New York, Random House, pp 24–123 (original work published in 1620)

Balkin JM (2015) The path of robotics law. Calif Law Rev 6:45–60

Balkin JM (2017) The three laws of robotics in the age of big data. Ohio State Law J 78:1217–1241

Ball L (2016) Automating social network analysis: a power tool for counter-terrorism. Secur J 29: 147–168

Bayerisches Landeskriminalamt (2015) Abteilung V, Positionspapier zum Einsatz von PRECOBS bei der Bayerischen Polizei, Forum KI am 24./25.06.2015 beim BKA zum Thema Predictive Policing und geografische Kriminalitätsanalyse. https://www.bka.de/SharedDocs/Downloads/DE/Publikationen/ForumKI/ForumKI2015/kiforum2015EggerPositionspapier.pdf?__blob=publicationFile&v=1

Beebe N, Clark JG (2005) A hierarchical, objectives-based framework for the digital investigations process. Digit Investig 2(2):147–167

Brayne S (2017) Big data surveillance: the case of policing. Am Sociol Rev 82(5):977–1008

Brett A, Phillips M, Beary FJ III (1986) Predictive power of the polygraph: can the "Lie Detector" really detect liars? Lancet I(8480):544–547

Brighi R, Ferrazzano M (2021) Digital forensics: best practices and perspective. In: Caianiello M, Camon A (eds) Digital forensic evidence: towards common European standards in antifraud administrative and criminal investigations. Wolters Kluwer/CEDAM, Collezione di giustizia penale, pp 13–48. https://site.unibo.it/devices/en

Caianiello M (2019) Criminal process faced with the challenges of scientific and technological development. Eur J Crim Crim Law Crim Just 27(4):267–291

---

[65] See James and Gladyshev (2013), pp. 2 ff; Meyers and Rogers (2004), pp. 5 ff.

[66] Freely rephrasing Tolkien (2004), original work published in 1954, pp. 51 ff.

Caianiello M (2021) Dangerous liaisons. Potentialities and risks deriving from the interaction between artificial intelligence and preventive justice. Eur J Crim Crim Law Crim Just 29(1): 1–23

Contissa G, Lasagni G (2020) When it is (also) algorithms and AI that decide on criminal matters: in search for an effective remedy. Eur J Crim Crim Law Crim Just 28(3):280–304

Council of Europe (2017) Study on the human rights dimensions of automated data processing techniques (in particular algorithms) and possible regulatory implications, 6.10.2017. https://rm.coe.int/study-hr-dimension-of-automated-data-processing-incl-algorithms/168075b94a

De Miguel Beriain I (2018) Does the use of risk assessments in sentences respect the right to due process? A critical analysis of the Wisconsin v. Loomis ruling. Law Probab Risk 17:45–53

Deloitte (2018) The case for artificial intelligence in combating money laundering and terrorist financing. A deep dive into the application of machine learning technology, pp 1–40. https://www2.deloitte.com/id/en/pages/financial-advisory/articles/the-case-for-artificial-intelligence-in-combating-money-laundering-and-terrorist-financing.html

Deskus C (2018) Fifth amendment limitations on criminal algorithmic decision-making. N Y Univ J Legis Public Policy 21:237–286

Dror IE, Charlton D, Péron AE (2006) Contextual information renders experts vulnerable to making erroneous identifications. Forensic Sci Int CLVI(1):74–78

Eagleman D (2015) The brain. The story of you. Pantheon Books/Canongate Books, New York/Edinburgh

Epp CR, Maynard-Moody S, Haider-Markel D (2014) Pulled over: how police stops define race and citizenship. University of Chicago Press, Chicago

Ferguson AG (2018) Illuminating black data policing. Ohio State J Crim Law 15:503–525

Findley K, Scott M (2006) The multiple dimensions of tunnel vision in criminal cases. Wisconsin Law Rev MMVI(108):291–397

Fizaine J, Clarke N (2013) A crime-dependent automated search engine for digital forensics. Adv Commun Comput Netw Secur 10:73–87

Floridi L (2014) The 4th revolution. How the infoshpere is reshaping human reality. Oxford University Press, New York

Forza A (2018) La psicologia nel processo penale. Giuffrè, Milano

Freeman K (2016) Algorithmic injustice: how the Wisconsin Supreme Court failed to protect due process rights in State v. Loomis. NCJL Technol 18:75–106

Ganesch V (2018) A cyber crime evidence collection and multiagent digital investigation toolkit. IJCRT 6(1):94–99

Garapon A, Lassègue J (2018) Justice digitale: révolution graphique et rupture anthropologique. PUF, Paris

Garfinkel S (2009) Automating disk forensic processing with SleuthKit, XML and Python. In: Proceedings of the fourth IEEE international workshop on systematic approaches to digital forensic engineering, pp 73–84

Gialuz M (2019) Quando la giustizia penale incontra l'intelligenza artificiale: luci e ombre dei rischi assessment tools tra Stati uniti ed Europa. Dir pen cont. 29.05.2019. https://archiviodpc.dirittopenaleuomo.org/d/6702-quando-la-giustizia-penale-incontra-l-intelligenza-artificiale-luci-e-ombre-dei-risk-assessment-too

Gonçalves Evangelista JR, Sassi RJ, Romero M, Napolitano D (2020) Systematic Literature Review to Investigate the Application of Open Source Intelligence (OSINT) with artificial intelligence. J Appl Secur Res, pp 1–25

Goodfellow R, McDaniel P, Papernot N (2018) Making machine learning robust against adversarial inputs. Commun ACM 61(7):56–66

Guidotti R, Monreale A, Ruggieri S, Turini F, Giannotti F, Pedreschi D (2018) A survey of methods for explaining Black Box models. ACM Comput Surv 51(5), Article 93, 42 pp

Guimerà R, Sales-Pardo M (2011) Justice blocks and predictability of U.S. Supreme Court votes. PLoS ONE 6(11):e27188m. https://journals.plos.org/plosone/article?id=10.1371/journal.pone.0027188

Henderson SE (2018) A few criminal justice big data rules. Ohio State J Crim Law 15:527–541

Hildebrandt M (2015) Smart technologies and the end(s) of law. Novel entanglements of law and technology. Edward Elgar, Cheltenham

Hindriks KV (2014) The shaping of the agent-oriented mindset: twenty years of engineering MAS. In: Dalpiaz F, Dix J, van Riemsdijk MB (eds) Engineering multi-agent systems, second international workshop, EMAS 2014, Paris, France, May 5–6, 2014. Revised selected papers. Springer, Cham, pp 1–14

Hoelz BWP, Ghedini Ralha C, Geeverghese R (2009) Artificial intelligence applied to computer forensics. In: Proceedings of the 2009 ACM symposium on applied computing, pp 883–888

Huq AZ (2019) Racial equity in algorithmic criminal justice. Duke Law J 6(68):1043–1134

IBM (2019) Fighting financial crime with AI. How cognitive solutions are changing the way institutions manage AML compliance, fraud and conduct surveillance, pp 1–18. https://www.acfcs.org/fighting-financial-crime-with-ai-how-cognitive-solutions-are-changing-the-way-insti tutions-manage-aml-compliance-fraud-and-conduct-surveillance-new-ibm-whitepaper/

Isaac WS (2018) Hope, hype, and fear: the promise and potential pitfalls of artificial intelligence in criminal justice. Ohio State J Crim Law 15:543

James J, Gladyshev P (2013) Challenges with automation in digital forensic investigations, Digital Forensic Investigation Research Group, University College Dublin, Ireland. https://arxiv.org/ftp/arxiv/papers/1303/1303.4498.pdf

Joh EE (2014) Policing by numbers: big data and the fourth amendment. Wash Law Rev 89:35–68

Joh EE (2018) Automated policing. Ohio State J Crim Law 15:559

Kahneman D, Sibony O, Sunstein CR (2021) Noise: a flaw in hu-man judgment. Little Brown Spark, New York

Karabiyik U, Aggarwal S (2016) Advanced automated disk investigation toolkit. In: Peterson G, Shenoi S (eds) Advances in digital forensics, XII. DigitalForensics 2016. IFIP advances in information and communication technology, vol 484. Springer, Cham, pp 379–396

Katz DM, Bommarito MJ II, Blackman J (2017) A general approach for predicting the behavior of the Supreme Court of the United States. PLoS ONE 12(4):e0174698. https://journals.plos.org/plosone/article?id=10.1371/journal.pone.0174698

Kroll JA, Huey J, Barocas S, Felten EW, Reidenberg JR, Robinson DG, Yu H (2017) Accountable algorithms. Univ Pa Law Rev 165:633–705

Lagioia F, Contissa G (2020) The strange case of Dr Watson: liability implications of AI evidence-based decision support systems in health care. Eur J Leg Stud 12:1–44

Lagioia F, Sartor G (2020) Artificial intelligence in the big data era: risks and opportunities. In: Cannataci J, Falce V, Pollicino O (eds) Legal challenges of big data. Edward Elgar, pp 280–307

Lange EJ (1975) The illusion of control. J Pers Soc Psychol 32(2):311–332

Larson J, Mattu S, Kirchner L, Angwin J (2016) How we analyzed the COMPAS recidivism algorithm. https://www.propublica.org/article/how-we-analyzed-the-compas-recidivism-algorithm

Lasagni G (2019) Banking supervision and criminal investigation. Comparing the EU and US experiences. Springer, Cham

Liao N, Tian S, Wang T (2009) Network forensics based on a fuzzy logic and expert system. Comput Commun 32(17):1881–1892

Liberatore F, Quijano-Sánchez L, Camacho-Collados M (2019) Applications of data science in policing: VeriPol as an investigation support tool. Eur Law Enforc Res Bull IV:89–96. https://www.cepol.europa.eu/sites/default/files/European_Law_Enforcement_Research_Bulletin_Spe cial_Conference_Edition_Nr4_web.pdf

Lightbourne J (2017) Damned lies & criminal sentencing using evidence-based tools. Duke Law Technol Rev 2017:327–343

Manes V (2020) L'oracolo algoritmico e la giustizia penale: al bivio tra tecnologia e tecnocrazia. In: Ruffolo U (a cura di) Intelligenza artificiale. Il diritto, i diritti, l'etica. Giuffrè, Milano

Martin DL (2002) Lessons about justice from the "Laboratory" of wrongful convictions: tunnel vision, the construction of guilt and informer evidence. UMKC Law Rev 70:847–864

Maxwell W, Bertrand A, Vamparys X (2020) Are AI-based Anti-Money Laundering (AML) systems compatible with European fundamental rights? ICML 2020 Law and Machine Learning Workshop. https://hal.archives-ouvertes.fr/hal-02884824v4/document

Meissner CA, Kassin SM (2004) You're guilty, so just confess! Cognitive and behavioural confirmation biases in the interrogation room. In: Lassiter GD (ed) Interrogations, confessions and entrapment. Springer, New York, pp 85–106

Meyers M, Rogers M (2004) Computer forensics: the need for standardization and certification. Int J Digit Evid 32(2):1–11

Miller K (2014) Total surveillance, big data, and predictive crime technology: privacy's perfect storm. J Technol Law Policy 19:105–146

Mutsaers P, van Nuenen T (2020) Predictively policed: the Dutch CAS case and its forerunners. https://www.researchgate.net/publication/346593158_Predictively_policed_The_Dutch_CAS_case_and_its_forerunners

Nickerson R (1998) Confirmation bias. A ubiquitous phenomenon in many guises. Rev Gen Psycol 2(2):175–220

Niller E (2019) Can AI be a fair judge in court? Estonia thinks so. Wired, 25 March 2019. https://www.wired.com/story/can-ai-be-fair-judge-court-estonia-thinks-so/

O'Neil C (2016) Weapons of math destruction: how big data increases inequality and threatens democracy. Crown Publishers, New York

Oswald M, Grace J, Urwin S, Barnes GC (2018) Algorithmic risk assessment policing models: lessons from the Durham hart model and 'Experimental' proportionality. Inf Commun Technol Law 27(2):223–250

Panagiotou A, Ghita B, Shiaeles S, Bendiab K (2019) FaceWallGraph: using machine learning for profiling user behaviour from Facebook Wall. In: Galinina O, Andreev S, Koucheryavy Y, Balandin S (eds) Internet of Things, smart spaces, and next generation networks and systems - 19th international conference, NEW2AN 2019, and 12th conference, ruSMART 2019, Proceedings. Lecture Notes in Computer Science, vol 11660, Springer, pp 125–134, 19th International Conference on Next Generation Teletraffic and Wired/Wireless Advanced Networks and Systems, NEW2AN 2019, and 12th Conference on Internet of Things and Smart Spaces, ruSMART 2019, St. Petersburg, Russian Federation, 26/08/1

Parodi C, Sellaroli V (2019) Sistema penale e intelligenza artificiale: molte speranze e qualche equivoco. Riv trim Dir pen cont 6:47–203

Pasquale F (2015) The Black Box Society: the secret algorithms that control money and information. Harvard University Press, Cambridge

Perry WL, McInnis B, Price CC, Smith SC, Hollywood JS (2013) Predictive policing. The role of crime forecasting in law enforcement operations, RAND. Safety and Justice Program, USA, Library of Congress, pp 1–155

Popper K (2002) The logic of scientific discovery, 2nd edn. Routledge (original work published in 1934)

Quattrocolo S (2020a) Artificial intelligence, computational modelling and criminal proceedings. A framework for a European legal discussion. Springer, Cham

Quattrocolo S (2020b) Speech at the debate of 20 October 2020, published in Processo penale e Intelligenza Artificiale, Position Paper/1., Fondazione Leonardo, pp 17 ff.

Raeder M (2003) What does innocence have to do with it? A commentary on wrongful convictions and rationality. Mich State Law Rev 2003:1315–1335

Rao AS, Georgeff MP (1991), Modeling rational agents within a BDI-architecture. In Allen J, Fikes R, Sandewall E (eds) Proceedings of the 2nd international conference on principles of knowledge representation and reasoning (KR 1991), Cambridge, USA, Morgan Kaufmann, April 22–25, pp 473–484

Recent Cases (2017) State v. Loomis, Wisconsin Supreme Court requires warning before use of algorithmic risk assessments in sentencing. Harv Law Rev 130:1530 ff. https://harvardlawreview.org/2017/03/state-v-loomis/

Rifkind M (2014) Report on the intelligence relating to the murder of Fusilier Lee Rigby. House of Commons, Williams Lea Group on behalf of the Controller of Her Majesty's Stationery Office

Roberts M, Driggs D, Thorpe M et al (2021) Common pitfalls and recommendations for using machine learning to detect and prognosticate for COVID-19 using chest radiographs and CT scans. Nat Mach Intell 3:199–217

Russell SJ, Norvig P (2010) Artificial intelligence: a modern approach, 3rd edn. Prentice Hall, Englewood Cliffs

Sartor G, Lagioia F (2020) Le decisioni algoritmiche tra etica e diritto, in Intelligenza artificiale. In: Ruffolo U (a cura di) Intelligenza artificiale. Il diritto, i diritti, l'etica. Milano, Giuffrè, pp 63–88

Scrivens R, Gaudette T, Davies G, Frank R (2019) Searching for extremist content online using the dark crawler and sentiment analysis. In: Deflem M, Silva DMD (eds) Methods of criminology and criminal justice research. Emerald Publishing, pp 179–194

Seidensticker K, Bode F, Stoffel F (2018) Predictive policing in Germany. https://www.researchgate.net/publication/332170526_Predictive_Policing_in_Germany

Stallard T, Levitt K (2003) Automated analysis for digital forensic science: semantic integrity checking. In: Proceedings of the nineteenth annual computer security applications conference, December 8–12. IEEE Computer Society, Washington, DC, pp 160–167

Steinbrook R (1992) The Polygraph Test: a flawed diagnostic method. N Engl J Med CCCXXVII (2):122–123

Sunstein CR (2019) Algorithms, correcting biases. Soc Res Int Q 86(2):499–511

Susskind R (2017) Tomorrow's lawyers. An introduction to your future, 2nd edn. Oxford University Press, Oxford

Tolkien JR (2004) The Lord of the Rings. Harper Collins Ebook (original work published in 1954)

Toor A (2016) Automated systems fight ISIS propaganda, but at what cost? The Verge http://www.theverge.com/2016/9/6/12811680/isis-propaganda-algorithm-facebook-twitter-google. Accessed 27 July 2021

Ubertis G (2020) Intelligenza artificiale, giustizia penale, controllo umano significativo. Riv Trim Dir pen cont 4:75–88

Vermaas O, Simons J, Meijer R (2010) Open computer forensic architecture a way to process terabytes of forensic disk images. In: Huebner E, Zanero S (eds) Open source software for digital forensics. Springer, New York, pp 45–67

Vogel B, Maillart JB (eds) (2020) National and International Anti-Money Laundering Law. Developing the architecture of criminal justice, regulation and data protection. Intersentia, Antwerp

Wason PC (1960) On the failure to eliminate hypotheses in a conceptual task. Q J Exp Psychol 12(3):129–140

Wooldridge M (2009) An introduction to multiagent systems, 2nd edn. Wiley, pp 1–453

Wooldridge M, Jennings NR (1995) Intelligent agents: theory and practice. Knowl Eng Rev 10: 115–152

Online Hearings and the Right to Effective Defence in Digitalised Trials

Antonella Falcone

Abstract This chapter focuses on practical and legal issues concerning online hearings in domestic and transnational criminal proceedings, where parties generally appear through videoconference or web conference. Remote attendance to the hearings, indeed, cannot be considered as equivalent to the physical one and implies risks to the right to an effective defence in criminal proceedings. This latter can be undermined if new technologies are deployed in ways that do not satisfy specific needs of suspects and defendants. Certainly, outcomes vary, mostly depending on videoconferencing techniques, parties involved, or types of procedural activities being held on the occasion that the attendance is partly or fully virtual and, above all, on the legal systems' features. The fact-finding process may be also shaped differently under the ICTs influence; however, it is undisputed that the use of technological devices may never end up denying the fundamental values of the criminal procedure.

A. Falcone (✉)
Law Department, University of Messina, Messina, Italy
e-mail: antonella.falcone@unime.it

1 Introduction

In the digital era, recourse to information and communication technology tools (hereinafter, ICTs)[1] entails several advantages in the daily administration of criminal justice,[2] but it also raises a number of practical and legal problems for the fairness of the trial and, above all, for the right to an effective defence.[3]

One of the most troublesome issues concerns online hearings in both domestic and transnational criminal proceedings, where people involved generally appear through videoconference or web conference. Remote attendance to the hearings, indeed, cannot be considered as equivalent to the physical one thus posing risks to the right to be fairly heard.

This topic has drawn extraordinary interest during the worldwide outbreak of the COVID-19 pandemic, since many States had to suspend in-person proceedings or replace them with virtual attendance of (all) parties to the hearings.[4] However, legal practitioners and commentators have not unanimously welcomed the extensive use of virtual connections.[5] Some of them warned that, under the excuse of the health emergency, new criminal procedural models, affecting the steady core of criminal justice,[6] could be introduced.[7]

---

[1] ICTs encompass videoconferencing platforms, case management systems (CMSs), digital communication and data exchange platforms, artificial intelligence (hereinafter, AI) and machine-learning technologies.

[2] See Council of the European Union (2020), Access to justice: seizing the opportunities of digitalization, Council Conclusions 11599/20, Brussels, 8 October 2020; European Commission (2020), Digitalization of justice in the European Union: A toolbox of opportunities, COM/2020/710 final, Brussels, 2 December 2020. Within the CoE, the European Commission for the Efficiency of Justice (CEPEJ) has sustained the digital transformation of the judiciary and the implementation of digital justice. See https://www.coe.int/en/web/cepej/cepej-work/quality-of-justice. EU also has promoted the development of e-justice over the last decade. See the current 2019–2023 Action Plan European e-Justice (2019/C 96/05).

[3] Gibbs (2017), pp. 1–35.

[4] For an examination of the challenges that the European Courts faced during the first wave of the health emergency, see the OCSE report, The functioning of Courts in the Covid-19 pandemic: A Primer, 2 November 2020, available online at https://www.osce.org/odihr/469170.

[5] The topic has drawn different critical positions. See, among the others, Manes and Trevi (2020); Gialuz and Della Torre (2020). On the contrary Susskind, calling for change, urged a new mindset in thinking about the future of courts; Susskind (2019). After the Covid-19 outbreak, this author fostered a "new website designed to help judges, lawyers, court officials, litigants, court technologists to share their experiences of remote alternatives to traditional court hearings", available online at https://remotecourts.org.

[6] State intervention in criminal procedural law deriving from "exceptional dangerous situations" is common. In Italy, for example, the so-called "security packages" coped with unreal urgent criminal phenomena through the introduction of penalties, limitations of guarantees and freezing or the exclusion of prison law benefits. See Orlandi (2020), pp. 7 ff; Mazza (2020), p. 1.

[7] For example, see the letter sent by *"Camere penali"* to the Italian Ministry of Justice Alfonso Bonafede of 15 April 2020, https://www.camerepenali.it/public/file/Documenti/2020-04-15-Lettera-MinistroBonafede.pdf. In Spain, the *"Asociacion Libre de Abogados y Abogadas"* (ALA)

Certainly, ICTs have brought about significant changes on both traditional roles of professionals (lawyers, prosecutors, judges) and individuals (suspects, defendants, witnesses, victims and even third parties) involved in criminal proceedings[8] and on the fact-finding process.[9]

Based on this, we should examine how online hearings can be harmonised with procedural law systems characterised by rights and safeguards and whether "virtual attendance" to the hearings can be partially equated to the physical participation without worsening the defence rights,[10] such as the right to be present at hearings, to prepare the one's defence in an adequate timeframe and adequate facilities, to the access to a lawyer, as well as the submission and examination of evidence, to the access to witnesses, to the right to translation and interpretation.

After some introductory remarks, the paper will address the use of online hearings at the national, international, and transnational levels, before and during the Pandemic. In so doing, relevant case law will be examined and examples of specific legal systems, where available, will serve as exemplifications. Finally, we will expose some critical observations.

---

has asked the Spanish Supreme Court to ensure the rights of the defendant to obtain proper legal assistance, www.fairtrials.org.

[8] Susskind (2017), p. 11. See also Jeuland (2019) p. 194 about the use of AI in trials. This author has stressed the importance of considering both the individual interests of the parties and their rational and emotional complexity, thus justifying the need for a "principle of attendance" that gives parties the right to ask for a physical attendance at the hearing to express themselves properly. This assumption has been shared by the French *Conseil d'État* which, during the recent Pandemic, suspended the use of videoconferencing in criminal hearings for the most serious crimes in the *Cours d'Assises* and *Cours criminelles* alleging a "serious and manifestly illegal violation of the rights of defence and of the right to a fair process". Cf. *Conseil d'État*, rulings nos. 446712, 446724, 446728, 446736, 446816 of 27 November 2020, available online at https://www.conseil-etat.fr/actualites/actualites/le-juge-des-referes-suspend-la-possibilite-d-utiliser-la-visio-conference-lors-des-audiences-devant-les-cours-d-assises-et-les-cours-criminelles.

[9] Rudnev and Pechegin (2019), highlight a "transformation of the evidentiary theoretical model" because of digitalisation of proceedings and "the emergence of new types of evidence, suggesting their gradation in legal force, even in an adversarial framework". This approach was developed for the first time in judicial practice of the International Criminal Court, which built a "hierarchy of evidence inherent in the inquisitorial form of the process in historical retrospect". 6th International Conference on Social, economic, and academic leadership (ICSEAL-6-2019), p. 324.

[10] For example, to meet the security interests that characterise types of charges and of authors, Italy establishes a legislative *fictio* equating the place of the audio-visual connection "to the courtroom" (Art. 146-*bis*, para. 5, CCP).

2   General Remarks and Definitions

To properly tackle the issues regarding the effectiveness of the defence right in the digitalised trials, we should clarify the meaning of the term "hearing" in advance.[11]

In criminal proceedings, "hearing" usually indicates a session before a judge involving a specific question before the trial itself (for example, the preliminary hearing[12]) or a court session where primarily evidence is introduced before a judge or a jury (*bench trial*), called upon to convict or acquit the accused.

The term normally refers to as a "space" of confrontation between the parties, who preferably should have the opportunity to present and defend their arguments in conditions of equality of arms before an independent and impartial judge.[13] In particular, this notion fits the adversarial model[14] and presupposes the respect of defence rights in both pre-trial and trial-hearings,[15] although in different terms.

Furthermore, a "hearing" can relate to instances of examination of witnesses, defendants, and private parties in the criminal trial or to interrogation of persons of interest in the case or suspects during the preliminary investigations.

This paper pays particular attention to online hearings held during the trial phase and to the role of defendants in this context.

---

[11] To identify the correct understanding is a matter of legal translation in terms of intercultural activity, since the legal system of a country is, perhaps, the most authentic expression of its culture. In the specific case of English, translation is particularly difficult, due to the conceptual and terminological features of the Anglo-American legal systems compared to the European ones and to the spread of English as a "*lingua franca*" or a "language of communication" in a multilingual scenario. On this topic, see Ruggieri et al. (2013).

[12] We should also bear in mind hearings held to formalise the indictment; to discuss of pre-trial procedural measures or coercive measures; hearings regarding the closure of the investigation or in which the defendant incriminates himself (abbreviated) or asks for alternatives to criminal proceedings (conditional suspensions of the proceedings and reparations agreements).

[13] This concept allows some exceptions. For example, in Strasbourg case law, the hearing that follows the "appeal on the point of law" may exclude the presence of the accused if only legal issues must be discussed. Another exception may be that of *in camera* hearings, where the attendance of the defendant can be excluded.

[14] See ECtHR, *Borgers v. Belgium*, judgment of 30 October 1991, App. No. 12005/86; ECtHR, *Makhfi v. France*, judgment of 19 October 2014, App. No. 59335/00; ECtHR, *Khuzv v. Ukraine*, judgment of 21 October 2010, App. No. 45783/05; ECtHR, *Diriöz v. Turkey*, judgment of 31 May 2012, App. No. 38560/04.

[15] The Strasburg judges have broadened the scope of the concept of "accusation", under Art. 3 (a) ECHR, thus strengthening the protection of the defence rights in the pre-trial phase. Indeed, as outlined by the European Court of Human Rights, the term "accusation" consists of "official notification issued to an individual by the competent authority in which affirms that he has committed a crime" or "other measures that lead to the same consequences and that substantially influence the situation of the suspect". See ECtHR, *Öztürk v. Germany*, 21 February 1984, App. No. 8544/79; ECtHR, *Kamasinski v. Austria*, 19 December 1989, App. No. 9783/82; ECtHR, *Drassich v. Italy*, 11 December 2007, App. No. 25575/04; ECtHR, *Mattei v. France*, 19 December 2006, App. No. 34043/02; ECtHR, *Pellisier and Sassi v. France*, 25 March 1999, App. No. 25444/94.

In addition, given that new ICTs can be distinguished according to several criteria,[16] we must delimit the area of our interest. For the purposes of this study, the expression "courtroom technologies" seems to be appropriate because it includes both the "venues" in which, and modalities by which, justice is delivered.[17] This definition concerns technology used to introduce evidence at trial (so-called illustrative evidence[18]), computer-generated evidence (substantive evidence[19]) and technological means providing remote attendance in cases of testimony, examination, and recognition in criminal proceedings.[20]

Among the latter, video-teleconferencing (also defined as virtual[21] or remote[22]) displays situations in which judges, legal representatives, witnesses, accused and other parties do not gather physically at the same venue but through ICT tools.[23] Audio hearings, in turn, are carried out by telephone or by audio-only systems, while video hearings are mostly held online using Zoom, Microsoft Teams, Meet, Polycom, CISCO Webex, WebRTC, TrueConf, and so on. Moreover, they can be either with partial audio and video (blended or hybrid), when just some of the participants are connected, or with full audio and video, if all parties use audio or video transmissions.

Regardless of the terminology, video-teleconferencing (hereinafter, VTC) typically takes place instantly[24] and often presupposes an Internet connection. VTC, indeed, entails "the use of two-way simultaneous transmission of audio-visual information picked up by cameras and microphones on one hand communicated by monitor and speakers on the other hand".[25]

A further possibility is to record a (remote) hearing and play it back in a higher instance, during the appeal proceedings or the proceedings before the Supreme Court. Recording is generally called 'video link technology'. It is important to

---

[16] Channels, instruments, and types of transmitting data may convey the same contents differently and vice versa: for example, one may access a website throughout a telephone cord or a mobile phone, a laptop or a television.

[17] Lederer (2004).

[18] They concern the introduction of evidence at trial (power point, diagrams, charts, etc.).

[19] They include scientific animations.

[20] See Simonato (2014), p. 292.

[21] To define the term "virtual" is not easy, given that it comprises the idea of potential and theoretical facts or, instead, simulated or constructed to be real facts.

[22] On the semantic scope of the term remote imported in Italy from the Anglo-Saxon experience, see Amodio (2020), available at https://www.sistemapenale.it/it/opinioni/amodio-basta-storpiare-da-remoto, who pointed out that "while the Italian adjective 'remote' looks at the past because it refers to the distance in time, the English term 'remote' can designate an aptitude to project oneself into the future by overcoming the distance in space, thus operating in different places".

[23] Courts used remote technology even before internet when closed-circuit television (CCTV) facilitated remote appearances.

[24] See Lederer (2004), p. 18.

[25] See Garofano (2007), p. 683. The term remote, in addiction, encompasses papers hearings, that do not fall under the field of this investigation.

note that in several countries, such as in UK, video link evidence is synonymous with videoconferencing. Thus, "before issuing a request for mutual legal assistance for videoconferencing, States should clarify the terminology used in the executing countries".[26]

Interestingly, digital forensic researchers have explored the possibilities of using models of Extended Reality (XR), such as Augmented Reality (AR), Virtual Reality (VR), and Mixed Reality (MR) in the courtroom.

More than 10 years ago, Collaborative Virtual Environments (CVEs) had already been proposed as a substitute for videoconferencing.[27] CVEs are computer intermediated communication systems "that allow geographically separated individualities to interact verbally and nonverbally in a participated virtual space in real time". They work like videoconferences, however, as "instead of sending video signals over a network, they send information concerning the actions of digital models".[28] In order to do so, optic detectors and cameras track the movements of avatars[29] and render their actions via incorporations visible to other interactants of a virtual reality. Despite all this, "the applications of CVEs for collaboration and interaction of possibly many participants that may be spread over large distances has remained largely outside legal practice".[30]

Moreover, the Pandemic has shown growing interest—especially for commercial purposes—in the use of 3D light projections of people (holograms[31]) physically miles away in a different location. Although this technology is still evolving, it could provide a good solution to hear defendants and witnesses, whenever they cannot attend a court hearing personally.

3   Online Hearings Before and During the Pandemic: A Brief Overview

Before the pandemic period, the use of audio and video connections in criminal justice varied within and outside the European Union. A study conducted by the European Commission in relation to all the 27 Member States showed that the use of videoconferencing for hearings in criminal cases was possible, for all situations detected, only in 11 countries (42%), while this technology was partially allowed in

---

[26] Manual on Videoconferencing Legal and Practical Use in Criminal Cases, p. 13, available online at www.unodc.org.

[27] See Bailenson et al. (2006).

[28] Bailenson et al. (2006), p. 269.

[29] An avatar is the representation of a person in a virtual environment.

[30] See Erra et al. (2021), p. 2.

[31] Hologram is "a three-dimensional image reproduced from a pattern of interference produced by a split coherent beam of radiation (such a laser)". See https://www.merriam-webster.com/dictionary/hologram.

hearings in 14 countries (54%). Only in one Member State (4%), remote hearings were not possible in any of the explored scenarios.[32]

Germany—where the presence of the accused at trial is generally mandatory[33]—regulates videoconferencing for hearing witnesses whose safety could be at stake, as well as for children and vulnerable victims.[34] In Spain, interrogations, testimonies, confrontations, explorations, reports, ratification of the experts and hearings are carried out publicly before a judge or court with the presence or intervention of the parties, except in cases provided for by law.[35] In Italy, since the beginning of the nineties, the fight against serious crimes, such as mafia crimes, has given rise to video and audio usage in the criminal trial to question witnesses and defendants

---

[32] Read the results on https://ec.europa.eu/info/sites/default/files/swd_digitalisation_en.pdf.

[33] In a case regarding the enforcement of a EAW for the purpose of an execution of a sentence held *in absentia* in the issuing country, the German Constitutional Court has linked the attendance to the criminal process to the *Schuldprinzip* and, in turn, to the human dignity (Art. 1 GG). See *BVerG*, *Solange III*, ruling no. 2735/14 of 15 December 2015, in which it was questionable whether the complainant would have the opportunity of a new evidentiary hearing against the judgment *in absentia* at the appeal stage in Italy. Hong (2016) states that: "In Solange III the Constitutional Court rightly refers to the guilt principle in criminal law, that it has long since derived from human dignity. It could easily additionally have drawn on its rich case law on other specific rights, namely the rights to a fair trial Art. 2(1) in conjunction with [Art. 20(3) Basic Law] and the right to a hearing [Art. 103(1) Basic Law] to justify the conclusion, that the dignity core of these rights or, as the Court puts it, the 'minimum guarantees of the rights of the accused in criminal trials' have been violated". Cf. Pollicino and Bassini (2019), pp. 527 ff.; Demetrio Crespo and Sanz Hermida (2019), pp. 559 ff.

[34] §§ 58b, 247a (2) Criminal Procedural Code, *Gesetz zum Schutz von Zeugen bei Vernehmungen im Strafverfahren und zur Verbesserung des Opferschutzes*. See Rafaraci (1999), p. 247. Video hearings are also possible in civil lawsuits pursuant to section 128a of the German Code of Civil Procedure (ZPO).

[35] See Art. 229(1, 2), Judiciary Act. Since 2003 hearings by videoconference (Organic Law no. 13 of 24 October 2013, which added section 3 of Art. 229) the above mentioned procedural activities may be carried out through videoconference or another similar system that allows two-way and simultaneous communication of image and sound and visual, auditory and verbal interaction between two geographically distant people or groups of people, ensuring in any case the possibility of cross-examination in criminal hearings and confrontation of the parties and the safeguarding of the right of defence, when so agreed by the judge or court. The first Pandemic online hearings took place in May 2020. See Royal Law-Decree no. 16/2020, on Procedural and Organisational Measures to deal with COVID-19 in the Field of the Administration of Justice.

(Art. 147-*bis* CCP).[36] Belgium allows hearing of witnesses, experts and suspects throughout videoconferencing, although during the preliminary investigation.[37]

Outside Europe, Australia treats the hearing of vulnerable witnesses and those held in situation where it is helpful to reduce the shortcomings of the large geographical distances separately.[38] In the US, remote connections are used to hear vulnerable witnesses[39] or, during the initial appearance, when a suspect is brought before the court within 24 h after the arrest.[40]

During the Pandemic, the measures enacted to handle the health crisis have allowed for the first time to carry out criminal proceedings entirely through videoconferencing. The rules for remotely holding criminal hearings during the health emergency were mostly the result of agreements and memorandum signed by single judicial offices with representative bodies of lawyers and local criminal chambers. In Italy, for instance, the Superior Council for the Judiciary (*Consiglio superiore della magistratura*) on 5 March 2020 adopted guidelines to coordinate emergency organisational planning from all judicial offices.[41] In Spain, the "*Consejo General del Poder Judicial*" (CGPJ) launched similar recommendations. UK enacted a

---

[36] The Law-Decree no. 306/1992, converted with amendments in Law no. 356 of 7 August 1992, introduced the Art. 147-*bis* of the implementing rules to the CCP. After the *Capaci* massacre, the law provided for the remote examination to protect individuals admitted to the protection programs. In 1998, Art. 146-*bis* of the implementing rules to CCP also provided for the remote participation of the accused at the trial. The Law-Decree of 18 October 2001, then Law no. 438/2001, enriched the subjective conditions for the application of remote attendance, including the charge of crimes pursuant to Art. 51 para. 3-*bis* of the Criminal Code, as well as of crimes committed under Art. 407 (2)(o) and (4) CCP. After the Law-Decree no. 103/2017, remote participation is current available in relation to offenses for which the accused are free, as well as for those in which they are witnesses. On this topic see, Rivello (2017).

[37] Consultative Council of European Judges (CCJE), Statement of the President of the CCJE, The role of judges during and in the aftermath of the COVID-19 pandemic: lessons and challenges, CCJE (2020)2, Strasbourg, 24 June 2020, p. 2.

[38] Rowden et al. (2010).

[39] See the case *Maryland v. Craig* where the court feared that a 6-year-old child, who had suffered sexual and physical abuse, would have been more traumatised if forced to testify before the defendant. US Supreme Court, ruling no. 89-478 of 27 June 1990 available online at https://www.oyez.org/cases/1989/89-478. In particular, the use of VTC testimony in Federal criminal trials raises issues about the meaning of the (face-to-face) Confrontation Clause (VI Amendment) and about how VTCs can satisfy the clause's fundamental guarantee properly. "The Supreme Court has made it very clear that a defendant's right to confrontation may be satisfied absent a physical, face-to-face confrontation, but only where denial of such confrontation is necessary to further an important public policy". In *Coy v. Iowa*, for instance, Justice Scalia explained that "it is every defendant's right to a face-to-face encounter with an adverse witness which lies at the core of a defendant's confrontation rights", as that right serves "to ensure the integrity of the fact-finding process". *Coy v. Iowa*, 487 U.S. 1012, 1020-21 (1988). On this topic, see Robinson (2021).

[40] Evert-Jan van der Vlis, Ministry of Security and Justice, The Hague, Videoconferencing in criminal proceedings, p. 13, available online at http://www.videoconference-interpreting.net/wp-content/uploads/2014/04/02_vanderVlis.pdf.

[41] See http://www.csm.it.

detailed guidance for professional participants in all the stages of criminal hearings, including consulting between the defendant and his/her counsel.[42]

The advantages that online hearings have provided during the health emergency to the functioning of court systems and, in turn, to the rule of law cannot be underestimated.[43] Overall, suspects were questioned in the police station remotely by the prosecutor or judge and legal assistance was delivered either via telephone or video. In pre-trial detention, defendants took part in proceedings through online connections installed in detention rooms. Hearings conducted through videoconference were held to present evidence before courts, or to discuss matters in an adversarial way.[44]

4 Remote Hearings in the Field of International and Transnational Criminal Justice

Recourse to video and teleconferencing has increased not only in several countries for domestic cases, but also at the international and transnational level[45] where the transfer of the evidence gathered in the "best place" is recurrent.[46]

The International Criminal Tribunal for the former Yugoslavia (ICTY) allows for remote participation to protect victims and witnesses, pursuant to the Rules of Procedures and Evidence. In the well-known judgment *Prosecutor v. Tadić*, the Court held that testimony introduced by videoconference cannot be as reliable as testimony presented in the courtroom. This different degree of reliability did not represent a revival of the inquisitorial principle at the international level; rather, it represented a compromise solution between different legal systems.[47]

The Statute on the International Criminal Court provides for a similar solution, thus requiring the ICC Trial Chamber to seek a proper trade-off between conflicting interests with a view to avoiding potential risks for the rights of the accused.[48] In criminal proceedings before the ICC attendance is required.[49] However, pursuant to

---

[42] https://www.gov.uk/guidance/joining-a-criminal-hearing-on-video-as-a-professional.

[43] Also, the ICT method of transmitting documents and briefs, the remote access to procedural files (telework) are certainly to be welcomed because they simplify the proceedings, thus avoiding backlogs and assuring access to the justice.

[44] Sanders (2021), pp. 3 ff.

[45] Videoconference is usually defined "rogatory of the third type". See Pisani (2002), p. 981.

[46] See Buzzelli (2017), p. 326. According to this author, the "best place" is that in which it is appropriate or possible to gather evidence or where evidence is simply located (so-called delocalisation).

[47] ICTY, *Prosecutor v. Tadić*, Decision on the Defence Motions to Summon and Protect Defence Witnesses and on the Giving of Evidence via Video-link, judgment of 25 June 1996, para. 21; available at https://www.icty.org/x/cases/dokmanovic/tdec/en/80429VL2.htm.

[48] See Evert-Jan van der Vlis, Ministry of Security and Justice, The Hague, p. 14.

[49] See ICC, *Prosecutor v. Lubanga*, ruling no. ICC-01/04-01/06-2662 of 20 January 2011, para. 13.

Articles 68 and 69 of the Rome Statute, the Chambers of the Court may, to protect vulnerable victims and witnesses or an accused, conduct any part of the proceedings in camera or allow the presentation of evidence by electronic or other special means (including videoconference or technologies to change the voice or reveal only her silhouette).[50]

In addition, in the field of Transnational Criminal Justice, at the European level, the Convention on mutual legal assistance stipulates that Member States can use teleconference when performing cross-border witness and experts' hearings.[51] However, this occurs under the condition that the person to be heard has given consent. Hearings using videoconferencing are also admitted considering the suspects' rights, "provided that the Member States involved deemed this to be necessary, their judicial authorities agree thereto and the suspect consents".[52] The drafters of the Convention subjected remote hearing to the previous consent of the accused, while requiring agreements between the Member States to enable the examination by videoconference and to lay down the procedures for its execution. The Brussels Convention, moreover, only provides for that the examination can be conducted directly or in any case directed, in accordance with the provisions of national law, by the judicial authority of the requesting State, referring to national law as to the establishment of the modalities and the possibilities of involvement of the defence. Thus, the assistance of a lawyer may be lacking implying concerns, especially in relation to situations, such as that of the examination of a co-defendant. Consequentially, the person questioned by videoconference in a transnational investigation can be deprived of legal assistance in cases that in a national investigation would instead guarantee it according to the law of the requested State.[53]

Cross-border videoconferencing, moreover, could require the assistance of a good interpreter if suspects or defendants do not speak the language of the requesting State, although the right to an interpreter is guaranteed only if deemed necessary (Art. 10).

Within the EU area, these rules have been replaced by Article 24 (Hearing by videoconference or other audio-visual broadcast) and Article 25 (Hearing by teleconference) of Directive 2014/41/EU on the European Investigation Order (EIO, hereinafter) which was enacted to strengthen the project of a European community of law and precisely the development of a common area of freedom, security, and justice (AFSJ).

Indeed, protection of the defence rights of suspects and accused persons in criminal proceedings is a fundamental challenge for the Union to maintain mutual trust between Member States and confidence in the European Union within the AFSJ

---

[50] On this topic see Triffterer (2008), Ambos (2003), and Broomhall (2003).

[51] Article 11. See Evert-Jan van der Vlis, Ministry of Security and Justice, The Hague, p. 15.

[52] Article 10.

[53] See Ruggeri (2015), p. 152.

pursuant to Article 67 TFEU.[54] This consideration explains the existence of specific obligations [Art. 24(2)(e) EIO Directive] imposed to the prosecuting authority, such as that of informing the defendants heard by videoconference about their rights.[55]

5 Online Hearings: Risks and Advantages for Criminal Proceedings

5.1 The Pros of Video and Audio Usage in Criminal Hearings

Online hearings entail unquestionable advantages in the development of the criminal trial, but also risks for the fair trial rights. Among the former, there is the possibility of a better management of court systems, mainly in terms of reasonable duration of the proceedings and efficiency of justice. The European Court of Human Rights, for example, convicted Finland for violation of fairness, since the lack of suitable technical equipment made it impossible to use the instrument of videoconferencing to carry out an examination of the witnesses, imposing a series of delays and an unreasonable extension of the procedural time.[56]

From the viewpoint of lawyers, online connections provide them with more time to prepare the defence since they do not have to reach the courtrooms and to find themselves sucked into the traffic.

A managerial idea of justice, however, requires a great deal of coordination and costs to assemble all the participants. Additionally, it calls into question the fairness and constitutional rights implicated in the criminal proceedings.[57] Therefore, any limitations to the rights of defence should be sufficiently counterbalanced.

Online hearings also raise the issue of the fulfilment of the court's publicity since the virtual courtroom is quite like *in camera* hearing. During the Pandemic, for example, the US state Michigan have moved towards "open justice" using YouTube. On the contrary, some European countries, such as Germany and Switzerland, have

---

[54] See also the Directives on the rights to interpretation and translation (2010/64/EU), to information (2012/13/EU), to access to a lawyer (2013/48/EU), to legal aid (2016/1919/EU), on the presumption of innocence (2016/343/EU) and procedural safeguards for children suspected or accused in criminal proceedings (2016/800/EU).

[55] What might happen is that the person to be heard has different *status* in the issuing Member State (witness) and in the executing Member State (suspect). Consequently, the interrogated person should be informed of the rights—recognised in both States—as a witness and as a suspect.

[56] See ECtHR, *Taavitsainen v. Finland*, judgment of 8 December 2009, App. No. 25597/07.

[57] ECtHR, *Van Mechelen and others v. Netherlands*, judgment of 23 April 1997, App. Nos. 55/1996/674/861-864, para. 58 had already stated that: "Having regard to the place that the right to a fair administration of justice holds in a democratic society, any measures restricting the rights of the defence should be strictly necessary. If a less restrictive measure can suffice then that measure should be applied". See Daniele (2017), pp. 136 ff.

prohibited filming court sessions, fearing that live hearings could affect the behaviour of both parties and judges.[58]

Video and audio connections are instruments that may divide, but also get individuals closer and can protect those involved in criminal proceedings.[59] The above-mentioned examples highlight that video and audio links are used to a limited extent in domestic cases, mostly to facilitate remote appearances to courtrooms in cases of serious offences or to protect certain categories of people. One might think of vulnerable witnesses or people exposed to reprisal by the suspect and his/her accomplices, children and victims who suffered sexual abuse, ancillary services, and prisoners.[60]

In cross-border cases, recourse to videoconference may be beneficial for suspects and defendants when European arrest warrants (EAWs) or International Arrest warrants (IAWs) are not strictly necessary because they are simply ordered to secure physical presence in the requesting State and there is no serious risk of flight, especially in low and medium criminality. Some UE States, indeed, require the presence of suspects and defendants for specific acts, especially in the first interviews carried out during the investigation or pre-trail detention or when the exercise of defence rights presupposes physical presence. Under this perspective, remote participation can serve as an alternative to a temporary transfer of suspects and accused under the European Arrest Warrant [Art. 18(1)(a) and Art. 19FD 2002/584/JHA[61]] and the European Supervision Order [Art. 19(4) FD 2009/829/JHA[62]].

These considerations could be extended to EIO procedures. Can the European investigation order be used as alternative means to temporary transfer, thus ensuring the participation of the accused in a criminal trial? Recital 25 sets out that EIO Directive applies to all stages of criminal proceedings; hearing by videoconference in the trial phase, however, will certainly not be used by Member States whose national law requires the physical attendance of the accused at trial. Furthermore, the same provision cannot be invoked by States which can only use videoconferencing to gather evidence; nevertheless, they may execute EIOs from Member States where

---

[58] See Sanders (2021), p. 14.

[59] Buzzelli (2017), p. 326.

[60] Remote attendance guarantees the prisoners' human dignity as they avoid prison transport trips, strip searches and waiting in holding cells.

[61] "Where the European arrest warrant has been issued for the purpose of conducting a criminal prosecution, the executing judicial authority must: (a) either agree that the requested person should be heard according to Art. 19; (b) or agree to the temporary transfer of the requested person". "The requested person shall be heard by a judicial authority, assisted by another person designated in accordance with the law of the Member State of the requesting court".

[62] "With a view to hearing the person concerned, the procedure and conditions contained in instruments of international and European Union law that provide for the possibility of using telephone and videoconferences for hearing persons may be used *mutatis mutandis*, in particular where the legislation of the issuing State provides that a judicial hearing must be held before a decision referred to in Article 18(1) is taken".

online hearing is allowed, provided that the rights of the accused and the fundamental principles of the executing State are guaranteed [Art. 24(2)(b) EIO Directive].

Finally, online attendance could also facilitate the exercise of "dual defence" when the defendants cannot pay two lawyers to take part in the hearing in two Member States.[63]

5.2 Audio-Video Hearings and the Right to be Present at Trial. The Risks for the Defence and Right to Confrontation

Significantly, the right to be present at trial is widely acknowledged in the European and international standards as a fundamental guarantee of the right to a fair trial. It is connected to the right to a public hearing, the right to defend oneself, the right to cross examination, the right to be assisted by an interpreter if the language used in the hearing is not understood. All these rights, indeed, could be hardly implemented without recognising the accused's right to be present.[64]

However, while ICCPR and Arab Human Rights Charter recognise respectively "the right of a person to be tried in his presence"[65] and that "everyone charged with a criminal offence has the right to be tried in his presence",[66] the European Convention on Human Rights simply grants the right "to defend himself in person or through legal assistance of his own choosing".[67]

According to the European Court of Human Rights (ECtHR), the right to be present in court does not always imply the right of personal attendance and, thereby, online participation does not necessarily constitute a violation of the right to a fair trial.[68] Furthermore, the ECtHR has clarified that the Convention does not specify the concrete modalities of exercising the right to defend oneself personally or to have

---

[63] See Bargis (2016), pp. 40 ff.

[64] Ruggeri (2019), pp. 581 ff.

[65] Article14(3)(d) ICCPR.

[66] Article 16(3) Arab Human Rights Charter.

[67] Article 6(3)(c). Furthermore, Article 8 of American Convention on Human Rights recognises "the right of the accused to defend himself personally or to be assisted by legal counsel of his own choosing". See Quattrocolo (2020), pp. 108–109.

[68] It is interesting to note that Directive 2016/343/EU on the strengthening of certain aspects of the presumption of innocence and of the right to be present at the trial in criminal proceedings, stipulates that the right of the accused to attend the trial is based on the right to a fair trial as one of the fundamental principles of a democratic society; this right should be guaranteed throughout the Union and implies a real "right to be present at the trial" (Art. 8). See Ruggeri (2015), pp. 135 ff. This author warns that the Directive has recognised the right of the accused to participate personally in his own trial in an excessively flexible way and that it has excluded the right to personal attendance from the intermediate and incidental decisions, where typically fundamental freedoms of the individuals are heavily affected.

the assistance of the lawyer.[69] It has also dealt with videoconferencing on several occasions and has deemed remote attendance to court hearings generally in line with the Convention only when based upon the principles of necessity and proportionality and provided that defence safeguards are fulfilled.[70] This occurs, for instance, where the witnesses were abroad, and it was excessively burdensome to request their presence, or the persons to be heard were invalid, or their physical safety was in danger.[71]

Moreover, during the hearings, the accused must be granted the possibility to confer confidentially with his/her lawyer.[72] Yet remote access to defence, wherever it takes place (in a police station, prison, or court), can make it very challenging for suspects and accused persons to interact confidentially and effectively with their lawyer.[73] Private communication between them must take place, for example, over a secure phone line or mobile phone or, if possible, separate videoconferencing equipment. Appearing in video and audio proceedings from the same location could certainly facilitate communication. However, lawyers are far from the courtroom and the interaction is not so immediate even if they hired assistants to be present at the hearing. Similar concerns occur when an interpreter is required.

Another problem stems from the accused's right to question or have questioned witnesses against him. As known, videoconferences can result either in the video-link participation of the defendant or in a video-link testimony. Since remote

---

[69] ECtHR, *Viola v. Italy*, judgment of 5 October 2006, App. No. 45106/04.

[70] See ECtHR, *Sakhnovskiy v. Russia*, judgment of 2 November 2010, App. No. 21272/03; ECtHR, *Yevdokimov and Others v. Russia*, judgment of 16 February 2016, App. Nos. 27236/05, 44223/05, 53304/07, 40232/11, 60052/11, 6438/11, 14919/12, 19929/12, 42389/12, 57043/12 and 67481/12; ECtHR, *Gorbunov and Gorbachev v. Russia*, judgment of 1 March 2016, App. Nos. 43183/06 and 27412/07.

[71] ECtHR, *Zhukovskiy v. Ukraine*, judgment of 3 March 2011, App. No. 45783/05; ECtHR, *Lawless v. United Kingdom*, judgment of 16 October 2012, App. No. 25307/10; ECtHR, *Papadakis v. Macedonia*, judgment of 26 February 2013, App. No. 50254/07. On the topic, see Bachmaier Winter (2013), pp. 127–146.

[72] It is worth mentioning that while the American Convention on Human Rights enshrines the right to communicate freely and privately with the counsel, the ECHR does not contain such provision. Nevertheless, the ECtHR considers the attorney-client confidentiality a fundamental right that can be exceptionally excluded by specific circumstances, such as the cases of protecting witnesses or preventing collusions. See, ECtHR, *S. v. Switzerland*, judgment of 28 November 1991, App. Nos. 12629/87 and 13965/88; ECtHR, *Brennan v. United Kingdom*, judgment of 16 October 2001, App No. 39846/98. See Bachmaier Winter (2022), pp. 10 ff.

[73] For instance, in the *Sakhnovskiy v. Russia* and *Gorbunov* and *Gorbachev v. Russia* cases, the ECtHR found a breach of the ECHR based on the violation of the privacy of a video-conferencing system installed and operated by the Russian police, as the sole means ensuring a person in remand prison to communicate with his lawyer for an appeal hearing.

It should be noted that in Latin America, especially in Brazil, allowing remote hearings is a setback in the fight against torture in custody since the physical presence of a defence lawyer and a judicial authority can help to discover torture against detainees. See "Fair Trials calls for ban on videoconferencing in custody hearings", available online at https://www.fairtrials.org/articles/news/brazil-fair-trials-calls-ban-videoconferencing-custody-hearings/.

examination excludes the possibility of a physical confrontation between the accused or his/her lawyer and the witnesses, video-examination is obviously not comparable to the traditional confrontation held in the courtroom. "The camera cannot perceive, and the television screen cannot display many of the details that would be evident if the witness were physically in the courtroom".[74]

The ECtHR has established that Article (6)(3)(d) ECHR must be interpreted in the sense that it recognises the accused' s right to an adequate and sufficient opportunity to examine the accused (even before the trial).[75] Despite this, the Strasbourg judges have not considered cross-examination to take necessarily place at the same time as the examination of the witnesses.[76]

5.3   The Evolution of the Criminal Hearings. From the "Sacred Space" to the "Virtual Space"

In criminal trial, rituality and symbolism have been conceived to foster the fundamental values, such as the fairness. Also, the space where the trial takes place is "ritual" and lighting, background, clothing, tone, and posture of the participants to criminal process are of paramount importance.[77] Conversely, online hearing changes the typical background and implies consequences on both the "physical" relationship between the parties and the "sacred nature" of the criminal trial.[78] A telling example of the way judges, parties and lawyers interact with each other in virtual hearings is provided by a US hearing, where a lawyer of the 394th District Court in Texas found himself with a cat face filter while using the laptop of an assistant.[79]

Moreover, personal attendance helps parties to assume better the significance of the court proceedings, and thus tend to comply more with the rules in a formal hearing context,[80] while video or web hearings may offer more chances for distractions and losing concentration, as they become tiring. It has been stressed that defendants can suffer from the so-called 'psychological divide' and a feeling of

---

[74] Garofano (2007), p. 702.

[75] See Casiraghi (2019), pp. 1363 ff.; Ubertis (2017), pp. 207 ff.; Orlando (2021), pp. 1 ff.

[76] ECtHR, *Carta v. Italia*, judgment of 20 April 2006, App. No. 4548/02; ECtHR, *Hummer v. Germania*, judgment of 19 July 2012, App. No. 26171/07.

[77] Garapon and Lassègue (2018), pp. 168–169.

[78] Janin (2011), p. 18.

[79] Available online at https://edition.cnn.com/2021/02/09/us/cat-filter-lawyer-zoom-court-trnd/index.html.

[80] "The irruption of technology into the 'sacred space' (the *ieròs kùklos* of Achilles' shield, described in the 18th book of the Iliad) breaks the hieratic solemnity of the three ancient units of time, place and action taken from Greek tragedy". Di Chiara (2007), p. 21.

detachment. Moreover, the conditions of the environment in which the accused, witnesses and experts render statements are surely significant.[81]

Against this framework, we should focus on the impact of virtual connections on the principles of orality[82] and immediacy[83] and on the defence rights.

The principles of immediacy and orality are usually interpreted as the right of the accused to a decision on the merits based on evidence directly observed and heard by the adjudicating judge. This means that the ruling must rely upon the direct assessment of the evidence, being able to see the parties' behaviour and listen to their arguments, to evaluate non-verbal communications (real-time facial expressions, body demeanour, voice inflexions) and reliability of the outcomes of examination.

Even the most sophisticated software and instruments designed for videoconferences will never assure the immediacy, as well as the proximity and the reality expected. Consequentially, how judges assess the witness testimonies or the defendant's statements turns out to be distorted. For example, since in videoconferencing looking at both the camera lens and the image of the other participants simultaneously is extremely difficult, if not even impossible, this would thus compromise the impression of eye contact. Conversely, it has been noted that CVEs systems can track each avatar's movement in the virtual environment and render the appropriate looking direction.[84] To convey the mutual gaze between parties and to promote a more immersive and lifelike alternative to video call, a good solution could be the full body and real time 3D holographic telepresence projection, where the involved person, who might be on the other side of the world, is physically standing from a portal machine in a room.[85] This technology also allows a multiple location hologram teleconference and, in turn, the interaction with as many parties as needed within a virtual environment.[86]

---

[81] See the survey Fielding et al. (2020). Under a different perspective, however, there are examples of witness or defendant who make authentic statements only in a less formal backdrop, such as in the case of video-link.

[82] This principle comprises the modalities by which the person who renders statements must be questioned as well as the handling of the legal issues and the issue of final decision. In the daily court proceedings, however, many are the trials which require written memories instead of oral evidence to better illustrate complex and technical facts.

[83] Pursuant to the immediacy principle, the case needs to be adjudicated by the same judges who directed the hearing. Exceptions are admitted. For example, the Italian Court of Cassation, in the ruling No. 41736 of 30 May 2019, of the judge [Art. 525(2) CCP] has admitted that the statements made before a different judge can be used for the decision simply reading them out, regardless of the consent or dissent of the parties.

[84] Bailenson et al. (2006), pp. 269 ff.

[85] See, for example the technology developed by Portl, available at https://www.portlhologram. com. The portals cost from $60,000 each. For example, Microsoft hologram communication technology is based on a headset called HoloLens 2, which cost $3500 per unit.

[86] For more details, see https://virtualongroup.com/full-body-real-time-3d-holographic-telepresence-projection/.

In a near future, therefore, witnesses, defendants, and expertise could render real-time statements as 3D projections before a holographic judge.[87]

Despite the potential benefits for the immediacy and *contradictoire*, the use of XR-technology in criminal justice will be manly dependent on its difficult implementation and the costs of installation. In addition, since CVE and holographic telepresence are outside the legal practise, no one knows exactly how concrete the risk of abuse will be in criminal trials, and whether they can strengthen or, rather, weaken the defence rights.

One might consider that, regardless of the system used (VTC, VR or CVE), technical and network problems (i.e., framing of the screen, noises, interference, etc.) can influence the effectiveness of the defence rights and, above all, the gathering of both oral and documentary evidence.

Regarding VTC, should the procedural acts, which have been already carried out, be repeated? What would happen, if the lawyer did not have adequate hardware and software to ensure the remote connection? Can a duty of "technological compliance", including costs, be imposed on the lawyer without affecting the effectiveness of the defence?[88] As Browning put it, "should judges have a duty of tech competence?"[89]

According to the Italian Court of Cassation, technical problems related to video-conference that do not allow the replacement of the personally-appointed lawyer—unable to activate the remote hearing—with a court-appointed lawyer leads to the nullification of the decision for violations of the right of defence due to the absence of the party or the defender.[90]

Some concerns about technical arrangements are related to the use and management of the microphones. For example, during the Pandemic, an Italian criminal lawyer of the Milan bar was unlawfully silenced with a click by the judge trying to handle the overlapping voices in a moment of lively dialogue between the parties.[91]

As has been noted, judges play a pivotal role in coordinating the order in which the parties speak and in giving instructions to the accused, the witness, or the interpreter during the hearing. These dynamics, of course, are enhanced in the transnational online examinations as well, where the problems are intensified by a large divide in the levels of digitalisation and quality of interpretations.

Moreover, defendants should be granted access to any documents. If remote technology is to be used for hearings involving files, and especially for submission

---

[87] In China, since 2017, civil cases have been treating by AI in the form of a holographic judge. See https://www.cravath.com/a/web/11730/NYLJ%2012-30.pdf.

[88] See Aprati (2021), p. 136.

[89] Browning (2020).

[90] Italian Court of Cassation, judgment no. 16120 of 5 February 2021.

[91] Interview available on https://extremaratioassociazione.it/9293-2/.

of documentary evidence, "courtroom technology" must be capable of presenting a clear and fast picture to all participants.[92]

5.4 The Enhancement of VTC Technology in Criminal Hearings

Are the principle of immediacy and orality violated by video-teleconferencing? The answer to this question is not simple since the procedural activities are not all the same. "Some of them can be better performed by video-teleconference rather than in a traditional way;[93] others can be carried out using ITs, but they imply some complications".[94] It mostly depends on techniques used, parties involved, or types of activities being held, during proceedings, on the occasion that the attendance is partly or fully virtual and, above all, on the legal systems' features.

The scope of the principle of immediacy has been softened. Within the ECHR framework, for example, although the preference is for the cross-examination to take place at trial, what matters is that the accused has the effective opportunity to cross-examine the witnesses during the entire proceedings. As Bachmaier Winter held, "when it comes to the only and decisive proof, respect for the principle of immediacy is required, but in all other cases economy and efficiency will prevail over strict immediacy".[95]

Nevertheless, audio and video tools can represent added values to the judgment in comparison with the "instruments" we already know—essentially writing and orality—and, above all, concerning the dialectical principle of *audi et alteram partem*—which must be understood not only as a guarantee but also as an epistemological method.

Under this logic, remote connection tools could be useful, for example, when the adversarial principles are not guaranteed or are only guaranteed in formal ways or for procedural acts which, previously, could not have been carried out at all or needed long time to be carried out without the use of such technologies.

From this point of view, the use of videoconferences techniques can help in reducing the duration of the hearings, avoiding continuances, breaking the principle

---

[92] According to Daniele digital technology gives rise to mixed evidence where sounds and images are probative elements of the statements whose genuineness must be verified. Daniele (2012), p. 8.

[93] The videorecording of the preliminary investigation activities constitutes a guarantee for the suspect because it avoids incorrect behaviours of prosecutors, witnesses and people interested in the case being hired with a video recording.

[94] Gori and Pahladsingh (2020), p. 576.

[95] Bachmaier Winter (2019), p. 325. See also ECtHR, *Chmura v. Poland*, judgment of 3 July 2012, App. No. 18475/05, para. 50.

of concentration, and preventing the risk that judges are not present during the whole trial; or, worse, that they forget what they have heard in the main hearing.[96]

One might also consider the possibility of recording a videoconference occurred in the investigative phase or in the first instance trial and reproducing it later, during the trial or the appeal. To this aim, hyperlinks including real-time transcription of the video-audio files would be useful for all parties of the criminal proceedings, facilitating judges, prosecutors, and lawyers to easily find the most relevant items of the transcriptions. Likewise, the possibility of tagging or marking parts of the transcriptions should be granted to defendants, so that they can reread significant passages or replay the videorecording to prepare the defence.

6 Conclusion

Following Prof. Nobili's words recalling the terminology used by Robespierre, it could be argued that criminal proceedings which lack forms and rules can no longer be defined as acts of justice but rather as *"opérationes sublimes"*. Therefore, even if ICTs today strongly influence fact-finding, they can never revert the essential values governing the criminal trial.

In the light of the analysis conducted, the assumption that only the physical presence in the courtroom where the trial is held could ensure the effectiveness of the right of defence is debatable. This essay has proven that, under certain circumstances, online hearings can assure the defence rights virtually, allowing the defendant to see and be seen by the witness, and vice versa, and comply with the defendant's right to cross-examination. As noted, the principles of immediacy and orality acknowledge a broad and flexible notion, providing the possibility of practicing it or not depending on the peculiarities of each case or admitting its replacement with the recourse to videoconferencing. Interestingly, the use of technology can improve the standards of procedural guarantees, as in the case of videorecording.

Notwithstanding this, the examples mentioned above have shown that there are still risks that the right to an effective defence in criminal hearings can be undermined if new technologies are deployed in ways that do not satisfy the specific needs of suspects and defendants.

Firstly, States should include minimum provisions in their Code of Criminal Procedures to clarify the participant's responsibilities in ensuring the proper functioning of the current technological tools, and the distribution of costs among the parties involved in setting up a remote hearing. To this purpose, protocols arranged during the Covid-19 emergency could provide useful examples.[97]

---

[96] See Aprati (2021), pp. 138 ff.

[97] See, among the others, *Guia para la celebración de actuaciones judiciales telemáticas – Poder Judicial*, available online at www.poderjudicial.es.

Secondly, as far as possible videoconferencing techniques, whether in national or cross-border proceedings, should be standardised and have the same configurations and parameters, such as those regarding the type of connections (*e.g.*, IP or ISDN) and the video and audio quality.

Furthermore, steps must be taken to enhance the principles of legality, necessity, accessibility, and transparency. Based on this, provisions such as the one contained in the EIO Directive (Art. 24) that allows the judicial authorities—in the case of a hearing via videoconference—to agree from time to time on the modalities to exercise remote examination of the declarant, does not appear perfectly in line with the principle of legality, which instead requires the timely predetermination of the rules to follow.

In cases of remote appearance, it is necessary to assess if it is legally provided and proportionate to the circumstances, as that represented by the person's impossibility to be physically present.[98] This usually happens at international and transnational levels, where the virtual examination could be the only way to protect the fundamental rights of the declarants, notwithstanding the weakening of the epistemic value of the *contradictoire*. In this specific field, a helpful tool can be represented by consultations between the issuing and executing authorities, which must check the proportionality in relation to the investigative or prosecution scopes of transnational justice.[99]

In addition, one of the guarantees to be respected is the person's consent,[100] which must be free and unequivocal before the video-audio connection, but also at the beginning of the hearings. When assessing whether consent is freely given and fully informed, one might consider the condition of women, children, older persons, persons with disabilities, persons deprived of liberty, and all those who may be suffering a manipulating situation.[101]

States should provide legal remedies to challenge a decision on audio-video conferencing and, at the transnational level, in both the issuing and executing countries.

Until now, and mainly during the sanitary emergency, private video-system have been widely used in criminal hearings, although they are mostly destined to

---

[98] Regarding the remote examination, see Daniele (2017), pp. 134 ff., who underlines the necessity to apply a threefold test to check: the suitability of videoconferencing to protect a declarant's right of equal importance with respect to the cross-examination; the capacity to safeguard the essentiality of *contradictoire* and the necessity of using video and audio links, whenever the recourse to other means is not possible.

[99] See Bachmaier Winter (2015), who fosters a consultation procedure between the requesting and executing authority to check the proportionality of the OEI required by the Directive, p. 52.

[100] It is questionable if the consent must be personally rendered by the defendant or, rather, whether it can be expressed through the appointed lawyer. See Constitutional Court, ruling no. 342 of 22 July 1999.

[101] See Grio (2014), pp. 123–125 for a detailed investigation on the privilege against self-incrimination in the context of videoconference and the guarantee against pressure on the moral freedom of expression and thoughts.

enterprises and offices and not to criminal trials; therefore, user-friendly instruments designed by a legal task force are recommended to comply with the defence rights and, above all, of the right to privacy. Personal data must, indeed, be secure and free from interception or misuse. To this aim, videoconferencing platforms should generate unique access links that can be used once. The transmission should be also encrypted to prevent the identification of the locations of the videoconference, especially in case of examination of vulnerable victims and witnesses or defendant under protection.

Interestingly, on one hand, the climate crisis may discourage long-distance travelling and encourage the use of remote hearings for environmental reasons. On the other hand, virtual connections present significant environmental impact due to data storing and transferring around the world.[102] For instance, turning off the camera or reducing streaming quality can significantly decrease the damage but it still raises troublesome issues for the defence rights. Inevitably, interruptions and delays in transmissions, poor sound, and video quality are not conducive to the defence's position.[103]

VTCs have been valuable tools for courts amid the recent public health crisis. Although courts have reopened, many have suggested expanding the use of video-teleconferencing for fully remotely holding criminal hearing, as a permanent feature of the justice system.[104] However, extending these practices needs caution, evaluation, and further research on their potential effects on the steady core of criminal procedure.

All in all, we feel like Alice in Wonderland who "enters a fantastical world, by climbing through a mirror into the world that she can see beyond it: there she finds that, just like a reflection, everything is reversed" and "moving away from something brings you towards it". Thus, is everything reversed or is the mirror showing us what we have failed or refused to see? What is certainly true is that walking away from "virtual reality" will inevitably bring us toward it.

Insofar as courts look at the future, there is no going back.

---

[102] A new study conducted by researchers from Purdue University, Yale University and the Massachusetts Institute of Technology has revealed that "just one hour of videoconferencing or streaming emits 150–1,000 grams of carbon dioxide". However, this result must be compared with that of a gallon of gasoline burned from a car which emits about 8887 g. See Purdue University, "Turn off that camera during virtual meetings, environmental study says: Simple tips to go green with your internet use during a pandemic", available online at www.sciencedaily.com/releases/2021/01/210114134033.htm.

[103] We are aware that more study about this subject is needed. All efforts to balance the environmental concerns and the right of defence rely upon philosophical thoughts that emphasise the "dignity of nature" in opposition to the anthropocentric view of the world which has, rather, characterised western ethics since the ancient Greeks. See Kohn (2013).

[104] See Bannon and Adelstein (2020).

References

Ambos K (2003) International criminal procedure: "Adversarial", "Inquisitorial" or mixed? Int Crim Law Rev 3:1–37

Amodio E (2020) Smettiamo di storpiare l'italiano con il lugubre "da remoto". www.sistemapenale.it. Last accessed 22 Sept 2021

Aprati R (2021) Il distanziamento sociale: un nuovo paradigma per il processo penale? Sistema Penale 2:131–142

Bachmaier Winter L (2019) Principio de inmediación y confrontation paralelismos, diferencias y tendencias en la prueba testifica. In: Ambos K, Malarino E (eds) Fundamentos de derecho probatorio en materia penal. Tirant lo Blanch, Valencia, pp 279–331

Bachmaier Winter L (2013) Transnational criminal proceedings, witness evidence and confrontation: lessons from the ECtHR's case law. Utrecht Law Rev 9(4):127–146

Bachmaier Winter L (2015) Towards the transposition of directive 2014/41 regarding the European investigation order in criminal matters. Eucrim 2:47–59

Bachmaier Winter L (2022) *Lawyer-client privilege* en la jurisprudencia del Tribunal Europeo de Derechos Humanos. In: Bachmaier Winter L (ed) Investigación penal, secreto profesional del abogado, empresa y nuevas tecnologías. Retos y soluciones jurisprudenciales. Thomson-Aranzadi, Cizur Menor, pp 1–448

Bailenson JN, Blascovich J, Beall AC, Noveck B (2006) Courtroom applications of virtual environments, immersive virtual environments, and collaborative virtual environments. Law Police 28(2):249–270

Bannon A, Adelstein J (2020) The impact of video proceedings on fairness and access to justice in court. https://www.brennancenter.org/sites/default/files/2020-09/The%20Impact%20of%20Video%20Proceedings%20on%20Fairness%20and%20Access%20to%20Justice%20in%20Court.pdf

Bargis M (2016) Il diritto alla "*dual defence*" nel procedimento di esecuzione del mandato di arresto europeo: dalla direttiva 2013/48/UE alla direttiva (UE) 2016/1919. Diritto penale contemporaneo 3:40–50

Broomhall B (2003) International Justice and the International Criminal Court: between sovereignty and the rule of law, 1st edn. Oxford University Press

Browning JG (2020) Should judges have a duty of tech competence? St Mary's J Leg Malpract Ethics 10(2):176–196

Buzzelli S (2017) Le videoconferenze transnazionali. Processo penale e giustizia 2:326–335

Casiraghi R (2019) I nuovi approdi "europei" del diritto al confronto. Cass pen 3:1363–1376

Daniele M (2012) La formazione digitale delle prove dichiarative. L'esame a distanza tra regole interne e diritto sovranazionale. Giappichelli, Torino

Daniele M (2017) La partecipazione a distanza allargata, superfetazioni e squilibri del nuovo art. 146-*bis* disp. att. c.p.p. www.dirittopenalecontemporaneo.it. Last accessed 21 Sept 2021

Demetrio Crespo E, Sanz Hermida ÁM (2019) In absentia proceedings in the framework of a human rights-oriented criminal law. The perspective of substantive criminal law. In: Quattrocolo S, Ruggeri S (eds) Personal participation in criminal proceedings. Springer, Cham, pp 559–576

Di Chiara G (2007) Il canto delle sirene. Processo penale e modernità scientifico-tecnologica: prova dichiarativa e diagnostica della verità. Criminalia 1:1–23

Erra U, Capece N, Lettieri N, Fabiani E, Banterle F, Cignoni P, Dazzi P, Aleotti J, Monica R (2021) Collaborative visual environments for evidence taking in digital justice: a design concept. Frame@hpdc, pp 33–37

Fielding N, Braun S, Hieke G (2020) Video Enabled Justice Programme: University of Surrey Independent Evaluation, 4 May 2020. http://spccweb.thco.co.uk/media/4807/university-of-surrey-video-enabled-justice-final-report-ver-11.pdf

Garapon VA, Lassègue J (2018) Justice digitale. Révolution graphique et rupture anthropologique. Press Universitaires de France, Paris, pp 1–364

Garofano A (2007) Avoiding virtual justice: video-teleconference testimony in federal criminal trials. Catholic Univ Law Rev 56(2):683–714

Gialuz M, Della Torre J (2020) D.l. 28 ottobre 2020, n. 137 e processo penale: sulla "giustizia virtuale" servono maggiore cura e consapevolezza. www.legislazione penale.it. Last accessed 15 Nov 2021

Gibbs P (2017) Defendants on video – conveyor belt justice or a revolution in access? www. transformjustice.org.uk. Last accessed 22 Feb 2022

Gori P, Pahladsingh A (2020) Fundamental rights under Covid-19: an European perspective on videoconferencing in court. ERA Forum 2:561–577

Grio A (2014) The defendant's right in the hearing by videoconference. In: Ruggeri S (ed) Transnational evidence and multicultural inquiries in Europe. Springer, Cham, pp 119–126

Hong M (2016) Human dignity and constitutional identity: the Solange-III: decision of the German Constitutional Court. *Verfassungsblog*. www.verfassungsblog.de. Last accessed 30 Nov 2021

Janin M (2011) La Vsioconférence à l'épreuve du procès equitable. Les Cahiers de la Justice 2:13–27

Jeuland E (2019) Justice numériquem justice unique? Les Cahiers de la Justice 2:193–199

Kohn E (2013) How forests think: toward an anthropology beyond the human. University of California Press, Berkeley

Lederer FI (2004) Courtroom technology: for trial lawyers the future is now. Popular Media. https:// scholarship.law.wm.edu/popular_media/41. Last accessed 10 Oct 2021

Manes V, Trevi M (2020) Processo penale online: opinioni a confronto. www.dirittodidifesa.eu. Last accessed 25 Sept 2021

Mazza O (2020) Distopia del processo a distanza. Archivio penale 1:1–10

Orlandi R (2020) Una giustizia penale a misura di nemici? Rivista Italiana di Diritto e Procedura Penale 2:7–15

Orlando C (2021) Testimonianza de relato e diritto al confronto tra ordinamento interno e giurisprudenza europea. www.legislazionepenale.it

Pisani M (2002) Rogatorie internazionali e videoconferenze, in Riv. dir. proc., p 981

Pollicino O, Bassini M (2019) Personal participation and trials *In Absentia*. A comparative constitutional law perspective. In: Quattrocolo S, Ruggeri S (eds) Personal participation in criminal proceedings. Springer, Cham, pp 527–558

Quattrocolo S (2020) Partecipazione al processo e contraddittorio. Legislazione penale, pp 107–120

Rafaraci T (1999) I mezzi audiovisivi nel processo penale tedesco. In: Zappalà E (ed) L'esame e la partecipazione a distanza nei processi di criminalità organizzata. Giuffrè, Milano, pp 245 ff.

Rivello P (2017) La disciplina della partecipazione a distanza al procedimento penale alla luce delle modifiche apportate dalla Riforma Orlando. www.dirittopenalecontemporaneo.it. Last accessed 2 Sept 2021

Robinson D (2021) Confrontation during COVID: a fundamental right, virtually guaranteed. Univ Miami Race Soc Just Law Rev 1(12):115–140

Rowden E, Wallace A, Goodman-Delahunty J (2010) Sentencing by videolink: the western Australian experience. Judicial College of Australia and ANU Sentencing Conference, Canberra

Rudnev V, Pechegin D (2019) The impact of the leading digital technologies on criminal proceedings: a case of video conferencing. In: 6th International conference on social, economic, and academic leadership (ICSEAL-6-2019). Advances in Social Science, Education and Humanities Research, 441, pp 323–329

Ruggeri S (2015) Procedimento penale, diritto di difesa e garanzie partecipative nel diritto dell'Unione Europea. Diritto penale contemporaneo 4:130–160

Ruggeri S (2019) Personal participation in criminal proceedings. In: *Absentia* trials and *Inaudito Reo* procedures. Solution models and deficiencies in ECtHR case-law. Springer, Cham

Ruggieri F, Rafaraci T, Di Paolo G, Marcolini S, Belfiore R (eds) (2013) Processo Penale, Lingua e Unione Europea. Cedam, Padova

Sanders A (2021) Video-hearings in Europe before, during and after the covid-19 pandemic. Int J Court Adm 12(2):1–21

Simonato M (2014) Defence rights and the use of information technology in criminal procedure. Revue internationale de droit penal 1(85):261–310

Susskind R (2017) Tomorrow's lawyer. An introduction to your future, 2nd edn. University Press, Oxford

Susskind R (2019) Online courts and the future of justice. University Press, Oxford

Triffterer O (2008) Commentary on the Rome Statute of the International Criminal Court: observers' notes: article by article, 2nd edn. Beck, München

Ubertis G (2017) Sistema di procedura penale, I, Principi generali 4. Giuffrè, Milano

The Digital Transition in Criminal Trials: New Promises, New Risks, New Challenges

Stefano Ruggeri

Abstract There is probably no field of social life which has not undergone radical changes in light of the ongoing digital transition, and the consequent transformation of almost every human activity. Law enforcement and criminal procedure could not lag behind these phenomena. It is therefore no surprise that a shift towards to new digital techniques has more or less slowly characterised the evolution of every criminal justice system.

This contribution critically analyses the main results of the researches collected in this volume, with the aim of highlighting the tensions between conflicting interests and values, but also the difficult trade-offs that ICT instruments today require, if not always to improve, at least to maintain sustainable levels of fairness in the administration of criminal justice. Doubtless, investigative and procedural fairness remains the ultimate goal of modern criminal justice systems, and mostly of European case-laws, and this goal can surely not be abandoned in our digitalised world. Focusing on the new promises, the new risks, and finally the new challenges concerned with the digital transition in the fields of criminal proceedings and crime prevention provides a useful *fil rouge* to grasp the complexity of the ongoing evolution of criminal justice.

1 Introduction

There is probably no field of social life which has not undergone radical changes in light of the ongoing digital transition, and the consequent transformation of almost every human activity. Criminality is no exception. The availability of ever more sophisticated digital tools has led to the emergence of new offences with unprecedented seriousness and aggressiveness. Criminal organisations, in particular, have soon taken advantage of the widespread digitalisation of various economic sectors

S. Ruggeri (✉)
Law Department, University of Messina, Messina, Italy
e-mail: stefano.ruggeri@unime.it

213

by adapting their approaches to traditional criminal activities. Law enforcement and criminal procedure could not lag behind these phenomena. It is therefore no surprise that a shift towards to new digital techniques has more or less slowly characterised the evolution of every criminal justice system.

From a purely legal viewpoint, the digitalisation of criminal proceedings has not always been seen in positive terms, or at least it has often raised significant concerns, particularly as far as digital investigative measures are at stake which magnify the effects of already existing tools, or reveal totally new risks for individual rights. Such concerns are certainly justified in several situations, as a number of relevant digital instruments undeniably aggravates the potential of the criminal process itself to interfere with fundamental rights. A further relevant outcome of the use of information and communication technology (hereafter, ICT), which is strictly connected to such developments, has been the broadening of the intrinsically widespread intrusiveness of criminal proceedings and particularly of criminal inquiries, which can today impinge upon rights and freedoms of different people other than the person against suspicion of guilt has arisen.

Notwithstanding all this, the prejudices that still exist towards the in-depth transformations that digitalisation is producing in criminal justice systems are largely unjustified.[1] While digital tools undoubtedly raise worrisome questions regarding the effective granting of individual safeguards, we can however not overlook the benefits of a number of digital instruments which have become more and more frequent in criminal investigations, and even more perhaps, in court proceedings.

Such benefits should however not be viewed in terms of the enhancement of state-related or security-based interests, nor should digitalisation be acclaimed as a means of reviving some old-fashioned prosecutorial or punitive goals of the criminal process (*jus puniendi*, *Strafanspruch*, *pretesa punitiva*, etc.). Neither should we accept every effect of the increasing use of information technology in criminal proceedings as the inevitable result of the overall digital transition in our world, which is expected to bring about economic advantages in criminal justice too, from both a managerial and efficiency-oriented perspective.

If it is true that, as is widely acknowledged, the achievement of well-functioning e-justice today constitutes a public value,[2] this can surely be observed in the field of criminal investigation and even of crime prevention. Certainly, the enormous changes that are taking place in pre-trial inquiries can better satisfy the need for more reliable fact-finding than in the past. This outcome can prove particularly beneficial in various ways and from different viewpoints, which reveals the usefulness of a multifaceted approach to this problem matter. For instance, while the possibility of carrying out investigations with a higher degree of preciseness and exhaustiveness than in the past clearly reduces the risk of unnecessary criminal-law actions, this result can in turn not only contribute to better allocating procedural resources and avoiding the overload of the overall judicial system, but, even more

---

[1] See Galgani (2022), pp. 1 ff.

[2] *Ibid.*, p. 2.

relevantly, can prevent the irreparable consequences of the undue exposure to *jus terribile* of the individuals concerned.

At any rate, the deployment of ICT tools in criminal investigations and new digital arrangements in court proceedings sets enormous challenges, which cannot be underestimated in the ongoing process of human rights orientation of the European criminal justice systems. In particular, in the light of the digitalisation of a relevant set of procedural activities, there is a need not only to redefine the features of traditional rights (*e.g.*, the right to free communication, the right to legal assistance, etc.), but furthermore—and most importantly—to determine the scope of new rights whose effective protection consequently requires new safeguards (*e.g.*, the right to respect for digital privacy in relation to encrypted communications and data).

The studies collected in this volume reveal with clarity the tensions between conflicting interests and values, but also the difficult trade-offs that ICT instruments today require, if not always to improve, at least to maintain sustainable levels of fairness in the administration of criminal justice. Doubtless, since investigative and procedural fairness remains the ultimate goal of modern criminal justice systems, this goal can surely not be abandoned in our digitalised world. It would surely exceed the scope of this contribution to critically assess all the questions raised and the problems analysed in this book. Therefore, I have decided to devote this concluding chapter to three main perspectives, which could provide our readers with a *fil rouge* to grasp the complexity of the digital evolution of criminal justice. These perspectives respectively relate to the new promises, the new risks, and finally the new challenges concerned with the digital transition in the fields of criminal proceedings and crime prevention.

2   New Promises

In the light of these brief introductory remarks, it is apparent that talking about 'new promises' regarding the digital changes which are occurring in investigative practices and criminal trials could be somewhat misleading, at least if one thinks of future perspectives that have yet not materialised. The increasing recourse to information and communication technology has already opened perspectives that until recently seemed to be even unimaginable. This is particularly evident in the investigative phase. Worldwide, law enforcement bodies have had to rapidly adapt their techniques to the technological evolution of criminal activities, going even beyond the possibilities provided (and often the limits established) by the domestic or international law in force. It has been noted that the growth of criminal activities through the web has made digital measures almost indispensable for both crime prevention and criminal inquiries. But the enactment and spread of new investigative practices have in turn favoured the updating of domestic legislation with bottom-up approaches which, despite still being far from being completed, have already delivered significant results in several jurisdictions.[3]

Nobody can ignore the great contribution that ICT tools have made, and will certainly more and more make in a near future, to the ascertainment of facts implying knowledge that could otherwise not be achieved, or could only be achieved with considerable difficulties. In particular, *Orlando*'s study has shown that drones have already been deployed with enormous success in investigating the dynamics of human actions that are potentially relevant from a criminal law perspective, or situations that would not be investigated properly with human resources. But the advantages of such high-precision devices are not restricted to the field of crime control or criminal investigation, for they also provide extremely useful information in the context of investigations of a different nature, whose task is neither to prevent nor to detect any sort of criminal (or even civil) liability. For example, drones have proven indispensable tools for purposes of safety investigations in the event of aircraft accidents in open sea, mountains, or other inaccessible places.[4] There is no doubt that the proper carrying out of such investigations holds essential relevance to determine the effective need for instituting a criminal inquiry, and therefore to avoid that innocent individuals are exposed to the risk of undue criminal proceedings.

But the potential of such digital tools is not limited to these important functions; they also allow for crime scene reconstruction with the utmost accuracy of details, thanks to high-developed technologies.[5] As pointed out by *Militello*, recourse to remote sensing techniques (*e.g.* LiDAR) today proves especially beneficial for purposes of geographic analysis and reconstruction of facts and events with (potential) criminal-law relevance.[6] Data and images obtained by means of drones and satellites provide essential elements for the so-called 'forensic architecture'.[7] It is worth observing that these uses of ICT tools enhance the role of the criminal process as a context in which facts belonging to a past already lost are re-presented rather than simply found or discovered in the present through procedural arrangements.[8]

While such results are already visible in investigative practices, other scenarios are instead still a future perspective in different relevant fields. This is the case for virtual hearings in which 3D images are designed to overcome the shortcomings and limits of (already outdated) online hearings, as highlighted by *Falcone*.[9] To be sure, a new generation of digital trials with AI holograms is already a reality in some countries (*e.g.* China) in procedures that mainly regard internet-related property

---

[3] Several European countries—such as Germany, Italy, and Spain—provide clear examples of such phenomenon. See the contributions of Foti and Di Nuzzo with extensive references to cyber-intercepts, and search and seizure of digital evidence, respectively.

[4] Orlando, Sect. 3.

[5] *Ibid.*

[6] Militello, Sect. 2.2.

[7] Militello, Sect. 3.

[8] Capograssi (1959), p. 57; Ferrua (2017), pp. 16 ff.

[9] Falcone, Sect. 3.

cases, contract disputes regarding e-commerce, and so on. Holographic judges, however, will certainly not be accepted in a near future in modern legal systems which are increasingly committed to ensuring a more human criminal justice to satisfy human needs. By contrast, holographic hearings, despite being still far from being launched in criminal cases, could provide numerous advantages. For instance, they could enable attendance at trial in much more real terms than (already) traditional 2D online hearings, thus contributing to enhancing the participatory side of criminal proceedings. The achievement of such degree of digital realism, moreover, is also likely to improve the protection of global goods, *e.g.* by way of satisfying the environmental sustainability of criminal proceedings. Thus, the beneficial effects of ordinary 2D-remote hearings by reducing the pollution caused by long-distance travelled should not be overestimated, taking into account that "virtual connections present significant environmental impact due to data storing and transferring around the world".[10]

Another promising field in which digitalisation can bring about considerable advantages in criminal proceedings is that of MAS technology. As *Lasagni* has extensively pointed out, Multi-Agent Systems can significantly contribute to maintaining a certain degree of openness in criminal inquiries by way of at least delaying (if not neutralising) the so-called 'tunnel vision effect'.[11] The extent to which biases are avoided and the competent bodies can broaden their investigative perspectives by such means, however, largely depends on MAS's ability to elaborate the widest possible number of hypothesis regarding the reconstruction of the facts and the identification of suspects, as well as on the capability of the "system operational manager to solve divergences".[12] In this way, Multi-Agent Systems can prove extremely useful to enhance the role of falsification in criminal inquiries—furthermore, as a means not only to reach the truth,[13] but also and more interestingly, to reveal mistakes, detect false or inadequate trails, and so on. All in all, MAS technology surely reveals a field in which interaction between AI and human intelligence is essential to find sustainable solutions that highlight the real need for instituting a criminal process.

3 New Risks

Notwithstanding these and many other pros, we have noted that the use of information and communication technology entails enormous risks, especially where digital measures of investigation are to be adopted which are able to interfere with fundamental rights. Their intrusive potential is not comparable with that of traditional

---

[10]Falcone, Sect. 6.

[11]Lasagni, Sect. 4.1.

[12]*Ibid.*

[13]In this sense Lasagni, Sect. 5.

investigations. Therefore, the dangers for individual freedoms we have to face while dealing with ICT systems are surely without precedent. Even traditional investigative means, such as communication intercepts and searches, can today handle an incredible amount of data regarding an unpredictable number of people acting, and largely living, in the digital space, as widely stressed by *Foti* and *Di Nuzzo* respectively. This outcome magnifies the reach of law enforcement and of criminal law action itself.

In the light of this, the maintenance of classic terminology and procedural notions is probably more than questionable to fully understand the peculiarities and to tackle the problems concerned with new digital means of investigation. Otherwise we would remain ensnared in a frame of categories that are no longer able to properly face the challenges arising from new measures, or to equalise investigative tools which cannot share the same classification. Therefore, a new theoretical approach needs to be developed on the basis of new terminology, which reflects the real peculiarities of digital instruments of investigation.

If one looks at IT tools of investigation without prejudices concerned with legal concepts, the main common risk entailed by several digital measures of investigation is to give rise to uncontrolled forms of bulk surveillance in which data regarding everyone can not only be searched, intercepted, retained for purposes of crime control or criminal investigation, but can also be used even for criminal convictions. Yet, neither can such data often be deemed as entities with a well-defined probative value nor can they clearly be linked to specific goals. Even when a criminal inquiry has started, it is extremely difficult to define in advance what can be relevant to ascertain specific investigative hypothesis. In a *mare magnum* of digital data, any single piece can be considered as relevant, not just to prove any hypothesis of crime committed or attempted by anyone, but also, and much more relevantly, to define *ex post* the features of offences foreseen by vague, or anyway open and not clearly structured, criminal law provisions.[14]

European jurisprudences, despite some significant differences, show the clear awareness of the need for new approaches to counter such risks. In the landmark judgment *Digital Rights Ireland and Others*, the European Court of Justice focused on the effects of the lack of a duty of notification, which can give rise to a general

---

[14]This phenomenon, moreover, is of an extremely complex nature, and certainly is not only concerned with cybercrimes, or offences ascertained through digital instruments. Criminal law scholarship has long studied the repercussions on the *nullum crimen sine lege* principle of such interaction between procedural and substantive criminal law, whereby the scope of open-structured criminal law provisions is often largely dependent on the results of evidentiary procedures and fact-finding. The outcome is a clear procedural (re)definition of the characteristics of criminal offences, which can thus not be established *ex ante* but *ex post facto*, that is, during the criminal process and by means of procedural tools. Among others, criminal scholars at the University of Pisa have devoted a great part of their studies to this highly delicate topic, starting with Prof. Tullio Padovani: see Padovani (1999), pp. 527 ff. Cf. also Gargani (2017), p. 95; Gargani (2013), p. 844; Gargani (2016), pp. 81 ff.

"feeling that [...] private lives are the subject of constant surveillance".[15] In the light of this outcome, it appears to be inappropriate to simply refer to a digital version of already existing measures (*e.g.* interception of communication), which have largely become sophisticated forms of cyber surveillance, and should thus be treated as such.[16] Moreover, the risk of legitimising bulk digital surveillance is further enhanced by new measures without any parallelism with traditional investigations, *e.g.* Emotion Facial Recognition: as highlighted by *Neroni Rezende*, the danger of a long-lasting surveillance "is very much present for EFR implementations in the security domain".[17] Even more markedly, Strasbourg case-law has called for enhanced individual protection in cases of bulk surveillance. Significantly, in the recent judgment *Big Brother Watch and Others*, the Grand Chamber has called into question that "the acquisition of related communications data through bulk interception is necessarily less intrusive than the acquisition of content", so that "the interception, retention and searching of related communications data should be analysed by reference to the same safeguards as those applicable to content".[18]

4 New Challenges

The digitalisation of investigative practices and procedural activities in court trials, therefore, sets enormous challenges, which require new solution models. These must be able to look at the ongoing transformations, and even more at future perspectives, while maintaining untouched the axiological set-up on which a modern view of crime prevention and criminal process is founded.

A very delicate field in which we can not only observe the high potential but also the enormous risks entailed by the growing digitalisation is air and space law, which risks, moreover, have very relevant implications in the areas of crime control and criminal inquiries. As *Pellegrino* clearly held, satellites have already gained a crucial importance, if not always to prevent, anyway to detect and observe natural dangers, or to monitor climate changes, thus collecting relevant data that could also be essential to reconstruct the dynamics of criminal activities.[19] In several cases, the perspective provided by satellites renders such data a unique and unreplaceable information. Furthermore, satellites are today key tools to preserve safety and (cyber)security to avoid collisions in the outer space. This fundamental role of satellites, however, also reveals which risks arise from the lack of proper

---

[15] CJEU, *Digital Rights Ireland and Others*, judgement of 8 April 2014, Joined Cases C-293/12 and C-594/12, para. 37.

[16] In this sense see also Foti, Sect. 3.

[17] Neroni Rezende, Sect. 5.2.1.

[18] ECtHR, Grand Chamber, *Big Brother Watch and Others v. United Kingdom*, judgement of 25 May 2021, Appl. Nos. 58170/13, 62322/14 and 24960/15.

[19] Pellegrino, Sect. 2.

coordination by different national authorities, or even worse, from cyberattacks aimed at hacking satellites' computer systems. There is no doubt that the achievement of international law standards will be essential to tackle such huge problems.

In the field of preventive and criminal investigations, the most difficult challenges arise where digital measures with massive intrusive potential are needed. The main difficulty to ensure a fair deployment of such tools is probably not to proclaim the conditions under which interference should be allowed in abstract terms, but to guarantee full compliance with them in each concrete case involving the use of digital techniques impinging upon fundamental rights. Otherwise, even essential requirements, such as those expressed by the principles of lawfulness, necessity, and proportionality, threaten to become an empty shell.

This concern was certainly present to the European judges in *Big Brother Watch and Others*, so much so that the Grand Chamber not only confirmed the need to ensure the foreseeability of such intrusive interference by means of clear and detailed rules aimed at establishing the circumstances and conditions of surveillance,[20] but furthermore emphasised the importance of judicial oversight. However, placing the individual at the centre of the state's investigative action could lead us to consider even these fundamental requirements as limited and insufficient to ensure the fairness of digital inquiries. As Judge Pinto de Albuquerque rightly pointed out in his wide-ranging partially concurring and partially dissenting opinion,

> judicial oversight of the entire process would be meaningless if the categories of offences and activities and intercept subjects being monitored were not set out in the domestic law with the necessary degree of clarity and precision.[21]

This clear acknowledgment is of the utmost importance on several grounds, first of all since it focuses on the requirement of a clear definition by domestic law of the subjective direction of surveillance. This requirement, which had been expressly invoked by the Court more than 30 years ago in relation to telephone interception, cannot be deemed as outdated because of the enormous captative potential of digital tools. Respect for private and free communication is an individual right even in the digital era, and thus still today necessitates of "adequate safeguards against various possible abuses", starting with the definition of "the categories of people liable to have" their conversation intercepted and their digital lives subjected to constant surveillance on the basis of a judicial order.[22] The difficulties that lawmakers could encounter to fulfil this task due to the features of bulk surveillance, therefore, are not a good reason to justify a legal omission. On the contrary, the establishment of the subjective limits of interference in much more important in the digital than in the analogue era.

---

[20] ECtHR, Grand Chamber, *Big Brother Watch and Others v. United Kingdom*, para. 333. See recently, among others, Bachmaier Winter (2021), pp. 317 ff.

[21] Both quotations can be read in ECtHR, *Kruslin v. France*, judgment of 24 April 1990, Appl. No. 11801/85, para. 35.

[22] Para. 20.

The general failure by domestic lawmakers to define such limits, moreover, has led to another worrisome result. National judges are generally reluctant to take subjective elements into consideration while assessing the existence of *fumus delicti* as a precondition for a number of relevant means of investigation, remote computer searches, cyber investigation, digital surveillance, and so on. This approach, which is frequently justified by the fact that all such measures are ordinarily addressed against third parties too, and can be deployed even in criminal inquiries in which no suspect has already been identified,[23] is more than debatable. Not only does this interpretation largely overlook the relevance of subjective elements to define the features of the alleged offence,[24] but it furthermore ignores that all those measures—even more, if they are used massively—always affect fundamental rights of specific individuals.

The need for enhanced protection, moreover, should lead to strengthening the essential requirement of lawfulness, also in terms of legal foreseeability concerning the objective elements of the offences justifying digital investigations. I therefore fully share Pinto de Albuquerque's opinion also in the part regarding the need that domestic law establishes the categories of offences justifying digital interference, as well as the types of activities. As has noted, this necessity is not at all weakened—on the contrary, it has been reinforced—by the massive reach of certain digital means. Such enhancement of the principle of lawfulness approach would positively contribute to the evolution of procedural law in all those jurisdictions in which a considerable number of digital investigative means still lacks a clear legal basis, or is at best supported by general (and often generic) legal clauses.[25] But there is

---

[23] Some national legislation also provides indications that may appear to support this approach. For instance, Italian law distinguishes between a suspicion of guilt (*gravi indizi di colpevolezza*) as a condition for remand detention and further pre-trial restrictions on liberty and the right to free moment, and a suspicion of commission of the alleged offence (*gravi indizi di reato*) to justify telephone interception and today digital intercepts. See respectively Arts. 273 and 267 CPC. A great part of case law and legal scholarship shares the approach summarised in the text. See among others Negri (2004), pp. 107 ff., 112 f. I have already expressed my concerns about this interpretation in Ruggeri (2022), para. 2.1.

[24] In continental Europe, criminal law scholarship has long acknowledged the so-called *Doppelstellung* of criminal intent or negligence, that is, their double relevance as subjective elements and expressions of the structure of the alleged offence, which makes them essential elements for the complex assessment of *Tatbestandsmäßigkeit*. See among others, albeit with some differences, Jescheck and Weigend (1996), pp. 429 f.; Donini (1999), p. 257.

[25] This is the case for Italy, where the code of criminal procedure does not specifically regulate a number of relevant digital investigative techniques, which are still largely justified on the basis of general provisions, such as those laying down the principle of exhaustiveness of the prosecutorial inquiry and the admissibility of the so-called 'atypical evidence'. See Di Nuzzo, Sect. 4. I have also expressed some criticisms about this approach, not only since it frustrates the requirement of a clear and precise legal basis, but furthermore because of the inappropriateness of such general clauses, which are not able to justify any measure of investigation. In particular, the clause regarding atypical evidence relates to evidence-gathering procedures at trial, and is therefore by definition inadequate to legitimise the autonomous investigative intervention of law enforcement authorities in the pre-trial phase. Cf. Ruggeri (2021), pp. 854 f. Moreover, it should be taken into account that some important digital measures of investigation, such as search and seizure of digital evidence,

another worrisome implication of this set-up, which has led national authorities to often legitimise the use of lots of digital measures entailing very different investigative activities and in relation to every criminal offence. The awareness of the intrusive potential of ICT techniques, instead, calls for a clear abstract predetermination of the area of investigative intervention, in terms of the establishment of both the serious offences justifying digital interference and the types of interference. This simple conclusion should therefore lead to ruling out the possibility of resorting to measures such cyber intercepts, remote computer searches, seizure of digital evidence, or bulk surveillance, without a legal basis that specifically defines these essential requirements.

While such conditions are surely essential to ensure the effectiveness of judicial oversight, they might not be sufficient however. Judicial control does not necessarily entail an independent assessment of lawfulness, for several reasons. First of all, it depends on the functions of the competent judge in the relevant inquiries according to domestic law. In various countries in continental Europe (France, Portugal, Spain, etc.), investigative judges are still generally competent for investigations and evidence-gathering procedures prior to trial, which they often personally carry out. It is apparent that such responsibility does not provide the best conditions for impartial assessments regarding measures affecting fundamental rights. But relevant problems also arise in jurisdictions which have long replaced such judges with judicial authorities with the specific competence to ensure respect for fundamental rights; for instance, in Italy, the functions of these 'guarantor judges' are largely frustrated by the fact that they have no knowledge of the ongoing investigation carried out by law enforcement bodies, or even worse, they are solely given access to the information that public prosecutors decide to forward to them.

A good alternative would be to enact dialectical dynamics into the proceedings aimed at the enforcement of digital tools, with a view to avoiding the risk that the decision on the adoption of intrusive measures remains in the hands of the same authority, or worse still, of the same person. To this end, different competences should be set up and split between different bodies. A true dialectic, indeed, entails that the competence to request ICT measures intrusive potential should always be conferred to a body without decision-making powers (*e.g.* a public prosecutor). The responsibility for ordering such measures should in turn exclusively lie with a judge without investigative powers, unless urgent reasons require a different arrangement; and in no case, the judicial decision should overcome the limits of the request.

To ensure full compliance with the limits set out by law for digital interference, however, it is not sufficient that judges are excluded any direct investigative competences. Decision-makers should also be able to adequately carry out the complex tasks that domestic law and international human rights case-law imposes upon them. It is more than evident that the lack of proper knowledge about the stand of investigations would render even the fundamental principles of necessity and

---

today find a legal basis in cross-border cases through the implementation of the EIO Directive. See Di Nuzzo, Sect. 2.

proportionality, as observed, purely declamatory requirements, and any judicial oversight substantially and practically impossible.

The best solution to preserve a truly impartial control would probably be to entrust it to an *ad hoc* authority, be it either a single judge or a court, as provided for by the Swiss CPC, which, moreover, explicitly forbids members of the compulsory measures court to "sit as judge in the main hearing in the same case".[26] But even such model needs be reinforced by the acknowledgment of the full accessibility to the materials of the case by the competent judge or court.

One might object that since judges are in most jurisdictions generally required to give reasons for their decisions, the fulfilment of this obligation would jeopardise the secrecy of pre-trial investigations. Yet this is not a good reason to withhold relevant information from the judicial authority, which is responsible to verify the strict necessity of a specific measure and its proportionality in relation to the purposes of a specific procedure. There is little doubt that any investigative action which requires the use of digital interference entails enhanced responsibility, and therefore a clear risk-taking, on the part of the body in charge of the inquiry. The possibility for the judge to have full access the investigative file is therefore the price that public prosecutors should pay by deciding to apply for any form of digital interference with fundamental rights. Of course, the judicial control should be based on all the information obtained until the time of the request, with the result that, if the sought measure were denied because of exculpatory materials, these would be disclosed to the defence.

5 Conclusion

At the end of this research, we can definitively affirm that ICT systems have not only already opened unprecedented scenarios but also, and even more interestingly, let us view unimaginable perspectives that still today appear to belong to science fiction.

This is the case for holographic hearings. As has been noted, it seems highly problematic that hologram-judges can in a near future preside over criminal hearings, and can sentence someone to imprisonment. In spite of all their limits and possible mistakes, human decision-makers seem to provide a much better solution, not just because they can ensure a more reliable fact-finding but because a human decision is for now the best way of preserving the social sustainability of criminal justice through a truly fair balancing of conflicting values. Instead, hologram-based criminal trials bring considerable benefits, and could even contribute to restoring fundamental safeguards and principles that are already widely eroded in criminal proceedings, such as the principle of immediacy.[27]

---

[26] Art. 18(2) of the Swiss CPC.

[27] Falcone, Sect. 5.3.

Of course, the effectiveness of defence rights would anyway depend on several variables, and whenever defendants will also be enabled to holographic participation, specific technical arrangements will be necessary for various purposes, *e.g.* to preserve confidential communication with defence lawyers. A very promising perspective to enhance the level of digital realism could be to introduce into criminal trials Collaborative Virtual Environments (CVEs), that is, systems aimed at creating a virtual environment in which attendance of participants and non-parties will be assured by avatars.[28]

But even outside science fiction, the most traditional investigative practices can no longer be conducted without digital tools, which have become indispensable instruments for law enforcement and prosecutorial authorities in the key fields of crime control and criminal inquiry. The division line between these two areas has long been smoothed, and today appears to be widely eroded by the increasing investigative recourse to devices, such as drones, spyware, and so on. Unquestionably, most of ICT tools raise quite unsurmountable problems regarding essential safeguards of modern criminal justice, as well as new-generation fundamental rights. Cyber interception of encrypted communications stands out among investigative techniques for impinging on a number of new individual rights, which goes far beyond the right to data protection and the right to confidentiality and integrity of ICT systems, acknowledged by the German Federal Constitutional Court, as it can directly affect the core of the right to digital privacy, as rightly highlighted by *Foti.*[29]

In most cases, the problem is not to establish what science and technology can today achieve, or has already achieved, but which arrangements are compatible with human rights standards set out at either international or domestic law. The problem, in other words, is to define the legal limits of digital intervention rather than its practical potentialities. Therefore, *e.g.* whether a malware hiddenly installed allows an entire computer system or a whole set of digital data to be copied by means of a 'bitstream image technique' (bit-by-bit); to what extent and how many times all those data can be accessed; how many copies can be made; and ultimately, how long examination can last—all these questions are certainly not relevant for a lawyer from a purely technological viewpoint—we know that all this is technically possible, and will be much more feasible in the future—but because of the complicated legal questions that arise from all of them. It is also clear that facing the problems raised by ICT intrusive means of investigation by way of banning the use of the information obtained is not a proper solution; the real challenge is to find a way of avoiding digital interference, or at least reducing the risks of undue digital interference, and thus of abuses of digitalisation.

In sum, the challenges with which new-generation academics and legal practitioners will have to be confronted are quite unsurmountable ones. But while tackling the huge number of unprecedented problems, they are surely not alone, nor are they

---

[28] *Id.*, Sect. 2.
[29] Falcone, Sect. 5.3.

destined to navigate through (a)legal scenarios without clear coordinates and constantly at the mercy of technological developments. There are good reasons to assume that the best way of properly facing the ever newer legal questions raised by information and communication technology is to resort to the main principles and safeguards that have long governed criminal proceedings, and on the basis of which a modern view of a human rights-oriented criminal justice is solidly founded. The challenges of digitalisation can certainly not render them obsolete and outdated abstractions that need be abandoned. As happens in the field of transnational criminal justice, technological developments surely require changes and adaptations in approaching fundamental requirements, such as those of proportionality or minimum interference. But the core values expressed by such principles and safeguards must be jealously guarded and preserved, as it provides the guiding compass for lawyers of today and, even more, of tomorrow.

References

Bachmaier Winter L (2021) Proportionality, mass surveillance and criminal investigation: the Strasbourg Court facing Big Brother. In: Billis E, Knust N, Rui JP (eds) The principle of proportionality in crime control and criminal justice. Hart Publishing, Oxford, pp 317–335

Capograssi G (1959) Giudizio processo scienza verità. In: Capograssi G, Opere, vol 1, V. Giuffrè, Milano

Donini M (1999) Teoria del reato. In: Digesto delle Discipline Penalistiche, vol XIV. Utet, Torino

Ferrua P (2017) La prova nel processo penale. Volume I: Struttura e procedimento. Giappichelli, Torino

Galgani B (2022) Il processo penale in 'ambiente' digitale: ragioni e (ragionevoli) speranze. Questione giustizia, pp 1–15

Gargani A (2013) Processualizzazione del fatto e strumenti di garanzia: la prova della tipicità "oltre ogni ragionevole dubbio". La Legislazione penale, pp 839–858

Gargani A (2016) Crisi del diritto sostanziale e *vis expansiva* del processo. Criminalia, pp 303–327

Gargani A (2017) Fattispecie giudiziarie e dinamiche probatorie. Appunti sulla processualizzazione della tipicità penale. In: De Francesco G, Marzaduri E (a cura di) Il reato lungo gli impervi sentieri del processo. Giappichelli, Torino, pp 89–106

Jescheck H-H, Weigend T (1996) Lehrbuch des Strafrechts. Allgemeiner Teil, 5th edn. Duncker & Humblot, Berlin

Negri D (2004) Fumus commissi delicti. La prova per le fattispecie cautelari. Giappichelli, Torino

Padovani T (1999) Il crepuscolo della legalità. Riflessioni antistoriche sulle dimensioni processuali della legalità penale. Indice penale, pp 527–543

Ruggeri S (2021) Grundrechtseingriffe und neue digitale Ermittlungsmaßnahmen im italienischen Strafprozessrecht. Zeitschrift für die gesamte Strafrechtswissenschaft 133(3):843–860

Ruggeri S (2022) Le condizioni generali di ammissibilità dell'attività intercettativa al tempo delle comunicazioni digitali: la gravità indiziaria e l'assoluta indispensabilità per le indagini. In: Maggio P (2022) Intercettazioni e captatore informatico. La disciplina integrata dalle riforme. Giappichelli, Torino (forthcoming)

Milton Keynes UK
Ingram Content Group UK Ltd.
UKHW020800181023
430769UK00006B/220